Hans H. Hofstätter was born in 1928 in Basel, Switzerland. In 1939 he moved to Germany and in 1949 completed his final high school examination (Abitur). He studied art history, archeology, and German literature at universities in Basel, Munich, Paris, and Freiburg and received his Ph.D. under Professor Kurt Bauch after writing a thesis entitled, *"Die Entstehung des Neuen Stils in der französischen Malerei um 1890"* ("The Rise of the New Style in French Painting around 1890"). From 1956-61 he was an assistant to Professor Friedrich Gerke at the Institute for Art History, University of Mainz, and from 1961-71 chief editor for a southwest German art publisher. In 1973 he accepted the editorship for the periodical for Christian art and art history, *Das Münster.* Since 1974 he has been the director for the municipal museums of the city of Freiburg. In addition, he has also been a guest professor in the United States and a guest lecturer both inside Germany and abroad and has numerous papers and publications to his credit. Other works by Hans H. Hofstätter published by DuMont include: *Geschichte der europäischen Jugendstilmalerei ("History of European Art Nouveau Painting")* and *Symbolismus und die Kunst der Jahrhundertwende ("Symbolism and the Art of the Turn of the Century").*

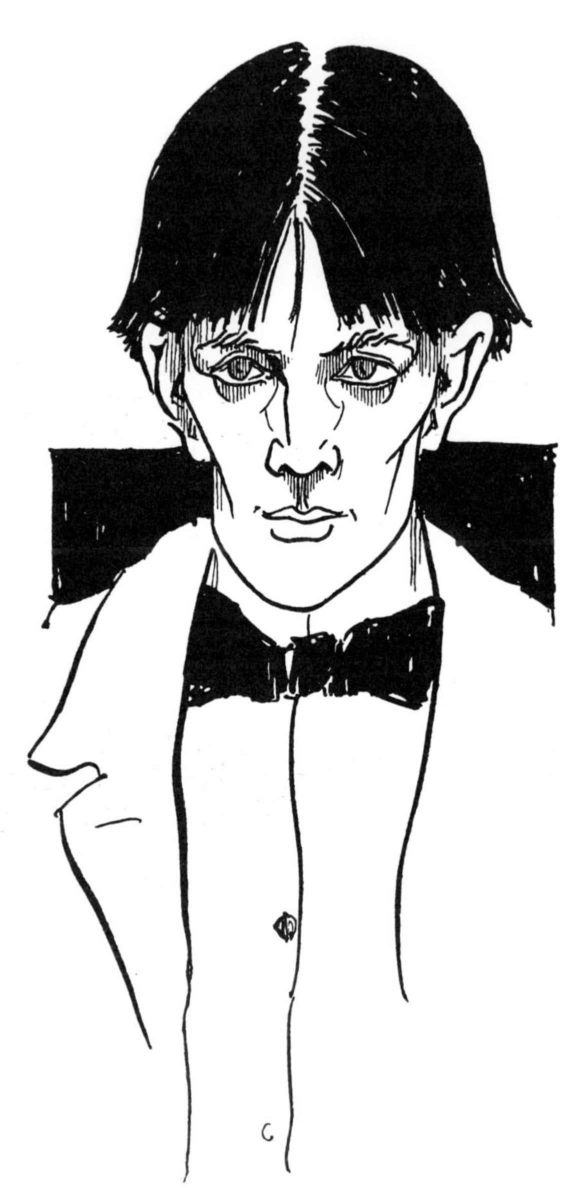

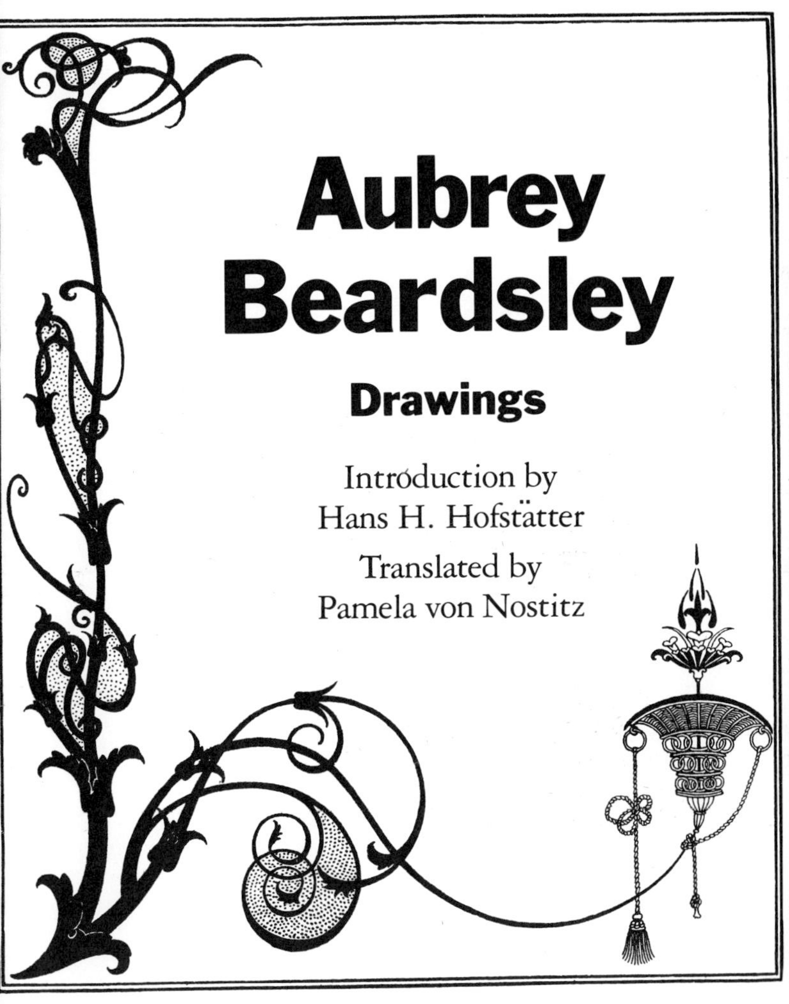

Aubrey Beardsley

Drawings

Introduction by
Hans H. Hofstätter

Translated by
Pamela von Nostitz

Barron's/Woodbury, New York

Front cover figure: *The Mask of the Red Death* (detail), 1895. Illustration for a story of the same name by Edgar Allan Poe.

First Publication

Printer: Gebr. Rasch and Co., Bramsche
Reproductions: Helio, Cologne

All inquiries should be addressed to:
Barron's Educational Series, Inc.
113 Crossways Park Drive
Woodbury, New York 11797

Library of Congress Cataloging in Publication Data

Beardsley, Aubrey Vincent, 1872-1898.
Drawings.

Translation of Zeichnungen.
Bibliography: p.
1. Beardsley, Aubrey Vincent, 1872-1898.
I. Hofstätter, Hans Hellmut, 1928-
II. Title
NC242.B3A4 1979 741.9′42 79-13369
ISBN 0-8120-2104-5

Library of Congress Catalog Card No. 79-13369
International Standard Book No. 0-8120-2104-5

PRINTED IN THE UNITED STATES OF AMERICA

CONTENTS

Bibliography

Beardsley, Aubrey. *The Letters of Aubrey Beardsley.* Eds. Henry Maas, J.L. Duncan, W.G. Good. London: Cassell, 1970.

Brophy, Brigid. *Beardsley and His World.* London: Thames & Hudson, 1976.

Brophy, Brigid. *Black and White: A Portrait of Aubrey Beardsley.* New York: Stein & Day, 1969.

Easton, Malcolm. *Aubrey and the Dying Lady, A Beardsley Riddle.* Boston: David R. Godine, 1972.

Marillier, H.C. *The Early Work of Aubrey Beardsley.* New York: Da Capo Press, 1967.

Reade, Brian. *Aubrey Beardsley.* New York: Viking Press, 1967.

Symons, Arthur. *The Art of Aubrey Beardsley.* New York: Boni and Liveright, Inc., 1918.

Introduction

"Morality is always the last refuge of people who cannot understand beauty."

Oscar Wilde

The wide diversification of art nouveau is remarkable, considering the short time span of scarcely two decades allotted for its development as an epoch. We are constantly encountering new artists who were active in this style. Each had his individual mode of expression, which was inextricably tied to his personality and distinguished his work from that of his fellow artists. A sustaining spirit was clearly present throughout this period and was shared by innumerable artists who realized their own potentialities through it. In the course of a few years the movement became widespread without the much longer preparatory period customary in the history of art. Generally, a standard was attained which did full justice to the demands of art.

In attempting to explain this phenomenon we encounter a set of closely related facts. On the one hand, the routine imitation of historical stylistic forms as practiced for decades had become insufficient. On the other hand, a distinct feeling of radical change in many fields had to emerge. The artistic sphere was fraught with the feeling of being at an end, while the innovations in other areas (technology, transportation, etc.) only slowly crystallized into artistic manifestations. Artists were seeking a refuge, an island on which one could survive and gather new powers, where demands could be fulfilled. This refuge was offered in the field of the decorative arts. The historical imitations of style were rooted in this field and had thus prepared the way. A margin of free play was also possible in this area, however, as it did not demand the highest artistic quality. Much more important were the requirements of function, as in arts and crafts, and ornamentation, in pictorial art as well as in book illustration. It is the latter subject with which we are primarily concerned.

In surveying as far as possible the profusion of illustrated and ornamented publications, a broader aspect emerges. We realize that this sound basis for various creative activities was established by only a few artists working largely independently of each other. It is precisely this medium through its mass production that assisted in making these prototypes known and facilitated or even invited their imitation or references to them. They struck the nerve of the times by first formulating in pictures what had been affecting many others. The material provocatively issued in these publications became common property in a short time, for its aesthetic content complied with the general aesthetic aims. In alluding to these prototypes we are referring above all to the Englishman Aubrey Beardsley and the Frenchman Henri de Toulouse-Lautrec, whose personal and artistic fates are characteristic of the entire state of the times. Their very bodily infirmities caused them to be outsiders, isolating them more and more from a society toward which they assumed a challenging position. They suffered from society's hostility and lack of understanding, which provoked them to issue new pronouncements against it. These in turn aroused more anger, since society refused to admit to the truth of its own reflected image. Oscar Wilde ingeniously and bitterly demonstrated this mirror battle to his readers in *Dorian Gray*. Both artists, Beardsley as well as Toulouse-Lautrec, were nearly shattered by their message, which was embraced and understood by few. However, their formal repertoire was exploited all the more for the aesthetic delight of their contemporaries.

Although one can compare the formal-aesthetic influence of Beardsley to that of Toulouse-Lautrec, from the standpoint of their sociological environments they may be regarded as antipodes. Toulouse-Lautrec's background was that of the bohemian artist, whom he soon came to embody. However, the impressionists and symbolists before and during his time had so amply provided scandals and shocked the public that he could almost feel secure in their tradition. This was not so for Beardsley in Victorian England, where people were forced into games of hide-and-seek, since the public prosecutor was quickly summoned whenever middle-class morality was presumed endangered. The paintings of the English Pre-Raphaelites bear striking witness to this with their disguise of contemporary problems in pictures of the love-crazed Rosamund, the lady of Shalott, the pernicious story of Paolo and Francesca, Helen of Troy, Venus verticordia, *The Awakening Conscience, The Stages of Cruelty,* and others. John Gordon Christian aptly pointed out that their "sentimentality, to which they unabashedly surrendered themselves and the hidden current of repressed sexuality, evident in so many of their pictures, seemed to embody the entire system of the Victorian ethic, against which the new century revolted." A new social type, the dandy, arose from this atmosphere in nineteenth-century England. While appearing to adapt to society, he secretly rebelled against it. Toward the end of the century the term came to mean a smug intellectual who, as a positive variant, resisted the vulgarizing levelling of cultural phenomena through his tools of irony and sarcasm, while maintaining a passive position. Powerless to seek new paths or change direction, he is related to the decadent, a term that at this time underwent a reevaluation, as his underlying behavior seemed the only possibility open to him. Such behavior is rooted in the consciousness of crisis and decline, for which compensation was sought only in a passionate aestheticism, a savoring of profligate beauty, the sensuously refined, and the glorification of a world of art as opposed to a world of simple realistic values. This aim was openly acknowledged as in a leading article of an 1886 publication in a Parisian periodical with the provocative title, *Le Décadant:* "It would be nonsensical not to admit to the state of decadence which we have reached. Religion, morality and justice are on the point of decay . . . the refinement of desire, feeling, taste, luxury, pleasure . . . are symptoms of such an upheaval." It was first perceived in this form in France and England, and it was in this tense setting that Beardsley's destiny ran its course.

Beardsley was born on August 21, 1872, in Brighton. His mother fell ill with puerperal fever and had no sooner been delivered of her child than she received word of her husband's bankruptcy. She managed with her two children, Aubrey and his slightly older sister, by giving piano lessons, and she took care of Aubrey, who was sickly from the beginning, until his death. Later, her care was solely restricted to the maternal, as her income was extremely meager. He attended a boarding school near Brighton; his grandfather supposedly absorbed the costs. He began drawing at seven years, mainly caricatures of his teachers and fellow students, but by the age of nine consumption forced him to leave school temporarily. Since the financial situation at home was tight, he first earned money at eleven years by using his ability to draw, occasionally selling place cards, etc. During this time he and his sister lived with an aunt because of their mother's illness. He continued to attend school, where he made his first literary discoveries and was impressed above all by the tales of Edgar Allan Poe. In spite of new ailments he managed to pass the school certificate examination and before his sixteenth birthday in 1888, secured a temporary position as a clerk in the office of a London borough inspector. In 1889 he transferred as a clerk to the office of the Guardian Life and Fire Insurance Company on London's Lombard Street. He read much during his free time, attended the theater and concerts but drew little, concerning himself instead with literary endeavors. In one drawing he poked fun at himself as a writer. The drawing, entitled *Le débris d'un poète,* depicted him working on thick volumes as he sat on a stool in front of a high desk. In autumn of 1889, still in the first year of his new job, he suffered violent hemorrhages.

Confined to his sickroom and suffering immensely, he began to grow artistically more active. He produced drawings and short literary works, which were actually published in a periodical, and was paid for them. Significantly, the drawings were concerned with themes with which he was occupying himself at the time: Manon Lescaut (pl. 1), Madame Bovary, the lady of the camelias, and scenes from novels by Daudet, Balzac (pl. 2), Racine, and Dante (pls. 3, 4). This is significant because it has already become clear that Beardsley's inspiration was derived from literature. From the above list it is evident that Beardsley was chiefly concerned with French literature, which he could read effortlessly in the original language, thanks to the foreign language knowledge gained in school. To be sure, there remained little time for drawing, as the need to earn money left only the evening hours free. He reluctantly spent his days at the insurance office. This reluctance, which he self-pityingly and even rather coquettishly displayed, is characterized in a letter to an acquaintance: ". . . in miserable condition, with a sallow complexion and sunken, red eyes, long, red hair, a shuffling gait and poor carriage." This is mentioned because the outward image of the artist is inextricably connected with his work, which is to say it expresses his detachment from his environment. Detachment is the important prerequisite for the artistic inexorability of his drawings. The basic characteristics of Beardsley's image hardly changed during the ten remaining years in which he lived and drew, becoming at most more pronounced and decided. His shyness, arising from the awareness of his physical inferiority, was concealed by his arrogance. Arthur Symons, later his close literary colleague, described him in a letter as the thinnest young man he had ever seen, "unpleasant and affected." On the occasion of a soirée he began an afterdinner speech with the words: "I would like to speak about an interesting subject—myself." Later, whenever he appeared at concerts, the theater, or in company, he carried his conspicuous, gilt leather portfolio, which he opened in order to make notes or sketches, and he literally stinted himself for his extravagant clothing. As a result he constantly lived on the verge of overtaxation. The author Max Beerbohm recalled a dinner with Beardsley, who was the center of attraction. ". . . until he suddenly, practically in the middle of a sentence, fell asleep in his chair. He had over-exerted himself and his vitality had left him. I still see him before me, how he sat there with his head drooped down: the thin face, as white as the gardenia on his lapel, and the protruding, angular features; the hair, that constantly hung as a fringe on his brow and had such a peculiar color — like tortoise shell; the narrow, angular form and the long hands, in which there was so much power."

He sought the first confirmation of the artistic quality of his autodidactically created drawings from the well-known Pre-Raphaelite artist, Sir Edward Burne-Jones, whom he visited randomly one Sunday afternoon. After Burne-Jones had seen the drawings, he invited Beardsley to tea together with Oscar Wilde, who also happened to be present. The host spoke encouragingly about young Beardsley's drawings. He commented that they were full of ideas, poetry and imagination, and that, while he seldom or never advised anyone to choose art as a career, in this case he could not do otherwise.

This set the stage for Beardsley's artistic career. The greatest living English artist had given him courage, but he had also noticed what was lacking and moved Beardsley to attend evening courses at the Westminster School of Art to gain a solid foundation. "I know you are not afraid of the work," wrote Burne-Jones to Beardsley, "but you must not waver, because the necessary discipline of school lies so far away from your natural interests and inclinations. You must learn to master the grammar of your art, and if your exercises are stiff and prosaic, so much the better."

At the same time Beardsley extended his studies to foreign works of art. He visited the Royal Collection in Hampton Court. There he was inspired by Mantegna and became acquainted with works of contemporary artists, especially Whistler's famous Peacock Room in the London city hall. He rummaged through the secondhand bookshops in search of eighteenth-century French illustrations and in so doing also discovered Japanese woodblock prints in which he became interested. Their influence can be traced throughout his work. What money he did not need for living expenses and drawing supplies was henceforth invested in books, and in the following years he acquired a select library. At the same time his drawings, published in a small periodical, *The Bee,* met with modest success. To the detriment of his health, Beardsley worked after he came home from the insurance office, from nine o'clock until late in the night. A short stay in Paris, where he visited Puvis de Chavannes on Burne-Jones's recommendation, as well as the theater in Covent Garden, and a spontaneous enthusiasm for Richard Wagner brought variety into the otherwise monotonous life of a clerk.

After the encouragement from Burne-Jones, the second important outside impetus came through a book dealer who was familiar with Beardsley's graphic works. He told Beardsley that he could show some drawings to a publisher who had been searching for an artist to illustrate Malory's *Le Morte d'Arthur.* The publisher liked Beardsley's test drawings so much that he awarded him the contract. Beardsley now felt strong enough to give up his job with the insurance company and resigned. He wrote in a letter that if ever a person was in the wrong place, he was. He left the office and afterwards told his family. At first there was a spectacle, but of course, since he now experienced success so to speak and was talked about, they would become less sure of themselves and emphasize how much they were interested in his work. That was especially true of his devoted father.

This optimism, generated by the ability to determine the course of his life, contrasted with the pessimism arising from his doubts as to whether he could actually manage the work he had undertaken. He wrote that he was sure he was not up to it. Yet at the same time he knew it was his only chance. The book was to appear in monthly installments from the middle of 1893, and in eighteen months it would be complete with its twenty illustrations, some full page and some double page, plus 550 embellished initials, vignettes, and borders (compare pls. 14-22). Since Beardsley had not previously considered illustrating and laying out a book, he had to study how others had done it. His important model was still Burne-Jones, so he patterned his work closely on the examples Burne-Jones had compiled for the Kelmscott-Press in Hammersmith (London), which William Morris had founded in 1891. The design was strongly influenced by medieval book illumination, which in England was enriched by the newly discovered Celtic art of ornamentation. Each page, just like a chapter beginning, received asymmetrical embellished borders of varying widths, framing a large, rectangular center field (pls. 20, 22). The border was widest on the lower edge, narrower on the outer side, even narrower on top, and narrowest nearest the binding. The ornamentation of this border or of the border surrounding the lettering or picture at the beginning of the chapter was fashioned with interlace, composed of various intertwinings, entanglings, and other patterns. Beardsley invented new decorations for every border and developed a new sense for ornamentation. He sensitively harmonized the character of the ornament with the theme of the framed image and repeated it in simple form in the initial. He gradually freed himself from the naturalistic decorative motifs, as Burne-Jones had employed them, and strewed fantastic figurations between them. He did not uniformly fill the borders with the same ornamental motifs but created transitions between the varying forms of decoration on each side. Thus, both a new relationship between the frame and the enclosed space and a new epoch in the art of book illustration began.

For the small chapter beginnings, each numbered only with a Roman numeral, he designed small, vertical, rectangular illustrations which were completely filled except for the small space left free for the numeral (pls. 17-19, 21). In the full-page illustrations he adhered closely to the text, whereas in these smaller decorative motifs he freely paraphrased from the text or drew from his own imagination. The drawing with the three swans arose in this manner (pl. 19). Later, it became nothing short of a symbol of art nouveau. He also created images of naked ephebian youths with tender phalluses and thereby caused offense for the first time. All his drawings lack spatial depth and a sense of perspective and are clearly dependent upon the contrast between black and white areas which meet in a strikingly expressive line. This line can bend the figures in an elegant arabesque but can also coldly divide a figure from its background. This line is always more than a mere outline. It is already the celebrated line of the art nouveau style and expresses the character and nature of a figure. It not only defines the shape of a figure but also becomes part of its nature.

Apart from the natural similarities with all illustration, the art nouveau style is anything else but uniform. The extensive work on *Le Morte d'Arthur* forced Beardsley to seek and find his own style. He had seven styles, and in each, success, he once proudly professed, making a virtue out of necessity. Many pages owe much to Pre-Raphaelite models; some are naively simplified, frugal, and austere; some are governed by a sense of horror vacui, and their smallest spaces are encrusted with detail. Even Dürer's woodblock prints inspired him. Once, he even fashioned his initials, *AB,* after Dürer's monogram.

Beardsley once explained his method of working, expressing himself almost in parody. This explanation, of course, can not be applied to every picture, but the lovely and frequently reproduced *How Queen Guenever Made Her a Nun* (pl. 22) serves as an example. The picture depicts a large, black figure of a nun, reading a volume at a lecturn. Her habit broadly dominates the picture field. Beardsley explained that he had squirted a large spot of drawing ink on the picture and then drawn out from there, as chance had plotted the figure in the bud. This explanation may hold some truth but, more importantly, it seems to illustrate the general pictorial character of these pages. They were freely drawn and later etched, not carved in wood as were the orthodox works of the Kelmscott-Press. In contrast to the cold severity and finality of woodblock carving, the ink drawings offered possibilities which greatly facilitated the seismographical sensitization of the line. The surface contours can be corrected after their effect is tested. The black areas could be broadened with a brush wherever necessary, and zinc white could be used to blot out incorrect lines which could otherwise be scraped off with a penknife. Thus, a drawn picture better accommodates the inner conceptions and intentions of the artist than when a drawing is transferred into a woodcut by a foreign hand. Naturally, William Morris sharply criticized the imitation of his book art in such a deviant medium, but Beardsley confidently countered that Morris's work was nothing but an imitation of old things, but his was fresh and original.

With the success of *Le Morte d'Arthur* Beardsley became well known. So many possibilities were offered to him that he sometimes deplored the obligations to his publisher because they hindered him from accepting new tasks. These new tasks would offer him more freedom and more possibilities of self-realization than his work, which forced him to adhere to the designed plan for months.

In 1893 the first volume of the English art nouveau periodical, *The Studio*, appeared. It was read throughout the entire continent and contained some of Beardsley's first publications (compare pls. 12, 13). He also designed the cover and thereby demonstrated his sense for the functional aspect of a periodical title (pls. 10, 11). The title appears in the foliage of a tree of life, and the table of contents is compressed into the vacant white space beneath it to the right, so that passers-by looking at the magazine displayed in the bookshop would be informed of its content. A band of writing on the lower edge legibly noted the price (sixpence), the publication dates (monthly), and the address of the editor's office. The success of *The Studio,* one of the longest-lived art nouveau periodicals, was also a success for Beardsley. During the same period he received a contract to draw weekly for *The Pall Mall Budget* (compare pls. 7-9). This was followed by contracts for illustrating Lucian's *True History* (pls. 38, 39), *Bon Mots'* famous personalities (pl. 26), which Beardsley caricatured at the same time, and the first works for the cycle, *The Wagnerian.* In addition, the young man who had grown so famous gained entrance into the literary salons, where additional contacts were possible.

In 1893 Oscar Wilde's French version of *Salomé* appeared in Paris. Beardsley had drawn a picture of Wilde's *Salomé* which caught the attention of the author. Thereupon, he dedicated a volume of the French edition to Beardsley, with words to the effect: For Aubrey — for the only artist beside myself, who knows what the dance of the seven veils is and can see this invisible dance. It almost goes without saying that Beardsley received the contract for illustrating the English edition of the book (pls. 42-56).

However, Beardsley's drawings did not altogether adhere to Wilde's *Salomé*. As already evident in the chapter vignettes of *Arthur*, he repeatedly abandoned himself to associative inspirations upon reading the text and often perceived the contents much differently than the author. He depicted Herodias's daughter face to face with a pendulously breasted demon (pl. 43), designed fantastic garments for her such as the peacock skirt (pl. 45) and the black décolleté cape open to the navel (pl. 46). He placed a masked Pierrot in a modish Parisian hat at her toilette (pl. 51). An imp strikes up a dance (pl. 50), and neither naked breasts nor the tender phalluses of slender youths were omitted. Yet, the scenes which adhered closely to the text, such as the kiss of the decapitated head (pl. 53) or the dialogue between Salomé and John (pl. 55) are among the most impressive pages. Beardsley's final vignette of a naked Salomé being buried in a powder box by a Pierrot and a satyr may have alienated the author, as Beardsley's overall independence did not exactly delight him. He feared that the pictures' "shamelessness" (in fact, Beardsley had to touch up some pages) would attract more attention than the play itself. Later Max Beerbohm was heard to say that the play was first viewed in the right light through the drawings. The degree to which this relationship between the text and illustrations alienated Wilde from Beardsley is evident from the fact that the German translation of Wilde's play, published by Insel in 1903, carried illustrations by Marcus Behmer rather than those by Beardsley. Although Behmer was indeed influenced by Beardsley, he adhered more closely to the text. The friendship which might have arisen from the collaboration of Wilde and Beardsley already stood on a shaky foundation and could not endure another crisis (which will be discussed later).

Since the publication of the book Beardsley had become both established and notorious. He was boundlessly admired by some and sharply criticized by others. In 1893 the *London Figaro* stated that the drawings were a downright mockery of art. Beardsley felt obligated by this outcry to stage his life accordingly. As Julius Meier-Graefe reports, in his apartment hung "the most beautiful Japanese prints one could see in London together with the most detailed erotic works. They hung in simple frames on subdued wallpaper — all indecent, the unrestrained visions of Utamaro. If one, however, looked at these from a certain distance, they gave a very elegant, bright, and harmless impression." They were the prints Beardsley's friend, the painter Will Rothenstein, had obtained in Paris and sent to him because they were "so direct" that possessing them was painful to him.

Besides the blunt eroticism of the Japanese prints, Beardsley favored the representations of natural impossibilities, such as two men duelling with their exceedingly enlarged phalluses, while a girl, with her skirt tucked up and her legs spread apart, awaited the victor. The motif of the enlarged phallus was later employed by Beardsley in his *Lysistrata* illustrations, which are among the most bizarre he ever created (pls. 90-97). Beardsley basically rejected nature as a model and ideal of beauty and placed the artificial above nature, as did Whistler, who is said to have remarked that nature was always a horror to him. Besides the Japanese woodcut prints, Beardsley's models were above all French eighteenth-century illustrations, which he regarded as a standard for all pictorial art.

The preference for the artificial also characterized the way he worked, which he expressed in an interview. He believed he had to excuse himself a little, that it was the truth, but he confessed that he could not work in the daylight. He felt best when the lights burned in the city and so used to working in artificial light that if he wanted to work during the day he must pull down the blinds and have his candles before he began.

This corresponds to the description given by a young artist of a visit to Beardsley's atelier: "The windows were covered with black tapestries; the walls were dark, floor, carpet, and furniture black or nearly black; two altar candles in gilt bronze Empire candlesticks on a rococo table gave light. The table was also black, of the type which priests use. On the table lay pens, ink, brush, and opened razor, and a half-finished drawing." Not surprisingly, this description recalls another account of an apartment Huysmans gives in his book, *A Rebours (Against the Grain),* and the method of working under artificial light familiar to us from other symbolistic artists, such as Gustave Moreau.

Art critic Robert Ross had the rare opportunity of watching Beardsley draw and reported how he worked in these surroundings: "He sketched everything in pencil, at first covering the page with what appeared to be scribbling, constantly erasing and drawing new outlines, until the entire surface was studded with pencil strokes and erasure marks; on this chaotic base he draw with a gold pen and Chinese ink, often deviating from the pencil lines, which he afterwards carefully removed. In this manner every drawing was designed, constructed and completed on one and the same page."

Beardsley himself knew what the line in his pictures meant, since he had manipulated it into new paths for so long with so much patience and sensitivity. Beardsley noted that, apart from the grotesque aspects, he might well say that people especially liked the decorative element of his works, and that he might claim to some extent to control the line. He tried to extract as much as possible from a single curve or a straight line. Beardsley's early limitation of the space in which the line moves remained characteristic of all his drawings. First, he drew the frame. Its binding force is often emphasized by a double or, at times, even a triple edge. The lines assume their field of operation only inside this frame. They are prevented from swelling out beyond the border and forced to remit ascetically all excesses within the confined area. The artist often expressed his disappointment with the printed result. Beardsley felt that the etched line did not reproduce all the vibrations of the soul which were more strongly present in the drawn line. More often, he expressed disappointment in the change of format, especially in the reduction of size which disturbed the valence of the lines and surfaces. If the printed drawing was to be reduced in size, Beardsley would have preferred to have originally drawn it smaller and would have planned it differently, for, among other things, the mechanical reduction of size diminishes the distance between lines which can almost converge. This alters the desired tension produced by a precise interval. The sweep of a curved line must be drawn differently if it is to measure three centimeters or fifteen centimeters. This also demonstrates the importance of understanding Beardsley's drawings sympathetically in order to sense their spirit. Those who are familiar with only the printed versions will marvel at the originals and be surprised at how flat they appear in the mechanical reprints. Even the black surfaces possess a scarcely perceptible, yet pulsating liveliness in the original drawings.

By now Beardsley was entirely free and no longer bound to the pseudo-medieval tradition of the Pre-Raphaelites, from whom he disparagingly detached himself: "Do you know, I find the attempts of modern artists to return to the techniques and forms of the primitive craftsman just as foolish as if a grown man were to try to return to the clothing, behavior, and childish babbling of his infanthood. Nothing depresses me as much as a Gothic cathedral."

Although there were enough opportunities in the literary salons of London to make the acquaintance of people who, through similar convictions or commercial connections, could assist him, Beardsley made one of his most important acquaintances of these years in the waiting room of his doctor's office. He frequented the doctor's office almost as regularly as the salons in order to procure relief from the pain of his repeated hemorrhages. The man he met was the writer, Henry Harland, who had emigrated to England from America. Harland had not yet gained entrance to the salons and suffered from the same illness that plagued Beardsley, although not in such an advanced and painful stage. Their manner of appearing in public was similar. Each maintained a dandylike exclusivity in order to mask his physical infirmities. On New Year's Day, 1894, they sat in front of the fireplace at Harland's residence, where the fog was so dense that even in the room one's own hand was barely visible. On this occasion they formulated a plan to establish a literary-artistic periodical. A publisher could be found in the person of John Lane. Beardsley obtained a permanent position as art editor and was thus for the first time financially secure. Harland was given the secure post of literary editor. Above all, the magazine was to become a forum in which their own works were to be introduced to the public. The editors also wanted to gather all the artistic powers previously excluded from the gazettes and magazines by the reigning public taste. Beardsley wrote: "The idea has moved us, that many brilliant painters of tales and writers of pictures have not published their best things in conventional periodicals, either because they are not of immediate interest or because they are somewhat risqué."

The new magazine was called *The Yellow Book.* Although the title did not sound programmatic, it was considered unusual and provocative due to the yellow color of the cover. As with *The Studio,* the cover designed by Beardsley offered at a glance all the important information, such as the title, dates of publication, price, and sources, with the exception of the table of contents (pl. 57). A drawing in Beardsley's unmistakable black-and-white manner dominating the cover caught the eye at any given moment, especially here where the white contrasted against the yellow background. Also striking was the strict, formal arrangement of the title page with the larger band above and the narrower one under the title picture, which usually contained a literary relationship to a stylish lady. Among these appeared an imposing figure of a lady near a bookshelf; a lady receiving a blossom from a boy with an overflowing basket (pl. 68); a lady bending over a tray supported by Pierrot-like gnomes (pl. 72) on which books by Dickens, Shakespeare, and others (among them also a clearly visible literary project planned by Beardsley entitled, *Story of Venus and Tannhäuser*) are piled; a lady, reposing in a meadow as a faun reads to her from a book: drawings of incomparable taste, which we no longer find provocative. Beardsley never meant them to be provocative even if he did consciously seek to amuse. However, the fact alone that such a publication (for which Beardsley also designed the advertising posters) even appeared on the market had a provocative effect, since it made people aware of an intellectual "market gap" which would have been gladly overlooked. Among other things on Beardsley's posters was the following: "The aim of *The Yellow Book* is to as far as possible get away from the bad, old tradition of periodical literature and to offer an illustrated magazine, a beautiful product of the art of book illustration, modern and distinguished in its textual and pictorial content and at the same time popular in the best sense of the word. We are of the opinion that such a publication at present is distinguished by its absence." In the prospectus was supplementarily stated: "The collaborators will in many respects be more unrestrained than the limitations of the periodicals of the old style allowed for. . . . Indeed it will always strive to present itself as particular, pertinent and reserved, but it will be at the same time of a spirited modernity and not tremble before the disapproving glances of hypocrisy."

Obviously, this announcement must have challenged all the conventional periodicals, and their reaction was not long in coming. In a critique of the first issue, *The Times* wrote of a combination of English rowdyism and French lasciviousness. *The Westminster Gazette* even called for a parliamentary decree declaring this type of disturbance unlawful. *The World* wrote that Beardsley's illustrations looked like mad Japanese prints, and *Punch* called the entire thing filthy. A critic in *The National Observer* expressed his opinion of Beardsley's depictions of women, commenting that they resembled nothing on earth or in the firmament above the earth, or in the waters beneath the earth, with their lips, thicker than those of the Hottentots, their bodies, thin as a rail, their impossible pointed fingers and toes and their small eyes, which have all the form and charm of a snail robbed of its house.

In spite of, or because of, these critiques, *The Yellow Book*'s first publication in 1894 was a great success. Already during the first week of publication a second edition bearing the first number had to be printed and during the following week, a third. One drawing in particular, entitled *L'Education sentimentale,* (pl. 58), a perversion of Rousseau's book, aroused shock and enthusiasm. In the drawing a corpulent madame reads the rules of the house to one of her prostitutes, who stands before her. The girl's body is covered with a tight, pitch-black garment, the frilled ends of which reveal naked flesh. Beerbohm described the picture as follows: "The little one stands before her, her hands on her back, winking roguishly." Beardsley wrote in a letter that the uproar caused by *The Yellow Book* pleased him immensely. Again and again he was the target of attacks, with his "inexcusably far-fetched" pictures, which hardly ever illustrated texts but, rather, appeared as autonomous drawings. In the third issue Beardsley printed two drawings appealing to conventional taste. They were signed with an unfamiliar name. These, among all the illustrations, were sanctioned by the critics, who recommended to Beardsley that he let these expert drawings serve as an instructive example. Beardsley then gloatingly revealed to his critics that he had created both drawings.

Beardsley was at the pinnacle of his success. He had achieved material security and a degree of fame that strengthened his self-confidence, which was necessary, especially since the doctors had told him that he had only about five years to live. Beardsley pretended to manage his life and work effortlessly. He frequented cafés, mingled with artists and literary men, attended concerts and theater productions and never appeared to work at all. However, he worked through the night into the early morning hours and consequently suffered frequent catastrophic breakdowns. Then came the surprising collapse of *The Yellow Book,* which was just gaining ground when Beardsley pulled the rug from under it. The whole thing was based on a misunderstanding that the conventional press, which Beardsley had long since made into a tenacious opponent, maliciously played up.

While Lane, the publisher of both *The Yellow Book* and Oscar Wilde's works, was on a rather lengthy visit to America, Oscar Wilde was arrested. (Beardsley was originally supposed to accompany him but declined because of his health.) Wilde was reproached for moral offenses dealing with his fondness for young boys, which was an open secret. Beardsley's name was mentioned during the proceedings, but he was never involved in the trial. However, an incidental detail had more serious consequences. As Wilde was brought into the police station, he was carrying a book that happened to have a yellow cover. The book was the French novel, *Aphrodite,* by Pierre Louis, but no one wanted to know that. The press gave a detailed but different account: "Wilde took his buckskin gloves in one hand and grasped a cane in the other. Then he took a copy of *The Yellow Book* and placed it under his left arm." Wilde himself had never contributed to the magazine, but the press had among other things already apostrophized *The Yellow Book* as "Oscar Wilde among the magazines," and many people had already associated Wilde with Beardsley since their collaboration on *Salomé*. The public attacks against *The Yellow Book* became more and more vehement, and the publisher believed that by dismissing Beardsley as art editor he could save the magazine in which he had invested so much money. He telegraphed Beardsley's dismissal from Boston and announced that none of the material planned for the next edition would be used. When this expurgated edition appeared, a critic of *The Times* wrote of a general tone of striving for the healthy, as was hitherto unobserved. Yet another critic later remarked that after Beardsley's dismissal the magazine became gray and monotonous overnight, even if the now powerless and entirely serious periodical did manage to tortuously produce nine more issues. Finally, while sales continued to diminish, it was discontinued. *The Yellow Book* had existed for just four years. Beardsley was art editor for only one of those years (1894), when four issues were published. Together with his tubercular attacks Beardsley was plagued more and more frequently with another malady, intoxication, which was more difficult to hide than his tuberculosis.

Surprisingly, a new opportunity presented itself. Although it was overshadowed by the preceding events, it forced him to fulfill previously awakened expectations to which he had not unconditionally wanted to commit himself. It was Leonard

Smithers who offered Beardsley the new chance. Smithers had given up his law practice for the book business, where he dealt in bibliophilic rareties and especially "under the counter" erotica and pornography. Wilde also knew him and described him in a letter from prison to his friend, Reggie Turner: "His face, smoothly shaven, as becomes a priest, who serves the art of literature on the altar of God, is devastated and pale — not from the art of literature, rather from the men of letters, who have sentenced him to ruin, as he said, through their demands to be published by him. He loves first editions, especially in women: his passion is for small girls. He is the most cultured erotomaniac in all Europe. Besides he is delightful company and a nice man." He was a man of the world, as other descriptions characterize him, who constantly appeared in the company of dubious, often even ugly, ladies. Beardsley had made his acquaintance as far back as the heyday of *The Yellow Book,* as he looked over, borrowed or purchased books in his shop.

Beardsley's dismissal by Lane brought Smithers to the idea of founding an opposition magazine, and Beardsley was happy with such an offer, even if it yielded far less financially. He suggested the title, *The Savoy,* after a London hotel frequented by the members of the rich and fashionable world. Beardsley was able to entice fourteen of the total thirty-five collaborators of *The Yellow Book* to work for *The Savoy*. Again, Beardsley contested the layout (pls. 108-113, 115-120). However, Beardsley's illness delayed the hasty beginning of the new project. A sojourn in Dieppe with its stimulating sea climate renewed his will to work, but hemorrhages and exhaustion were also the results of this stimulating climate. Beardsley withdrew to Paris, accompanied by his mother and sister as always. Here he sought further collaborators for *The Savoy,* while working on another contract that promised success, the illustrations to Alexander Pope's *The Rape of the Lock*.

Pope's *The Rape of the Lock* was a parody of both poetry and aristocratic society. In reference to the rape of Helen as cause for the Trojan War, the rape of a lock of hair from the head of a distinguished lady became the point of departure for the battle for her virtue. He cleverly employed all the epic stylistic devices. The courteous vanities of the rococo society were as inflated as the self-images of the aristocrats. The verse epic thrives upon the contrast between imagined and actual reality. For Beardsley it was the artificiality of the first component that attracted him to the material. Beardsley's illustrations (compare pls. 98 - 106) revelled in the artificial, overrefined atmosphere of French rococo fantasies, for which his Paris visit offered the most multifarious stimuli and illustrative material. While working on this project he developed a new style, to which the drawings owe their great appeal. Beardsley no longer worked with his characteristic black surfaces, contrasting empty white spaces, and expressively drawn arabesquelike outlines; rather, he developed a style in which spaces cross-hatched into small sections and drawings composed of little dots give the appearance of grace and light. The atmosphere of the pictures with their beautiful women in deep décolleté, the buildings of hairdressers, the splendidly coiffed gentlemen in their richly patterned justaucorps, tight hose, and high heels, recalls Hofmannsthal's *Rosenkavalier,* which appeared approximately fifteen years later. Hofmannsthal may have been familiar with Beardsley's pictures. A relationship did at least exist between the two artists in that art nouveau legitimately adopted rococo motifs, which may also be strongly observed in Munich and Vienna. In these masterpieces Beardsley was successful in differentiating various media graphically, which, as in the *Cave of the Spleen* (pl. 104), appear in voluptuous diversity. The varying gray effects are only occasionally accentuated by small areas of pure black and white. The title page has a nearly sacred-solemn effect. An oval framed by candelabras bears a pair of open scissors and the shorn lock (pl. 106).

After Beardsley barely survived nearly fatal hemorrhages, he returned to London and continued work on *The Savoy.* The first issue was to be presented in time for Christmas, but since so much time had been lost because of Beardsley's illness, the deadline could not be met. In addition, the title page, in which Beardsley had vented his anger with *The Yellow Book,* had to be changed. It depicted a prominent lady strolling through a park and a small page running ahead of her. He is entirely naked under his open coat and is about to urinate on a *Yellow Book* beneath his spread legs (pl. 110). This seemed too risqué even for Smithers who was accustomed to piquant taste, so the drawing was rejected in this form. The extended deadline naturally impaired sales and was a bad omen for the magazine, which actually never did sell well.

It would be wrong, however, to believe that *The Savoy* was a pornographic rather than a literary periodical by reason of the publisher's character and the incidents surrounding the title page. *The Savoy* was clearly literary, as was printed in the prospectus appearing before the first issue:

> We hope that *The Savoy* will be an exclusive literary and artistic periodical. It aims to present literature in its written contributions and art in the form of its illustrations. In attaining this goal, we can only do our best and preserve the established hope that good writers and artists will be interested in seeing their works published alongside the works of other good writers and artists. Readers who expect from this magazine only very well-known or only very obscure names must be unfortunately disappointed. We have nothing against a celebrated artist who deserves to be celebrated, or nothing against an unknown of whom one has not yet seen enough, in order to become better acquainted with him for the time being. We demand from our collaborators nothing other than good work, and nothing but good work is what we are offering our readers. We are making this offer with confidence. We have no recipe and we do not wish any false unity of form or content. We have discovered a new position. We are not realists, not romantics, not symbolists. For us, all art is good that is good art. We hope to appeal to the tastes of intelligent people without having to be original just for originality's sake or clever for advertisement purposes, or timid for the sake of what happened yesterday. It is our intention to publish no verse that can not claim to be poetry, no belle-lettres that have no feeling for the beautiful in today's world, no criticism that lacks discernment and justice. We can hardly say more and are satisfied that we can hardly say less.

For the most part the critics reacted hostilely to the new project. Only the *Sunday Times* praised it as a *Yellow Book* without its childhood diseases, but it expressed the reservation that the English short story would probably never attain the standard of its French sister as in the short stories of Maupassant.

Meanwhile, Beardsley was pursuing his literary ambitions, writing partially in verse and partly in prose. The work with which he was most occupied was the legend of Tannhäuser, which he entitled, *Under the Hill*. The tale, which remains incomplete, thrived on erotic illustrations, including *The Toilette of Helen* (pl. 113), which corresponds with similar illustrations by Beardsley:

> Helen let her negligée glide behind her and raised herself to the mirror in an undefinable shower and fluttering of lace, trimmings and flounces. She was adorable long and slender, her back and shoulders were wonderfully drawn and the small malicious breasts, full of that irritating attractiveness, which no one can totally understand or fully enjoy. Her arms and hands were limber and small boned, and her legs were divinely long, twenty-two inches from the hip to the knee, and twenty-two inches from the knee to the heel, as befit a goddess. Whoever has seen Helen only in the Vatican, in the Louvre, in the Uffizi or in the British Museum, can not imagine how beautiful and sweet she looked in reality. . . . As her toilette was finished, all the doves gathered around her feet; she loved to have her ankles stroked with feathers; the dwarfs clapped their hands, stuck their fingers in their mouths and whistled. Sporion in the corner, looked up from his puzzle and trembled.

Abbé Fanfreluche, who sought out Helen in her closed world, was invited by Sporion to participate in a bacchanalia. Beardsley described himself in Sporion's image as a tall, slim, morally depraved young man with a slightly bent back, an uneasy gait, an oval, heartless face with olive skin which is drawn tightly over the bones, full, scarlet lips, Japanese slit eyes, and thick, golden hair.

The critical reviews of Beardsley's literary attempts were not good. They spoke of "phantastic twaddle, without coherence, art, or meaning — nothing but tiresome silliness, that yields nothing," and of pedantic pretentiousness. Yet, Beardsley did not give up and was more successful with another work, his *Ballad of a Barber,* for which he also drew the loveliest illustrations in the same dot technique as in *The Rape of the Lock,* albeit more frugally and cautiously (pl. 119). The ballad dealt with a hairdresser who could give the most boring creature an intelligent appearance. One day he had to dress the hair of the king's thirteen-year-old daughter who was as beautiful, "lyrical, and soft as a melody by Shubert." However, this beauty overwhelmed the hairdresser and induced him to destroy her: "He seized hold of a bottle of cologne and broke the neck with his hands. The princess let out a soft cry, the cut was sharp and deep: he left her as softly as a dream which leaves the sleeper to his sleep; smiling that all had gone so smoothly, he left the room on tiptoe. They hanged him on Meridian Street. They prayed in vain for Caroussel."

Beardsley never achieved more than indifferent success with his literary works even though he attracted attention through his elaborate wording and his carefully weighed images. In all cases the drawings remain more important. While working for *The Savoy* he also created major works which justified the fame he gained in these years. They include illustrations to *Rheingold* (pls. 122, 123), *Ali Baba* (pls. 131, 132), *Volpone* (pl. 137), *Pierrot of the Minute* (pl. 128), and above all Aristophanes' *Lysistrata,* a book which for generations of lawyers was the incarnation of bizarre pornography (pls. 90-97). Perhaps we can better appreciate the witty, sarcastic spirit of Beardsley's representations in the light of contemporary photographic pornography which reflects an empty society thriving on the phallus-cult of pure vanity. The exaggeration of the male organ is derived from the aforementioned Japanese prints. However, here it serves as an earmark of the spiritual impotence of its owner. It parallels the title page to Ben Johnson's *Volpone,* who prays before an altar of heaped, golden vanities — a knowledgeable continuation of the traditional *Vanitas* representations (pl. 137).

The production of these pictures was accompanied by the most grievous physical suffering. Beardsley had to cease work on *The Savoy* and thereby brought on its ruin. Trips to Brussels and to a spa brought temporary relief from his miseries but were followed by even more serious relapses. He wrote from Bascombe to his publisher: "Yesterday I lay hemorrhaging like a corpse. There seemed to be little hope for me and my lungs. Everyone here is friendly to me, flowers and fruit in abundance, which give me absolutely no pleasure. It has been a month now, since I was last able to leave my room and I fear it will be a while until I can even go to the dining hall. It is presumably an act of providence that sent such awful damp weather during this period. I am writing this letter clammy from head to toe."

It is not accidental that Beardsley occupied himself with the *Vanitas* pictures at this time. For some time he had been coming to terms with religious ideas, which were strengthened through the friendship of a recently converted son of a Russian Jewish emigrant, Marc-André Raffalovitch. He supported Beardsley financially, sent him books and introduced him to priests who instructed him in the Catholic teachings. On March 31, 1897, Beardsley made a confession, was accepted into the church and implored his publisher to destroy all obscene pictures, by which he meant above all the *Lysistrata* illustrations.

Considering his work, this religious transformation seems abrupt, and it is not even suggested in his letters. If we are aware, however, that an intellectual Catholicism was gaining ground at the same time that atheism was spreading in Europe, and even if we limit ourselves to the consideration of Beardsley's works, we realize that he was treading a narrow path between atheism and belief. Since both exerted their influence upon him, it was not impossible that he should turn to the latter.

Beardsley had not allowed himself to look into his own soul. The figure of the Pierrot, which extends throughout his creations in all periods as a leitmotif, is an example of this. Just as the Pierrot hides his true nature and sufferings from the world behind his unchanging costume and white painted face, Beardsley hid behind his dandyism and clever puns. Moreover, while producing his artistic creations he shielded himself from the environment, even from the light of day. Once, as a child he envisioned a bleeding crucifix falling off his bedroom wall. He related this in all seriousness and without his usual derision. He may have continued to repress this vision, which must have had an enduring influence on him, just as he may have repressed many religious ideas, clothing them in antitypes. The femme fatale, that sinful bearer of ruin, may have occupied him as a Madonna antitype, for the Madonna image also appears in his creations, not only on the Christmas card of 1896 with its nearly conventional mode of representation (pl. 114), but also in a concealed representation of the Annunciation, *The Mysterious Rose Garden* of 1894, in which a powerful, draped youth with a staff and lantern, whispers a message to a fearful, naked girl standing in front of a rose hedge (pl. 69). In an illustration to the *Ballad of a Barber* a Virgin and Child stand in the background on a chest for no apparent reason. Perhaps they are meant as a symbol of innocence (pl. 119). Around 1896 he drew the ascension of the Peruvian maiden, Santa Rosa, the Rose of Lima (pl. 117). Beardsley himself described in his novel fragment, *Under the Hill,* how the Holy Mary descended, kissed Rosa's forehead and quickly carried her off to heaven. Beardsley's early pictures were also full of religious or cultish allusions, beginning with the pictures of angels and demons in *Morte d'Arthur* and Salomé's desperate attempt to destroy the holy in the work bearing her name. Burning candelabra and altarlike superstructures are often pictured, and the toilettes of his femmes fatales almost recall altars of cultic celebration. On the frontispiece of *A Full and True Account of the Wonderful Mission of Earl Lavender,* dated about 1895, a ceremonial flogging of a naked young girl by a secularized priestess unmistakably refers to the frescoes of the Villa of Mysteries in Pompeii (pl. 86). One critic noted that Beardsley's people had a joyless depravity, as if that burden were a ceremonious social ritual. Beardsley's yearning for redemption is even more clearly evident in his work on the *Tannhäuser* material to which he returned time and time again. Its religious theme was a starting point for the shaping of the text: The knight Tannhäuser entangles himself in sin on the Venusberg, but he is overcome with repentence. He calls for the Virgin Mary's help, and she grants him a temporary return to the world. He makes a pilgrimage to the pope, throws himself at his feet, confesses and asks for the forgiveness of his sins. The pope denies him absolution and says he could no more hope for forgiveness than his papal scepter could produce blossoms. Tannhäuser returns to the Venusberg in despair. However, after three days the papal staff bears green leaves, and the pope orders a thorough search for Tannhäuser, but he can not be found. In Beardsley's drawing Tannhäuser wanders with searchingly outstretched hands through a thicket of thorns. He is represented as a bright figure against a dark landscape (pl. 76). We can see in Tannhäuser a self-portrait just as we can discover self-portraits in many of Beardsley's figures, from our knowledge of his psychological makeup.

In 1897 *A Book of Fifty Drawings by Aubrey Beardsley* was published in London with concluding words by Aymer Vallance. It was a book in memory of himself in which Beardsley collected his best works to be passed on (pl. 129). Three weeks before his death he wrote to a friend: "I am totally shattered and incapable of working. Please do not breathe a word of this to anyone. I have told the people here that I had a slight attack of rheumatism. I will, however, get down to work and at least write something, as long as I am in this condition that prevents me from drawing. And I had devised such great plans. The good saints are my only comfort and give me patience." Thus, the Pierrot-Beardsley hid his face from the world around him till the end, until he could hide nothing more. He died on March 16, 1898, at the age of twenty-five.

He had not only known in advance that he was about to die but had also sketched his death in a drawing in 1898, entitled *Pierrot's death* (pl. 121). He commented on the picture with a few words: "As it grew dark Pierrot fell into his last sleep. Then the comedians Arlechino, Pantaleone, il Dottore and Columbine tiptoed silently up the stairs, and lovingly carried the clown from Bergamo, clothed in white, away, no one knows where."

The Drawings

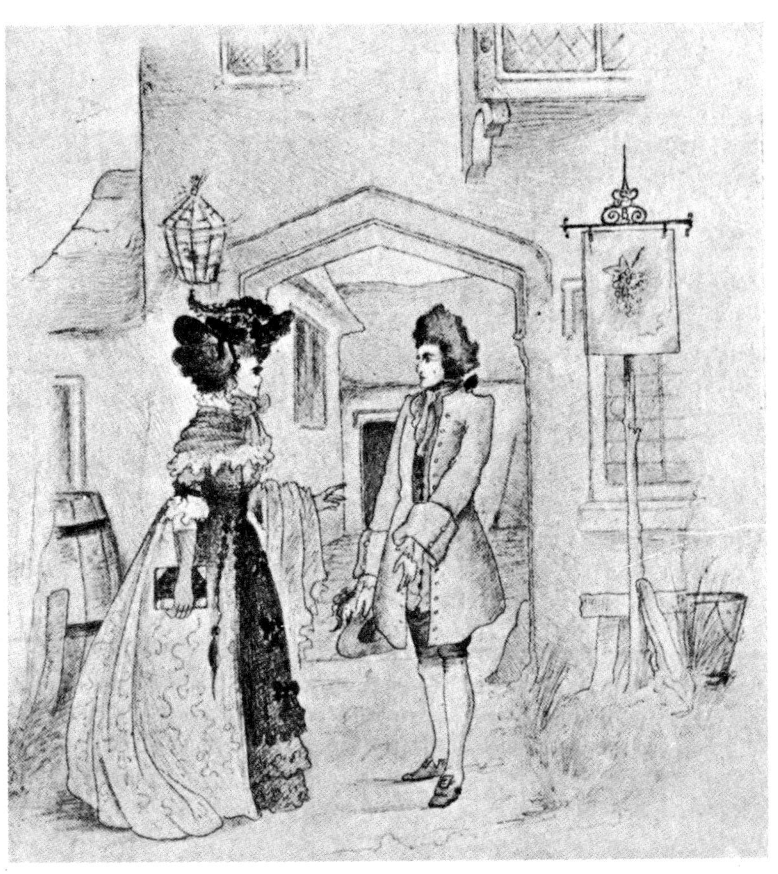

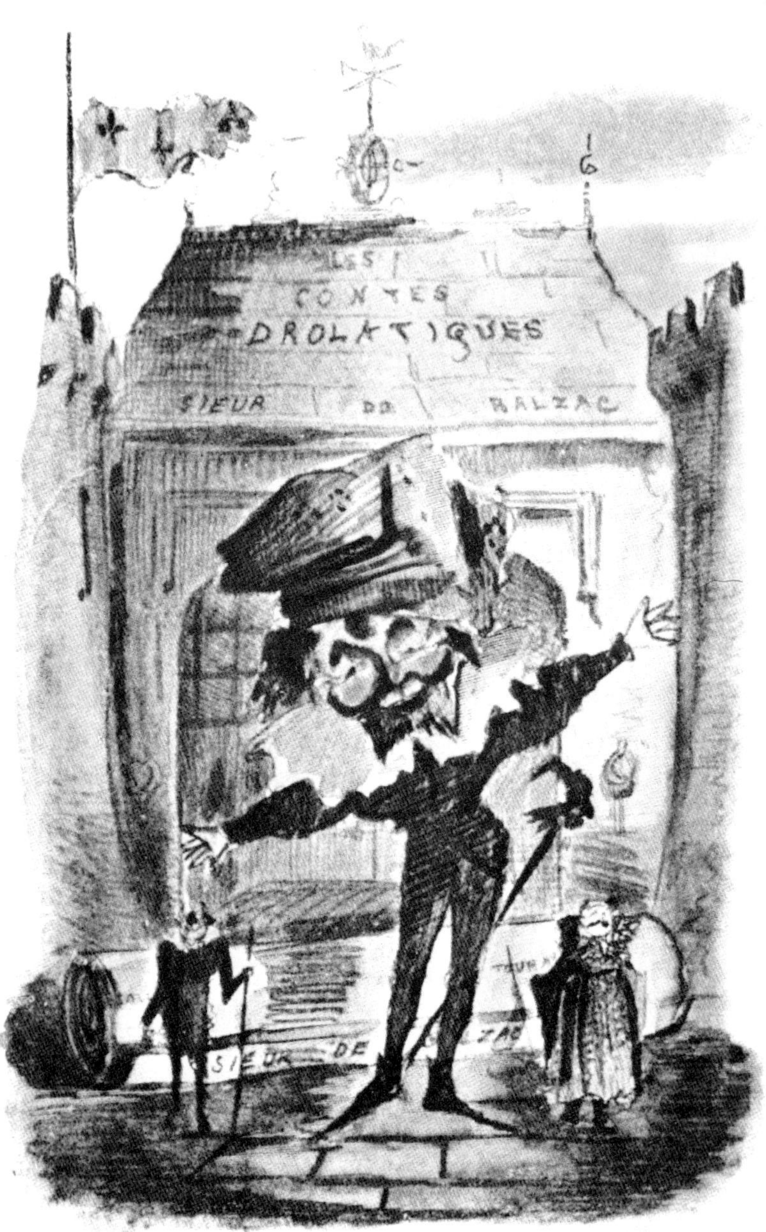
LES
CONTES
DROLATIQUES
SIEUR DE BALZAC
SIEUR DE

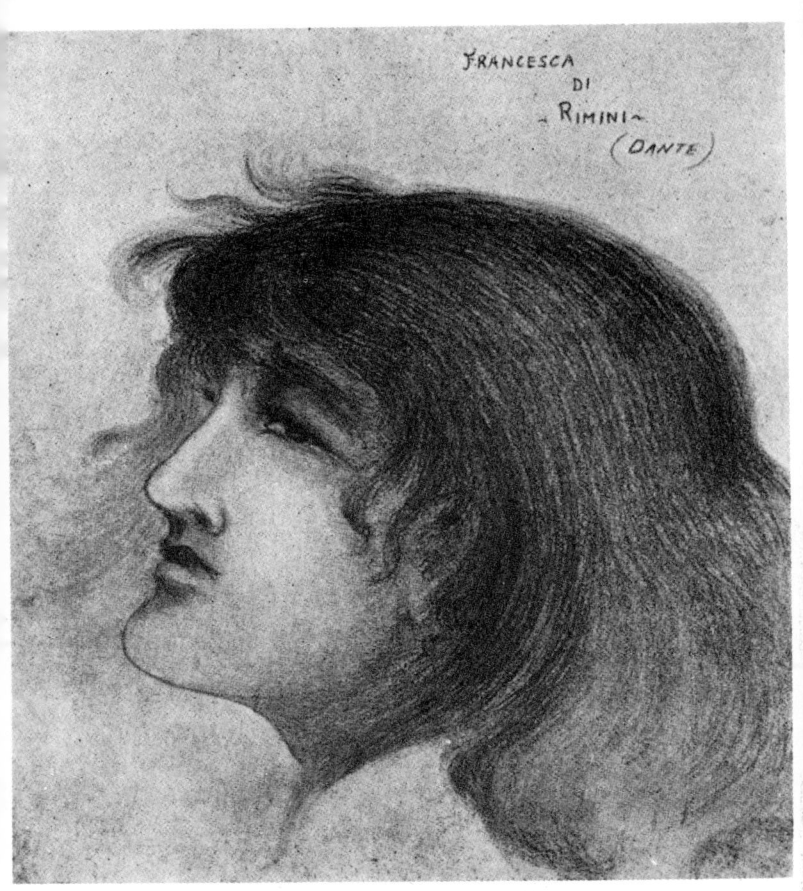
FRANCESCA
DI
RIMINI
(DANTE)

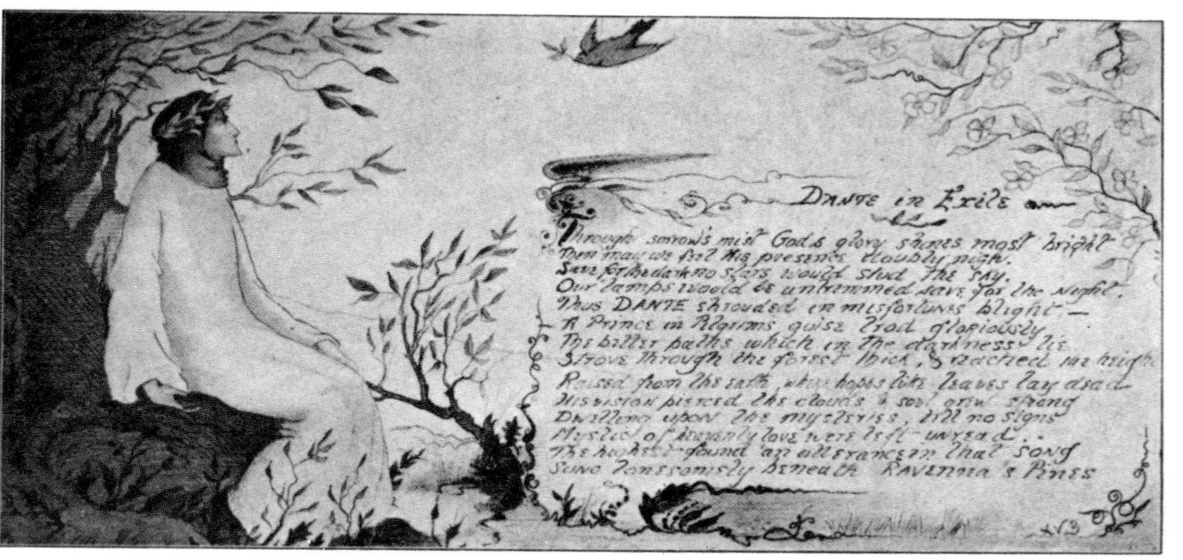
DANTE in Exile
Through sorrow's mist God's glory shines most bright
Then may we feel His presence doubly nigh.
Save for the dark no stars would stud the sky.
Our lamps would be untrimmed save for the night.
Thus DANTE shrouded in misfortune's blight—
A Prince in Pilgrim's guise trod gloriously
The bitter paths which in the darkness lie
Strove through the forest thick, & reached the height
Raised from the earth where hopes like leaves lay dead
His vision pierced the clouds & soul grew strong
Dwelling upon the mysteries, till no signs
Mystical of heavenly love were left unread.
The highest found an utterance in that song
Sung lonesomely beneath RAVENNA'S PINES

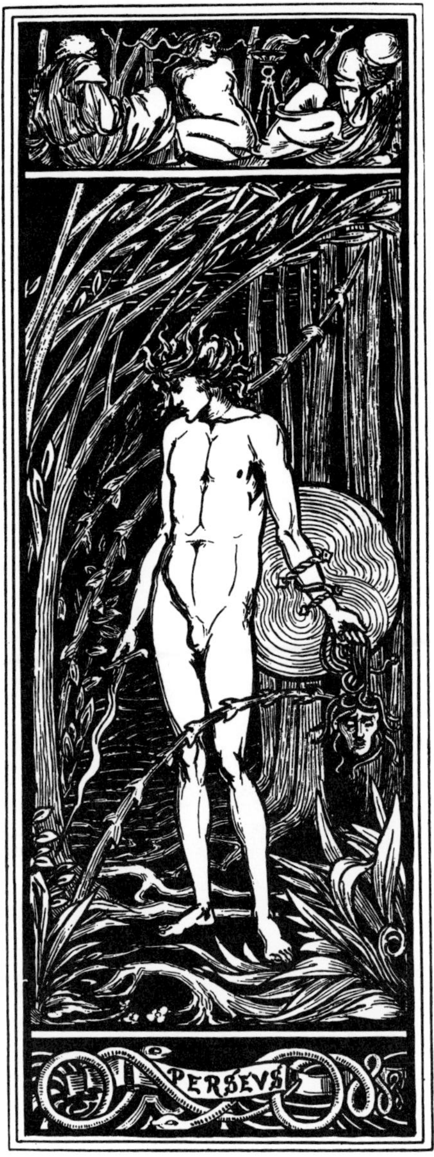
PERSEVS

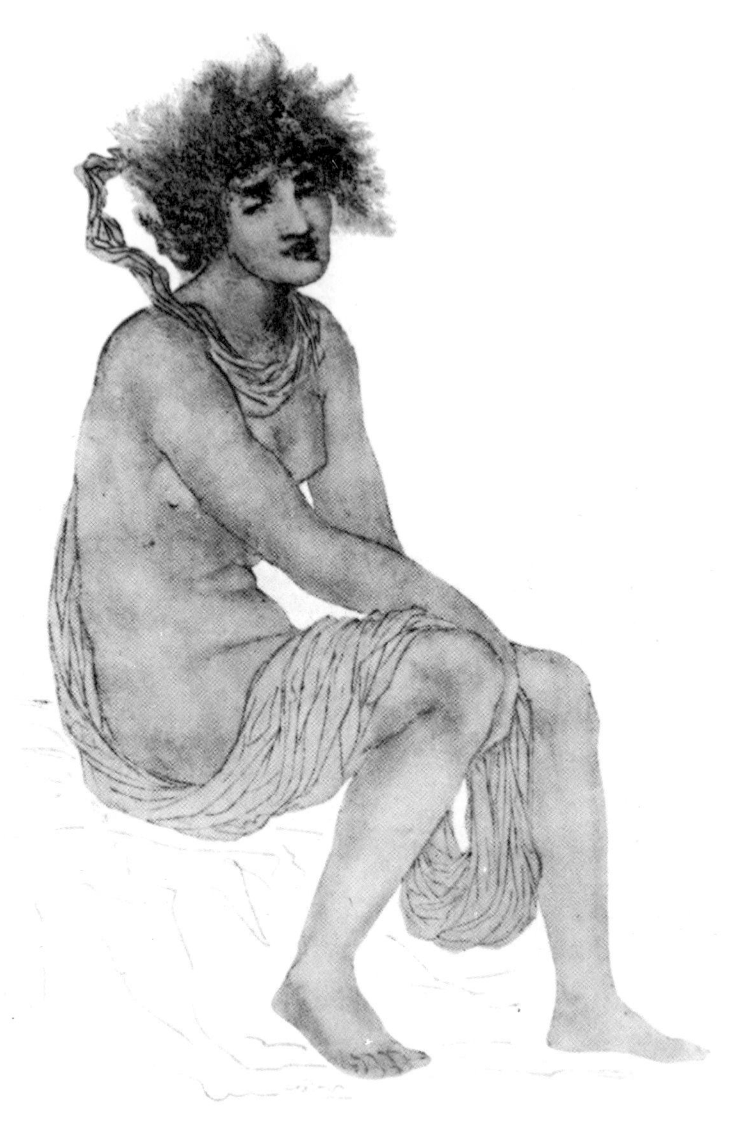

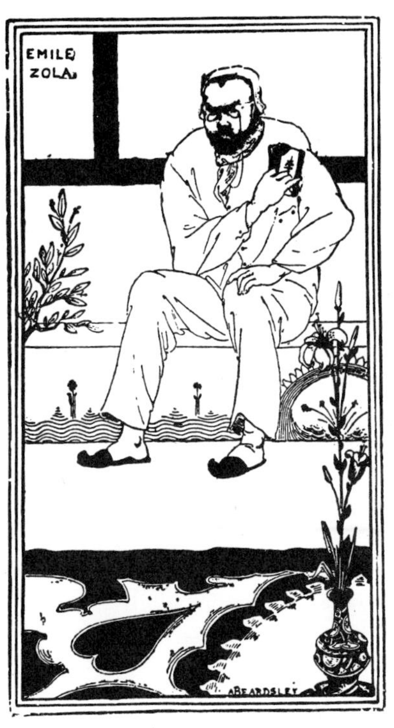
EMILE
ZOLA
A BEARDSLEY

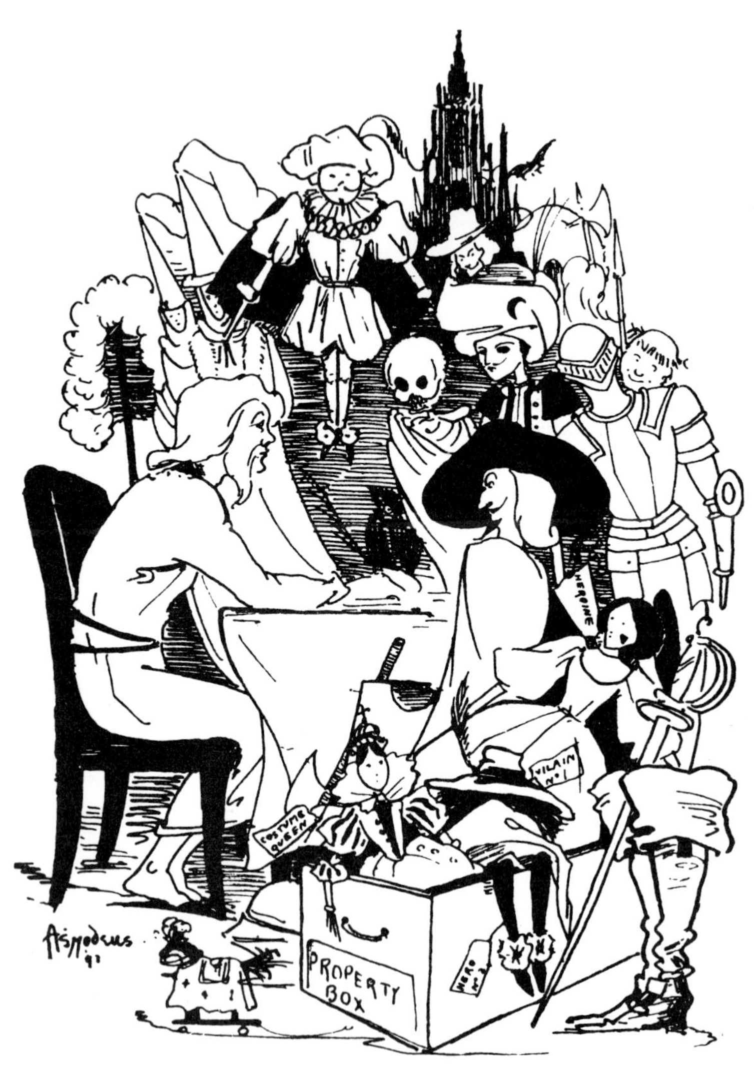
HEROINE
VILAIN No 1
COSTUME QUEEN
PROPERTY BOX
HERO
Asmodeus

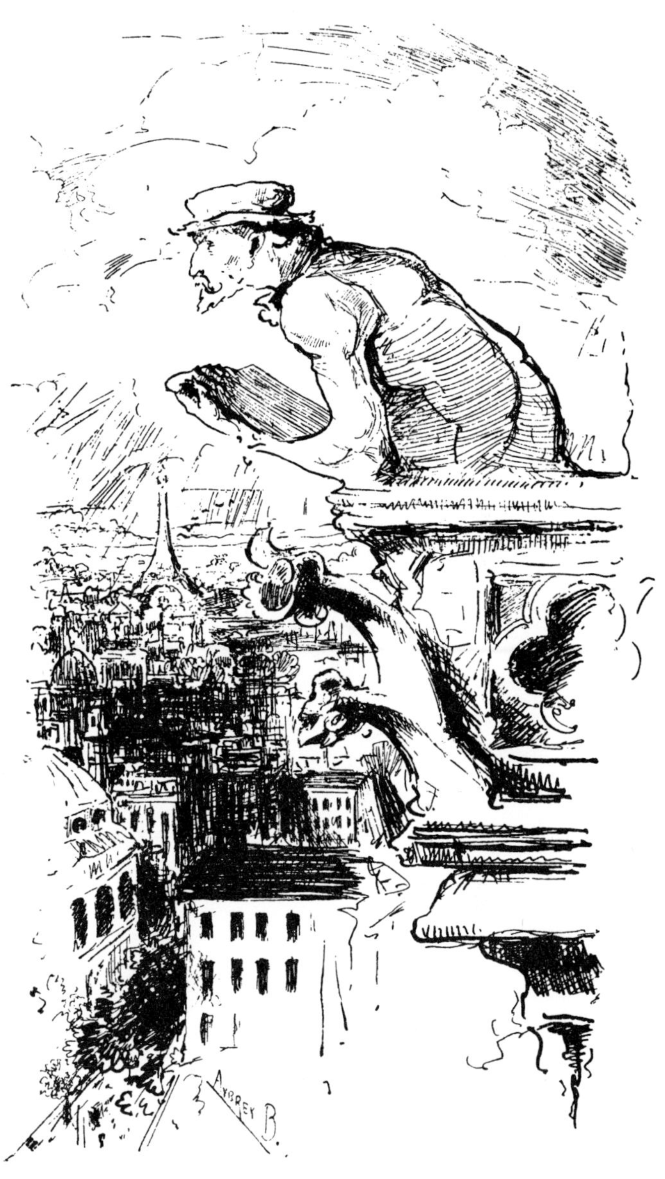
AUBREY B.

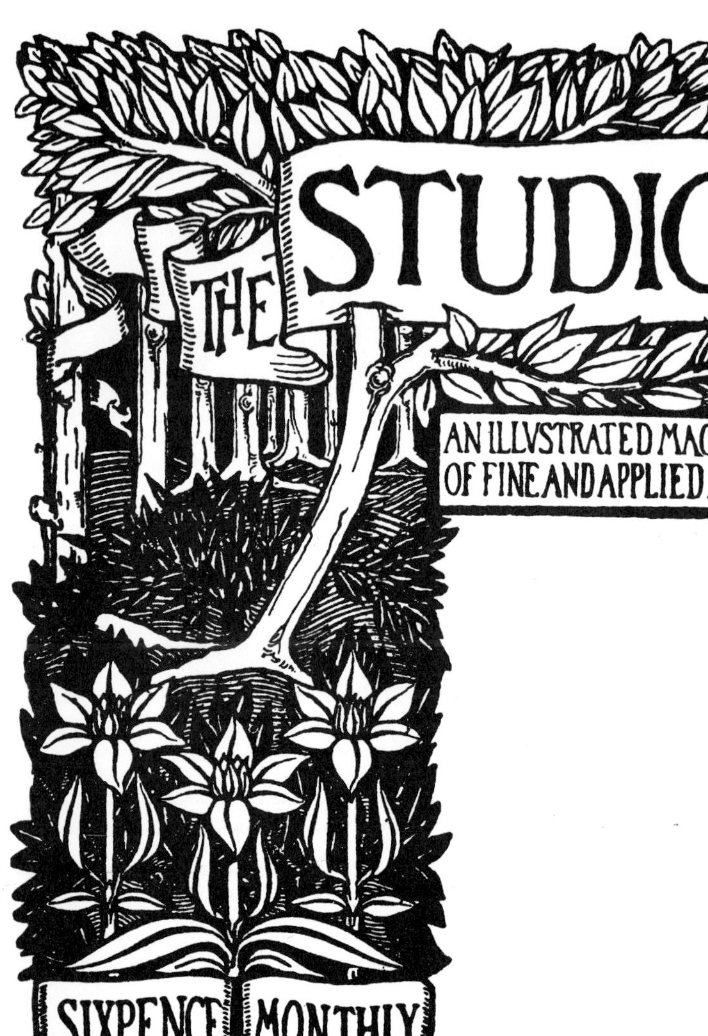
THE
STUDIO
AN ILLVSTRATED MAGAZINE
OF FINE AND APPLIED ART.
SIXPENCE
MONTHLY

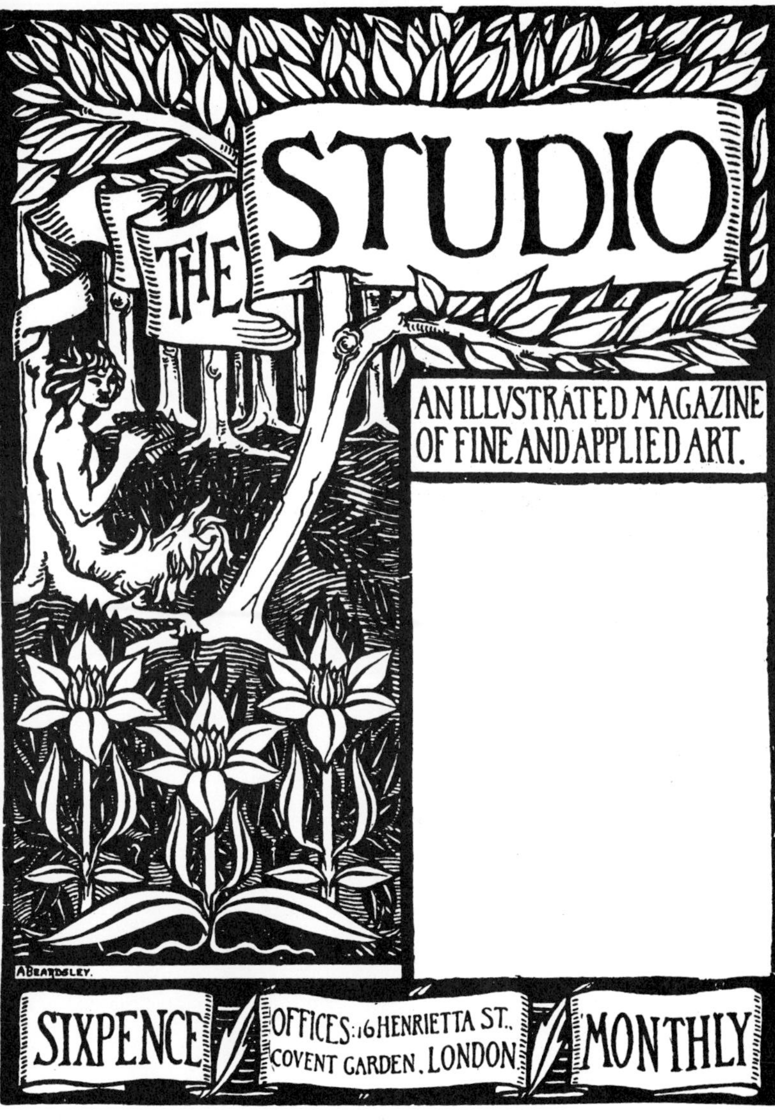
THE STUDIO
AN ILLUSTRATED MAGAZINE OF FINE AND APPLIED ART.
A BEARDSLEY.
SIXPENCE
OFFICES: 16 HENRIETTA ST., COVENT GARDEN, LONDON
MONTHLY

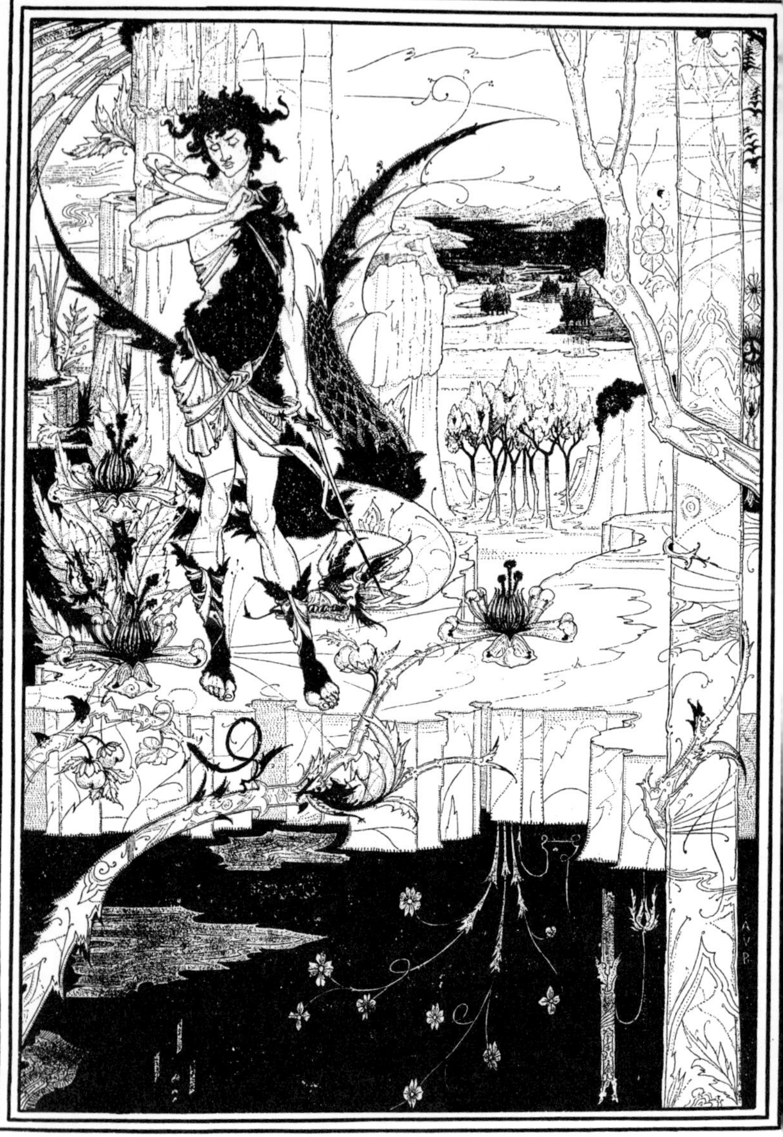

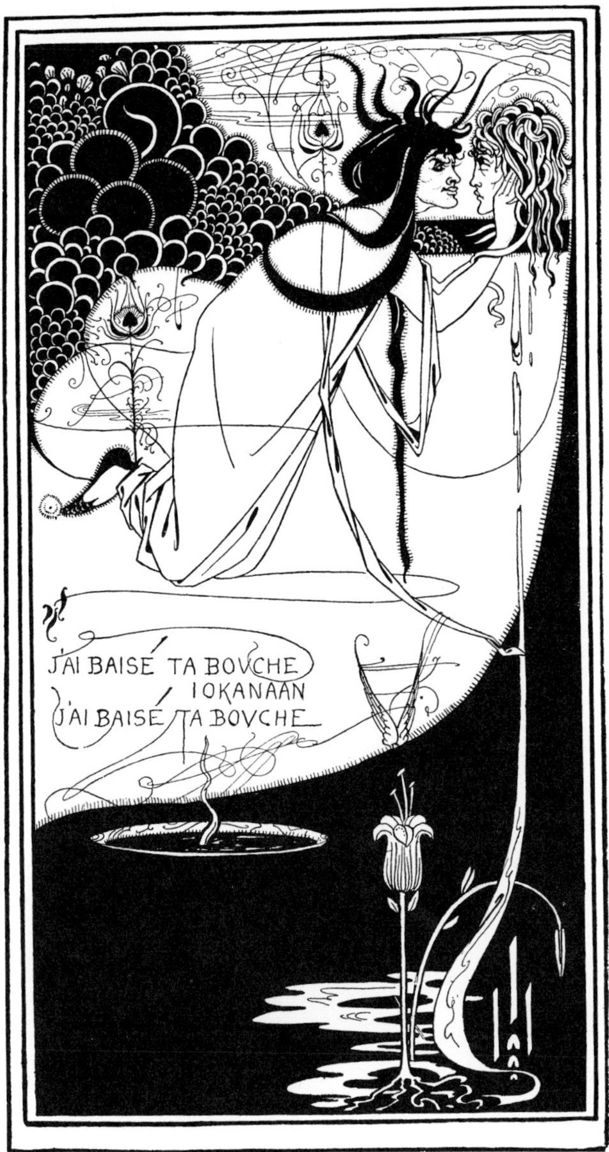
J'AI BAISÉ TA BOVCHE
IOKANAAN
J'AI BAISÉ TA BOVCHE

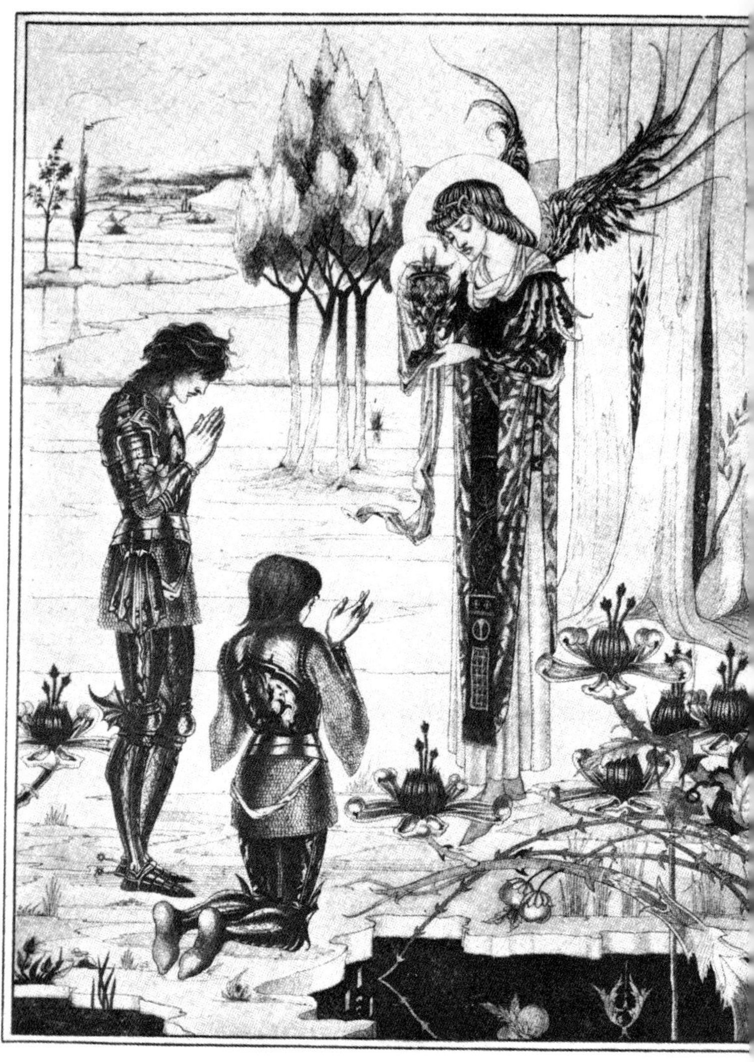

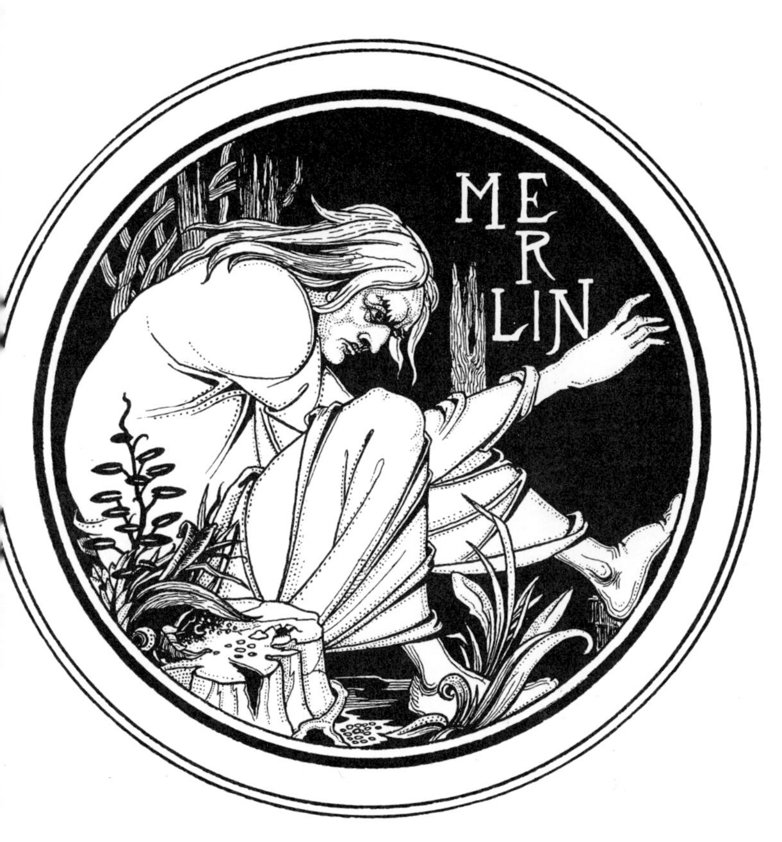
MERLIN

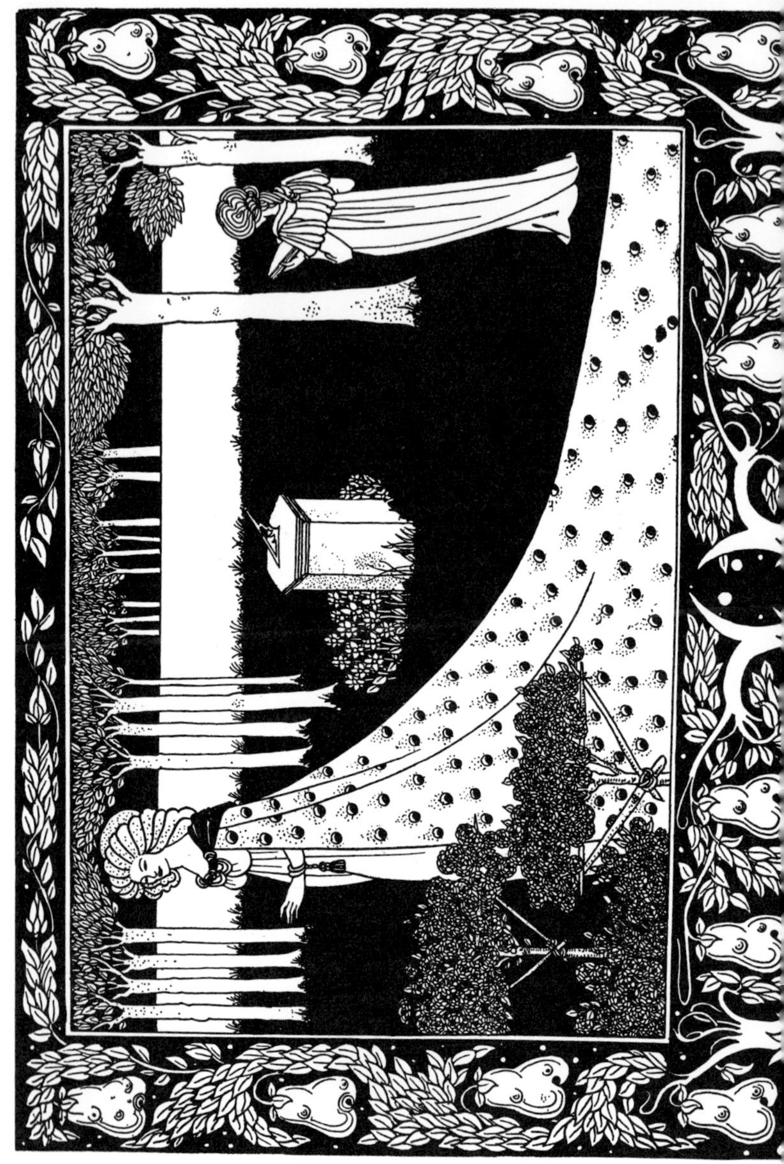

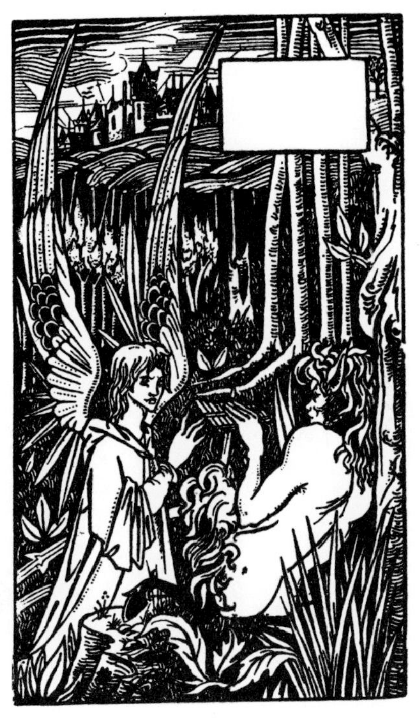

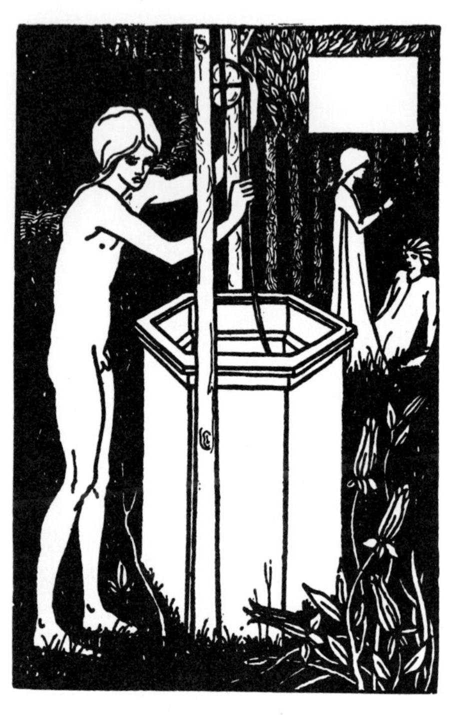

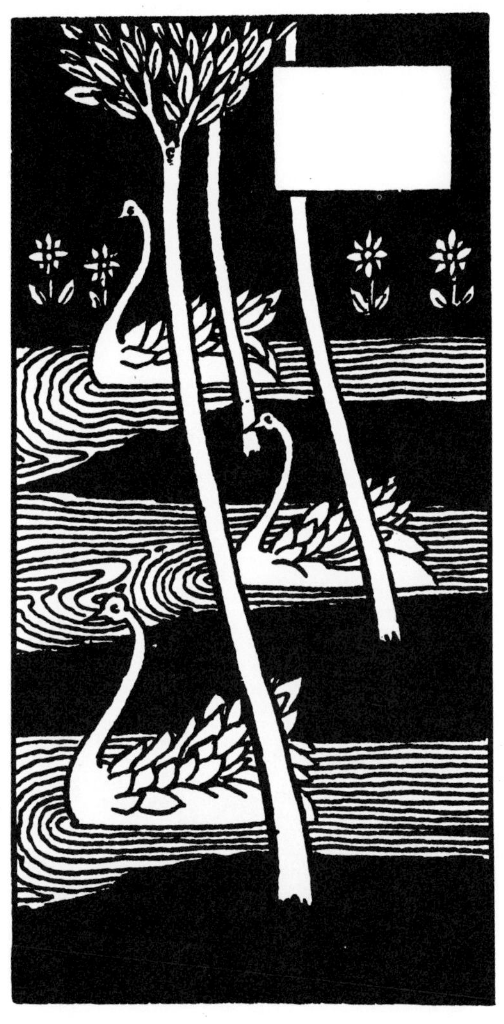

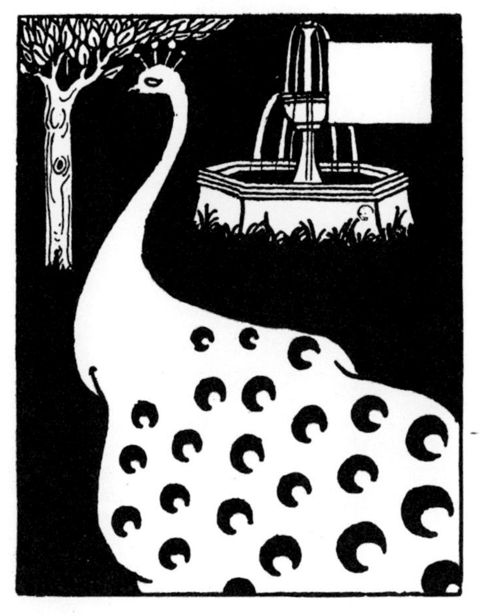

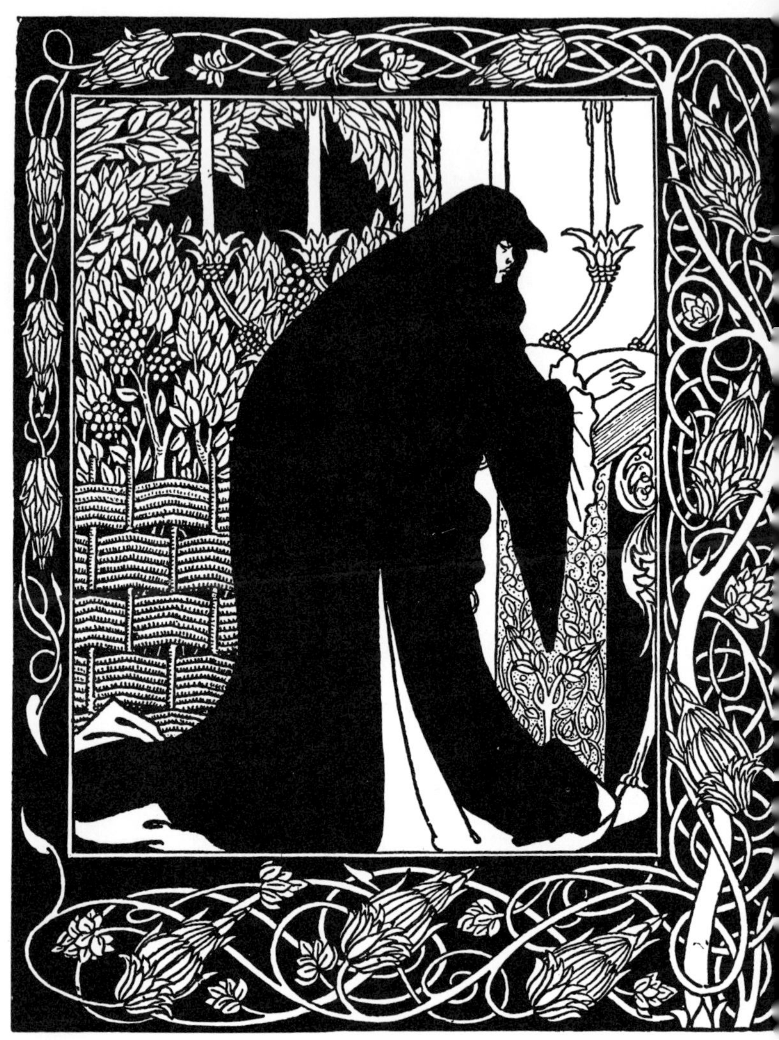

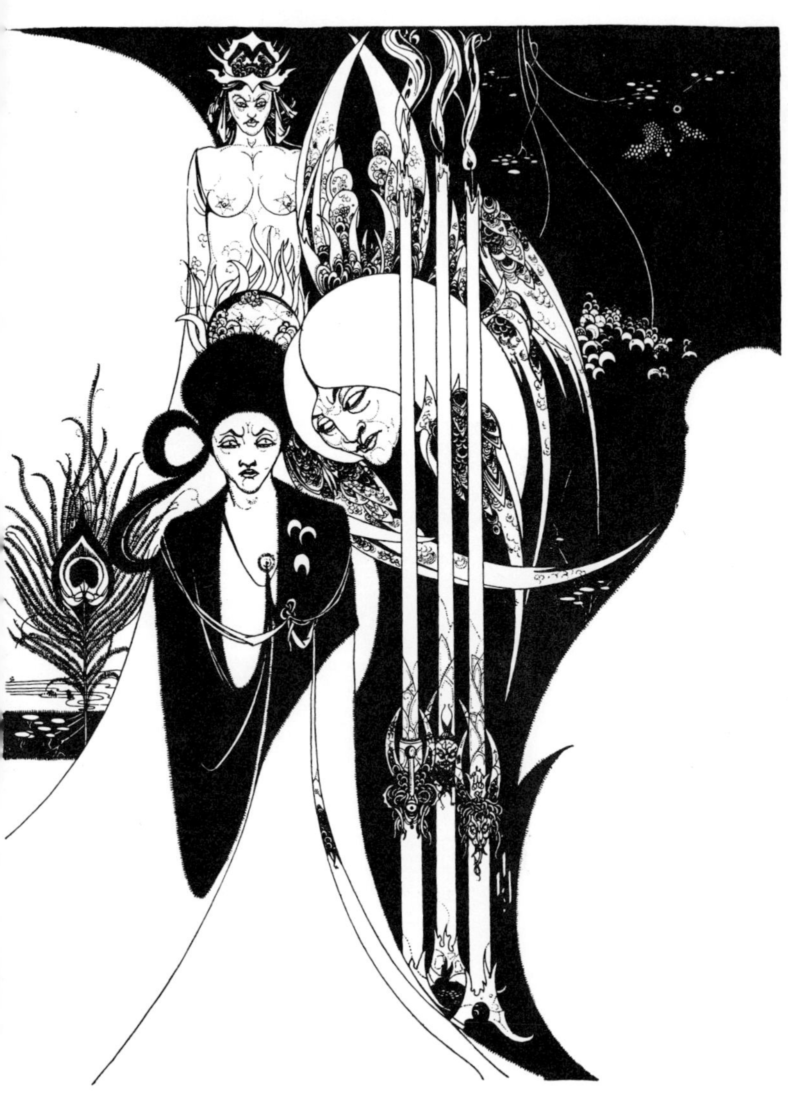

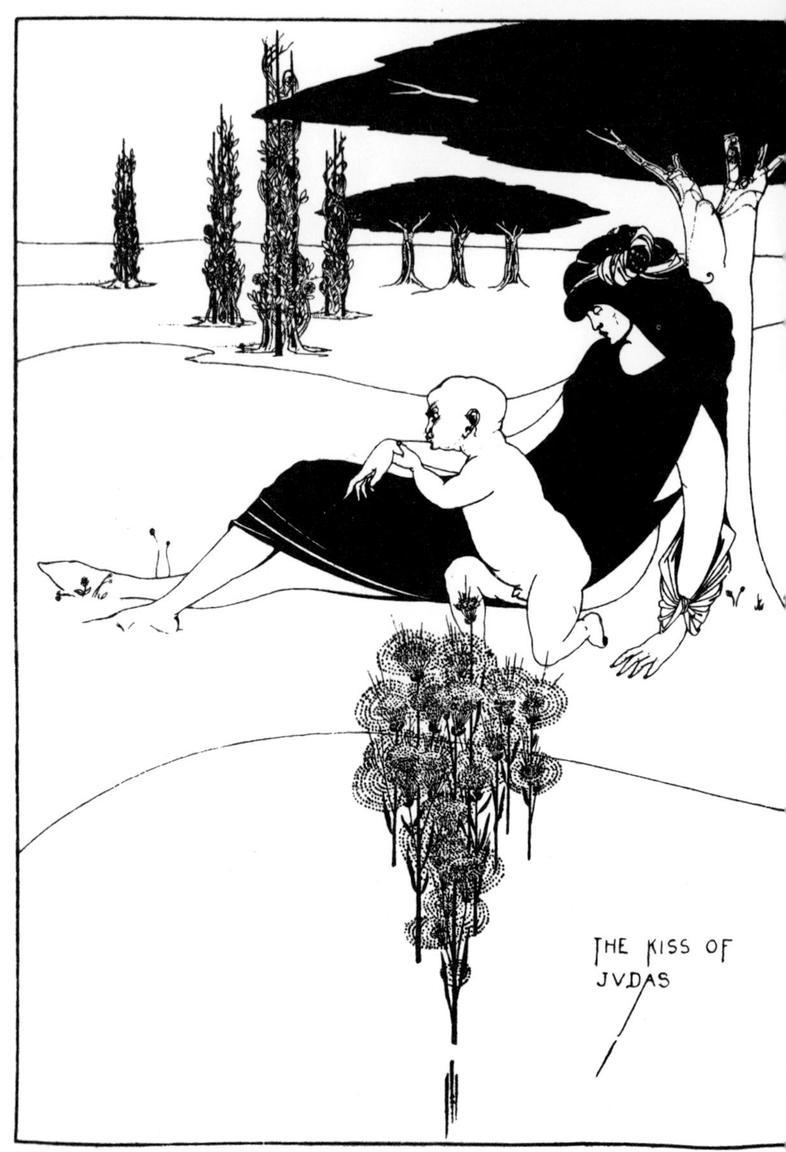
THE KISS OF
JVDAS

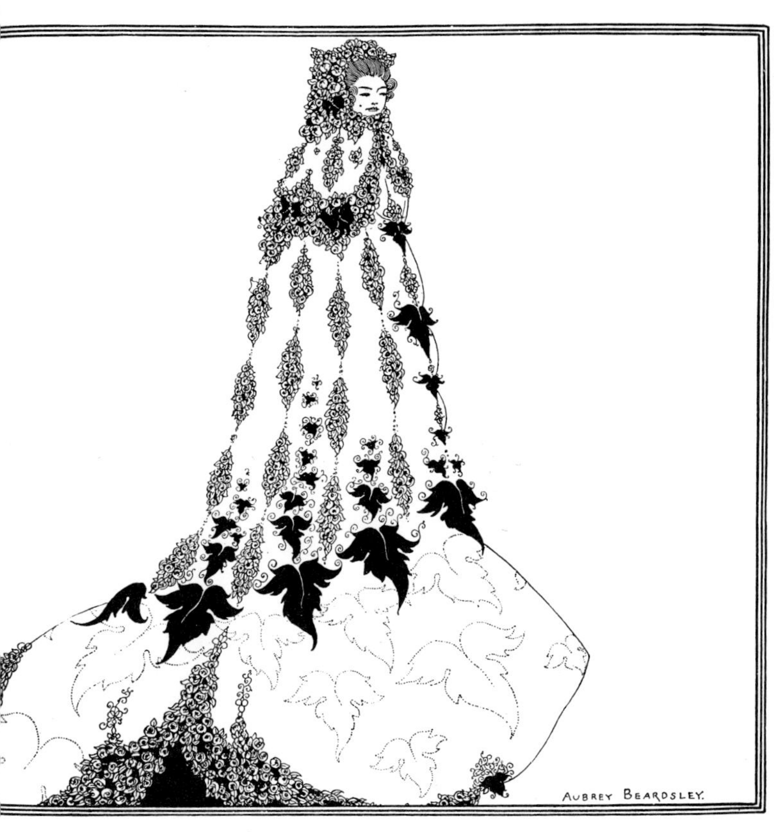
AUBREY BEARDSLEY.

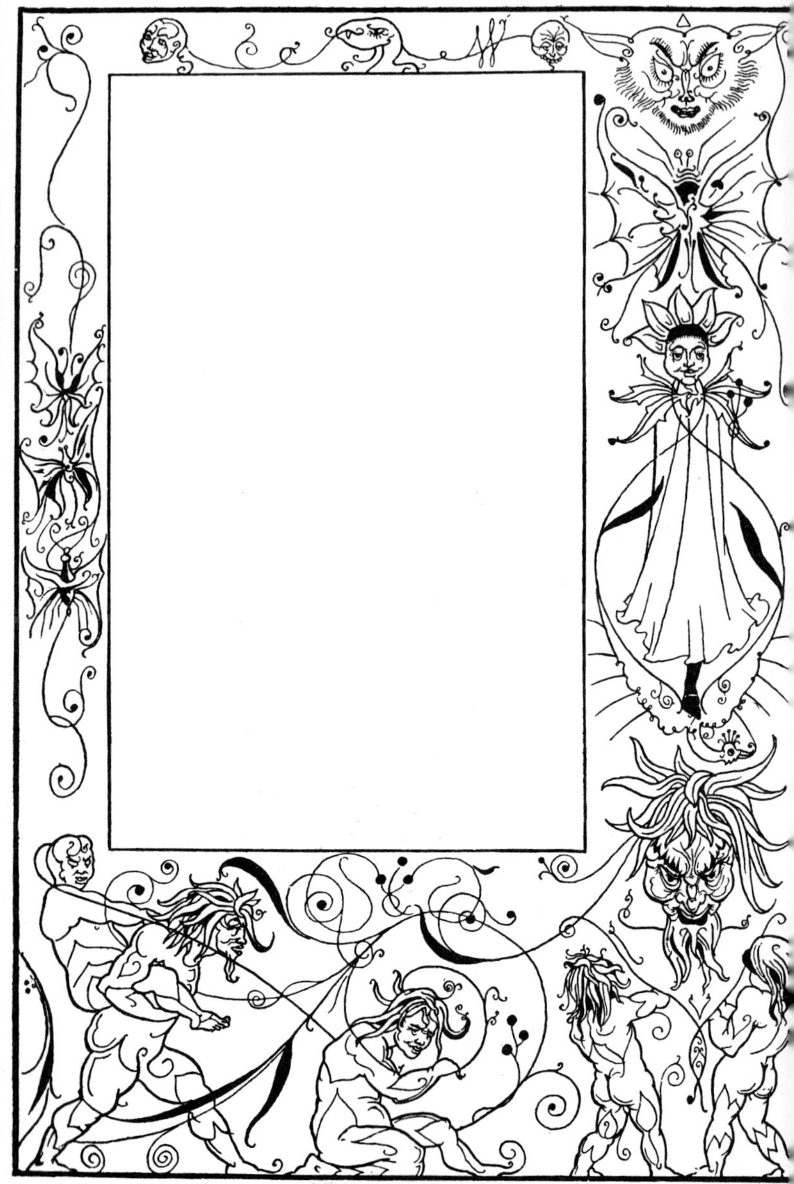

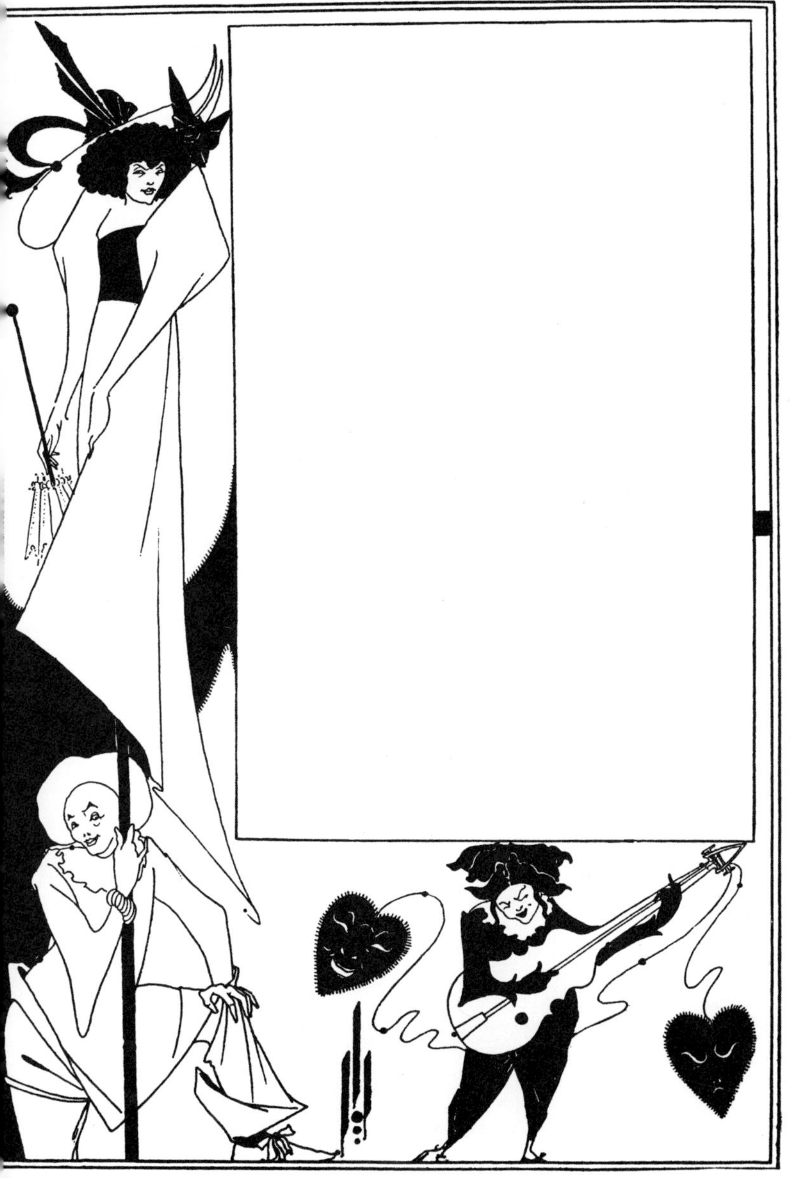

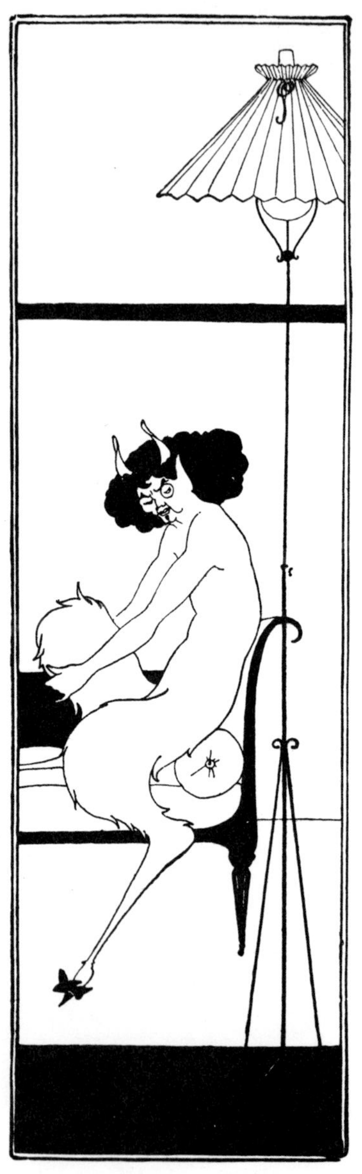

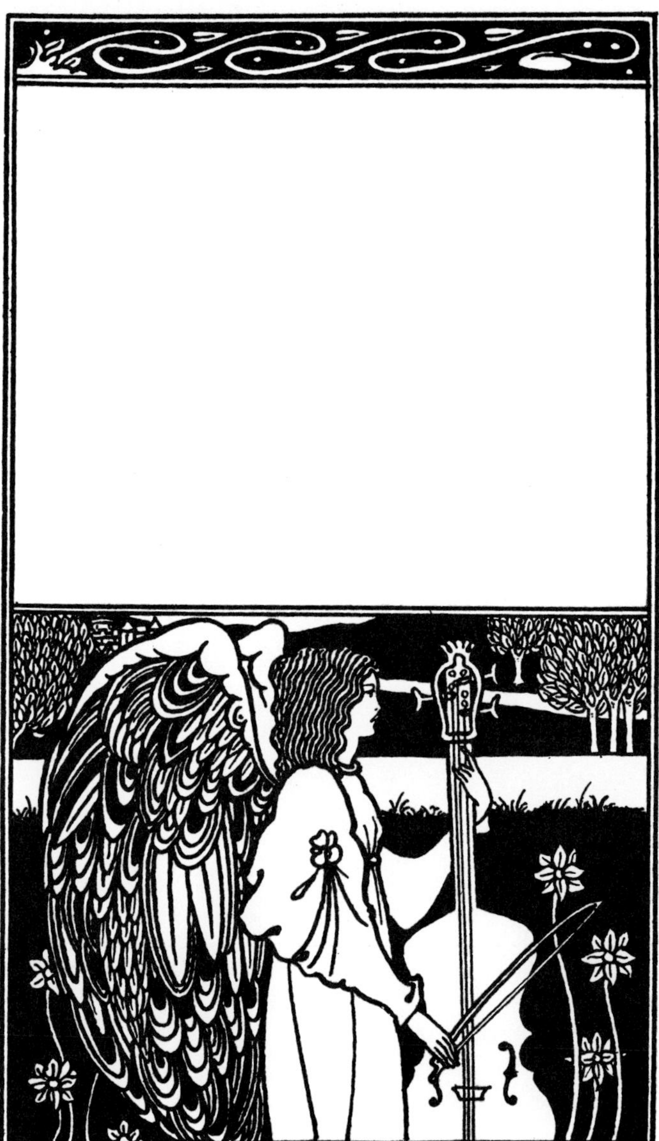

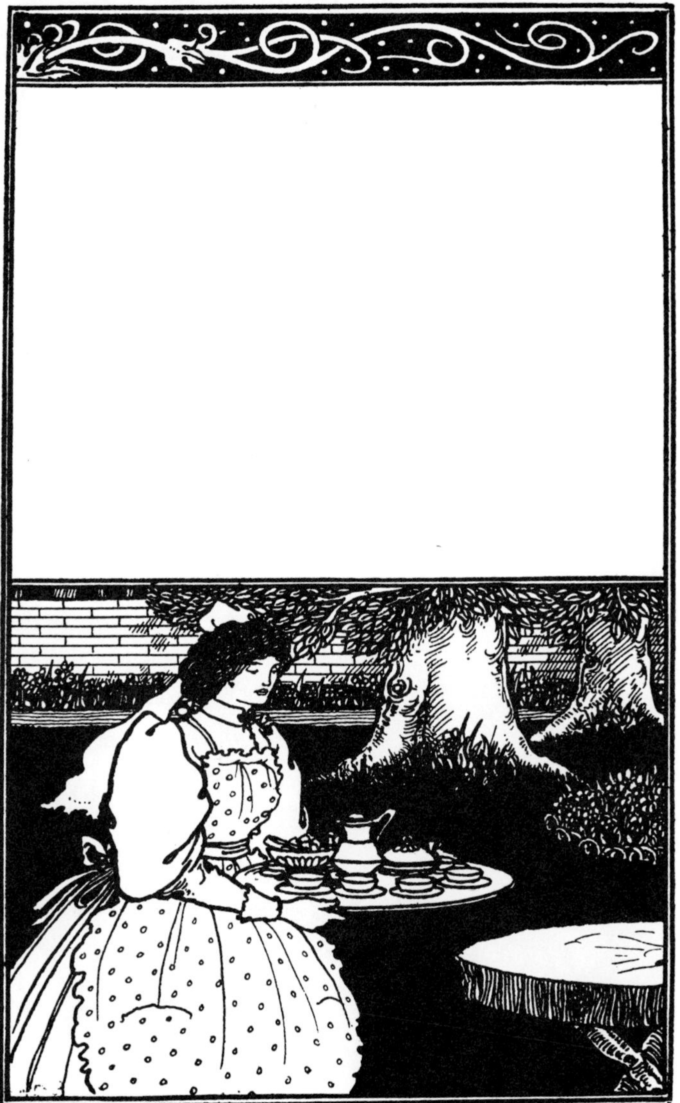

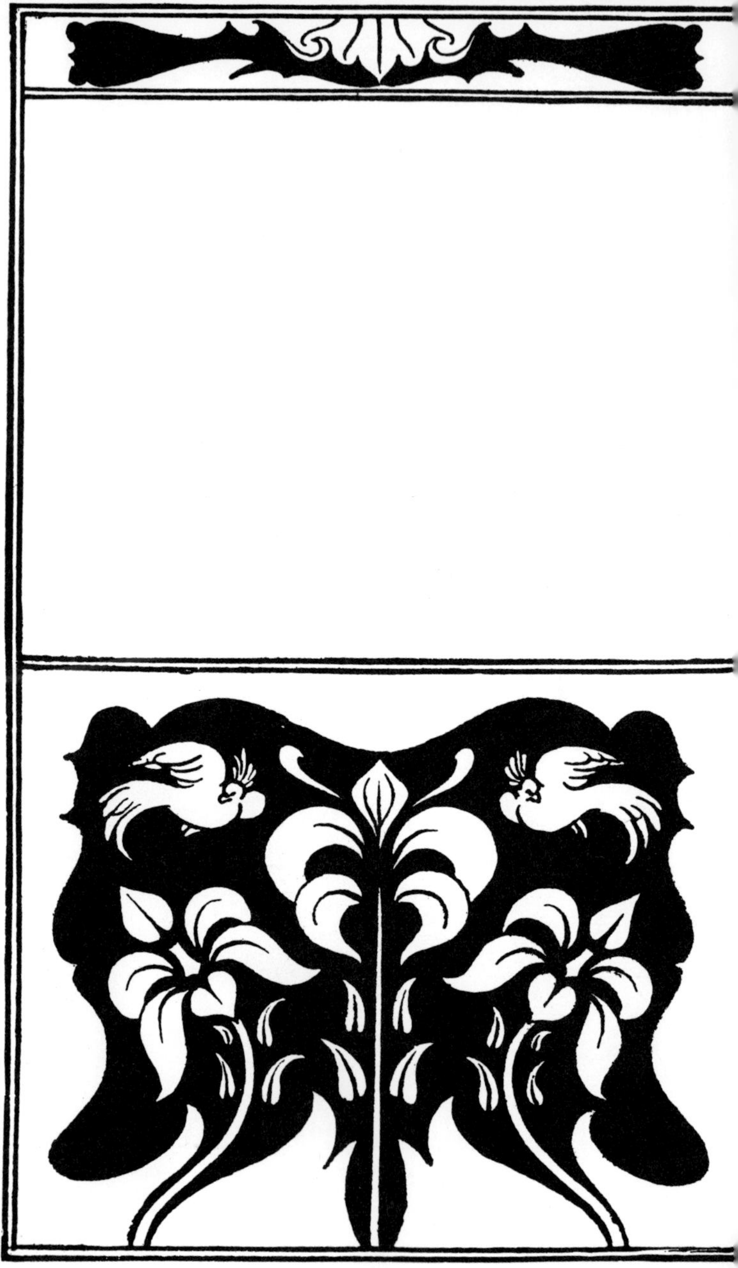

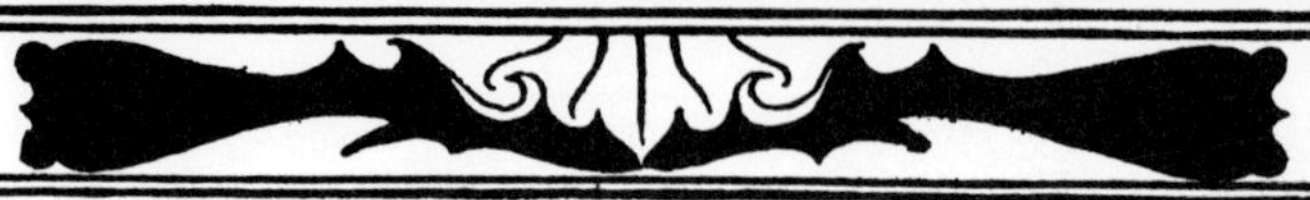

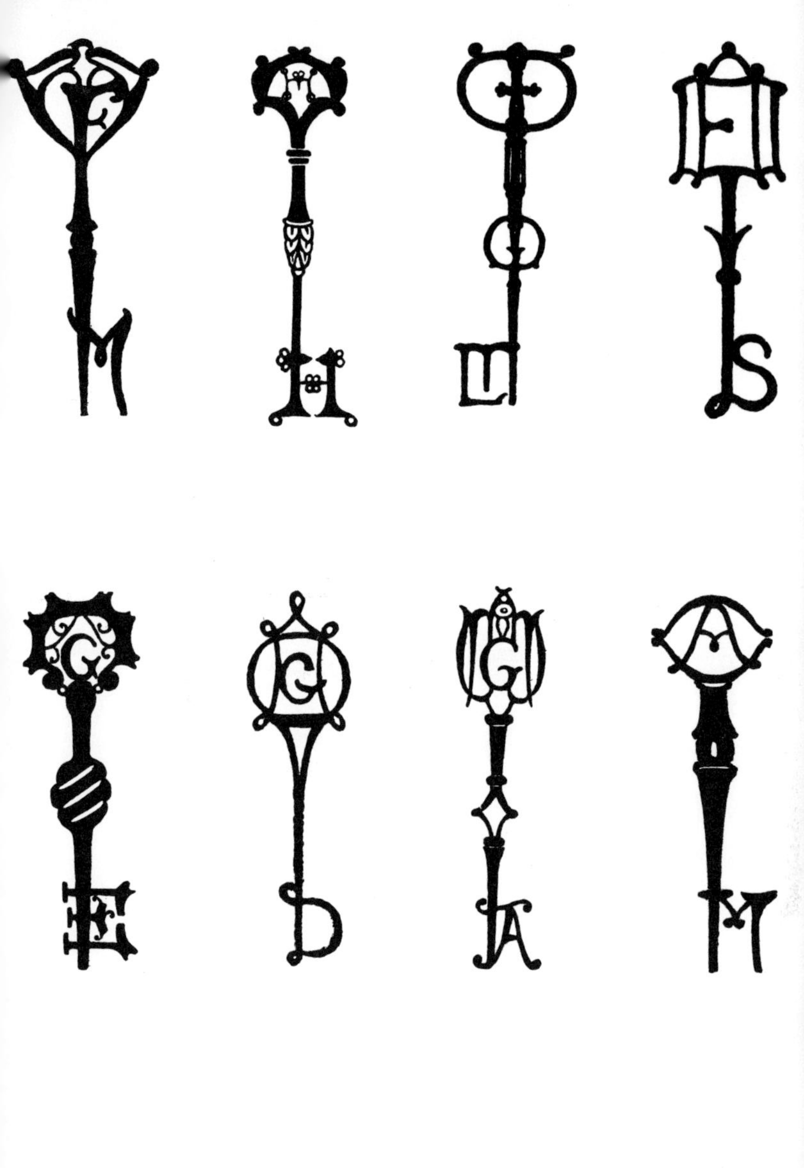

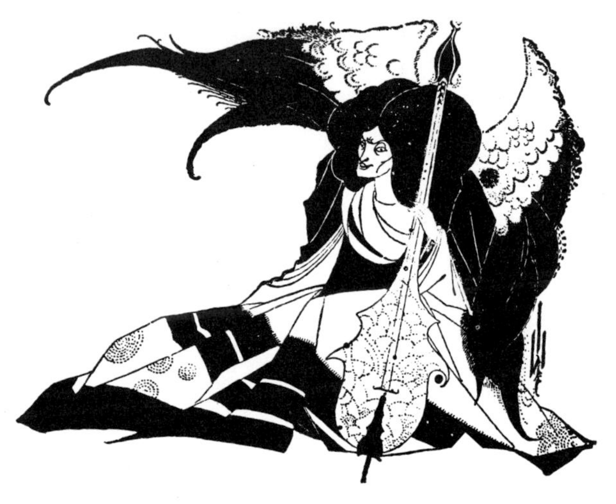

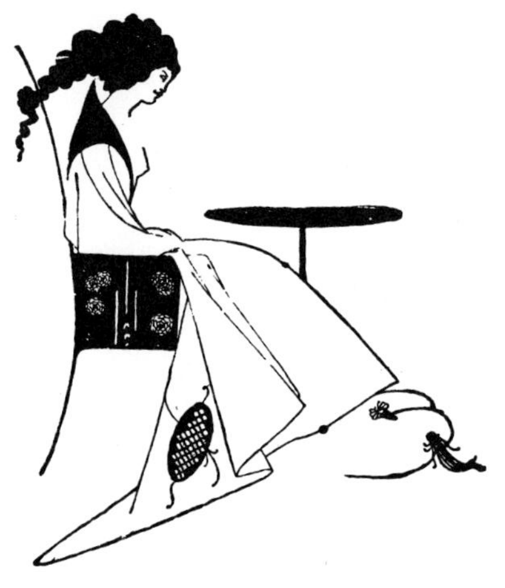

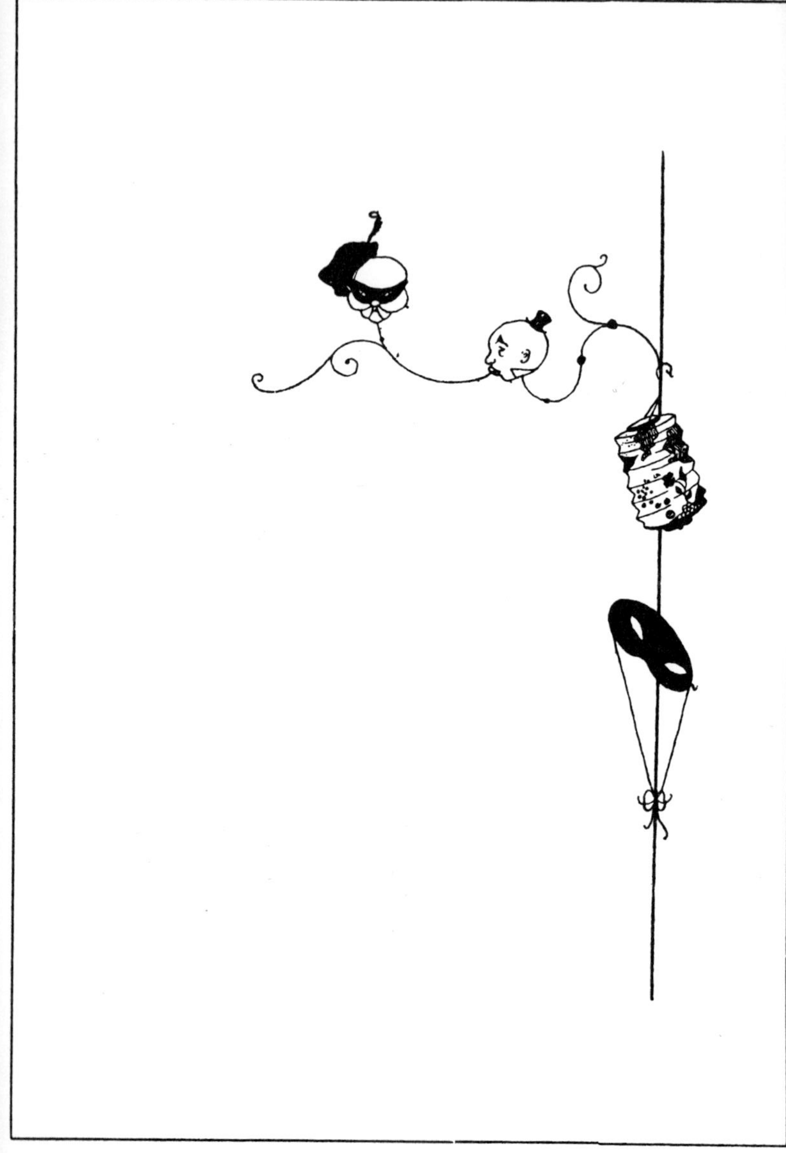

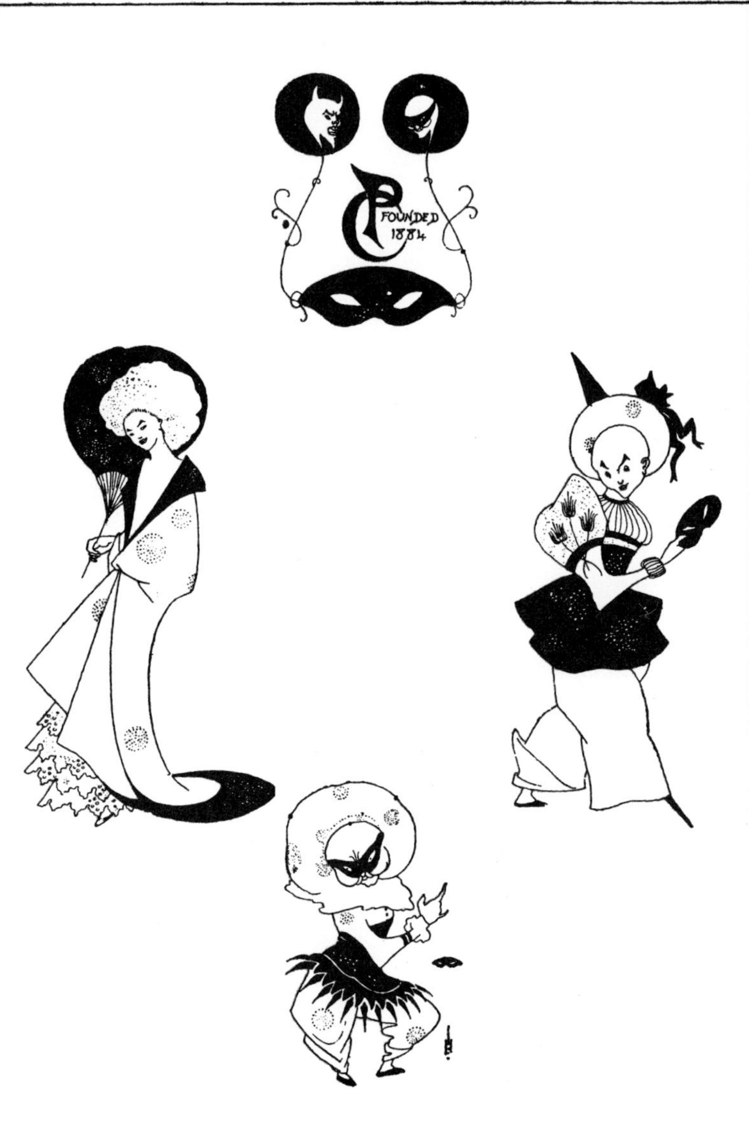
FOUNDED
1884

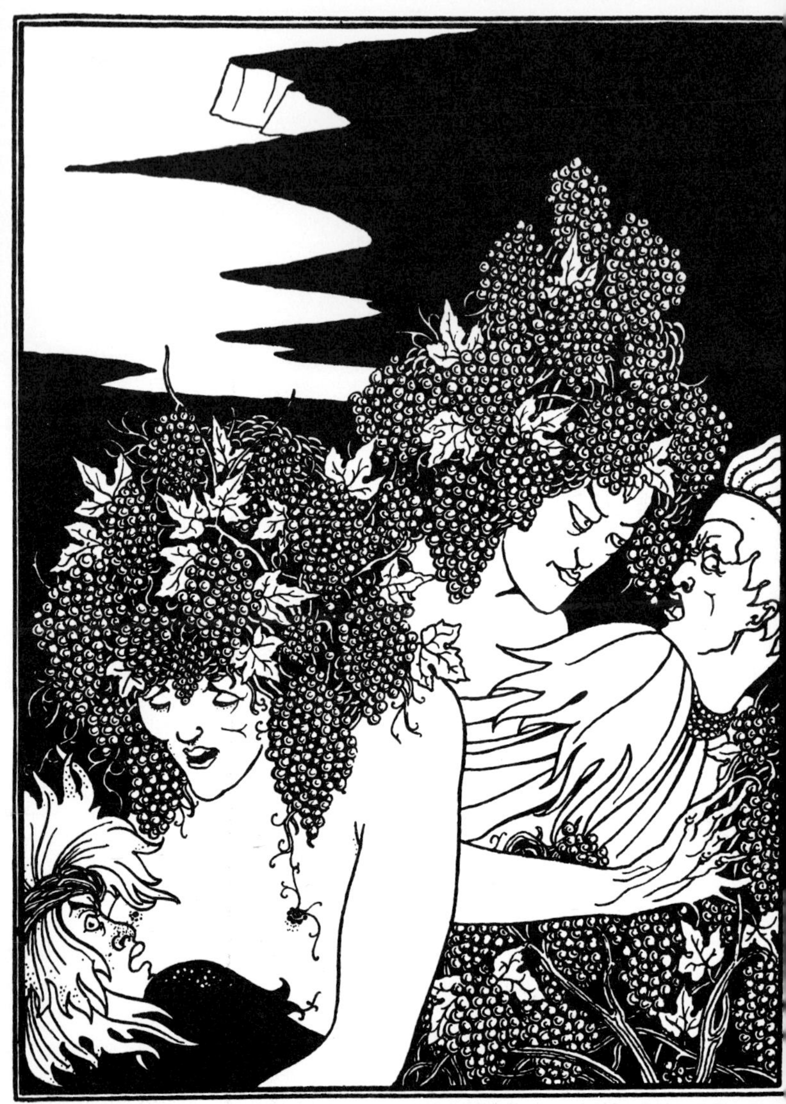

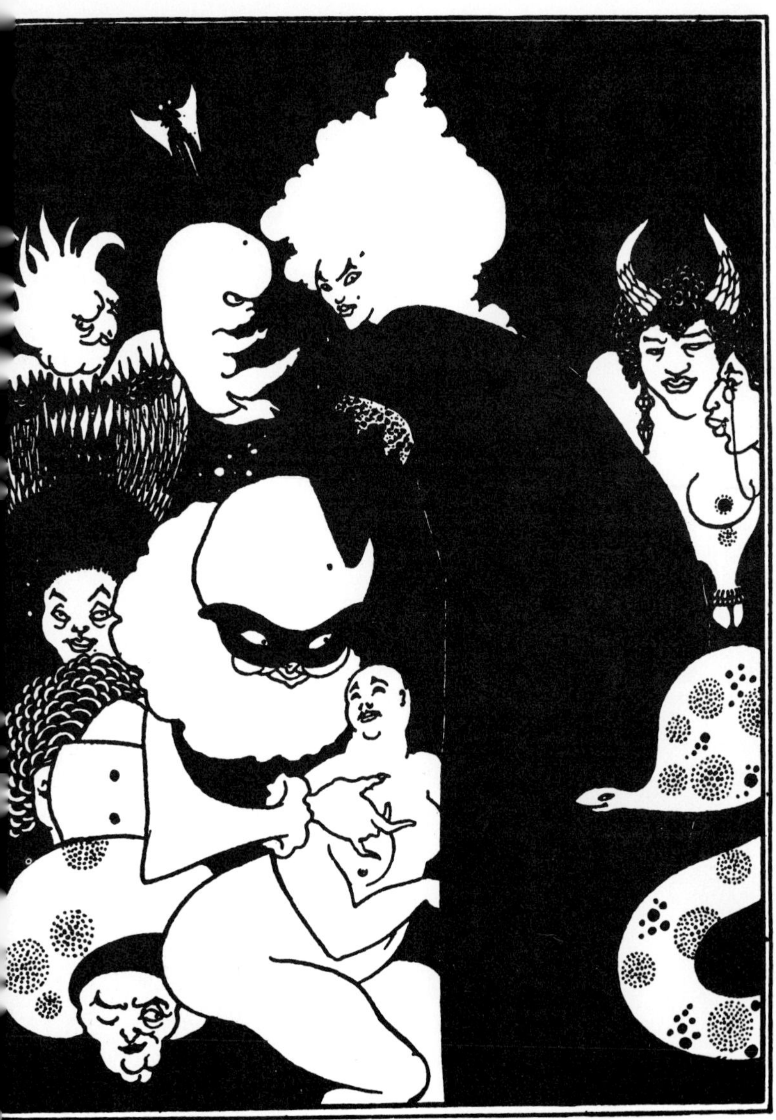

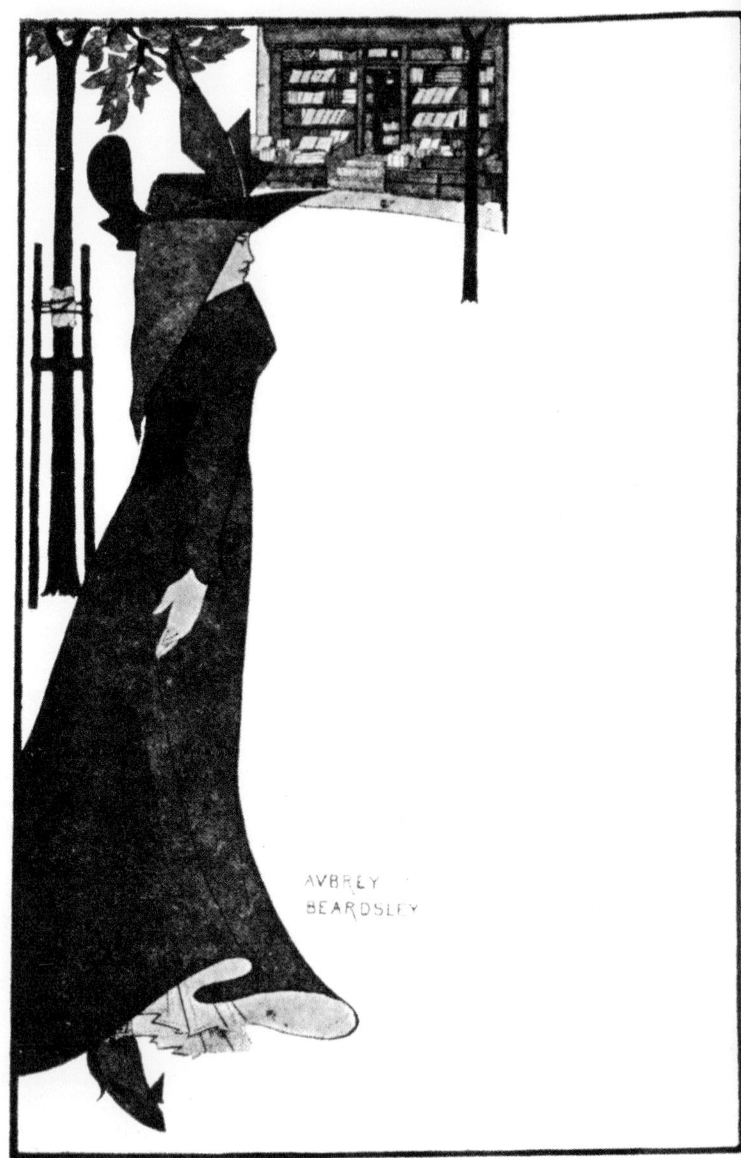
AVBREY
BEARDSLEY

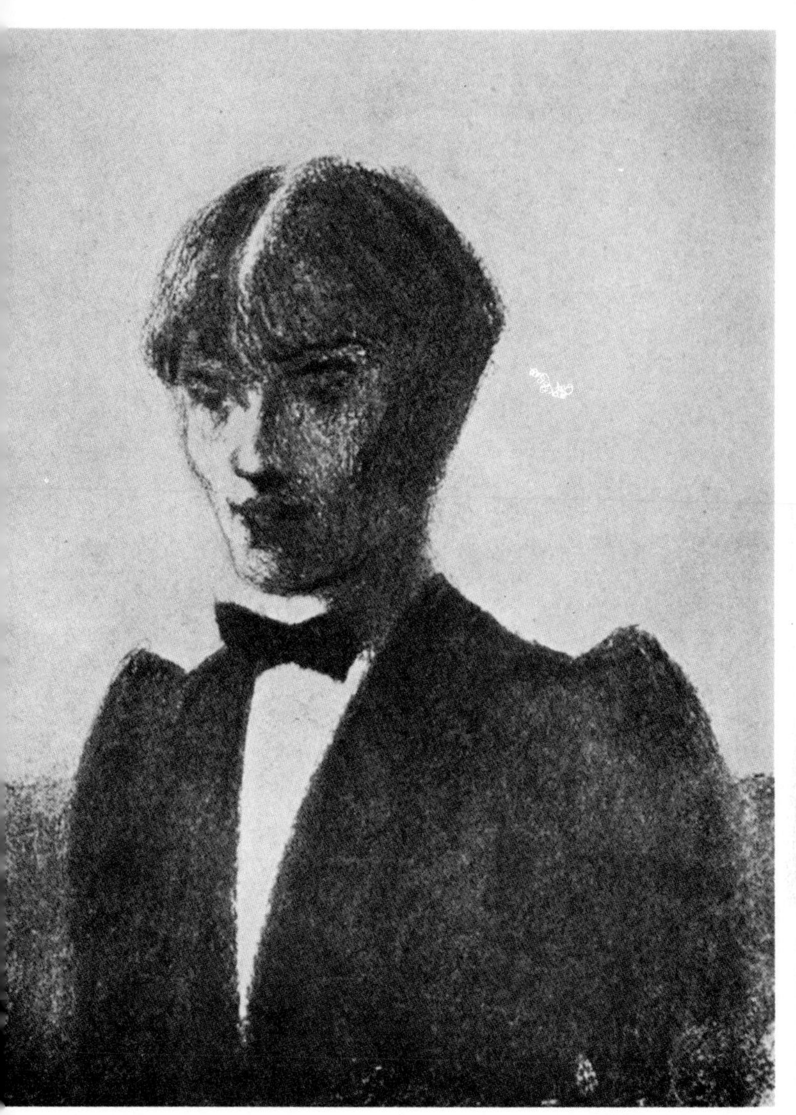

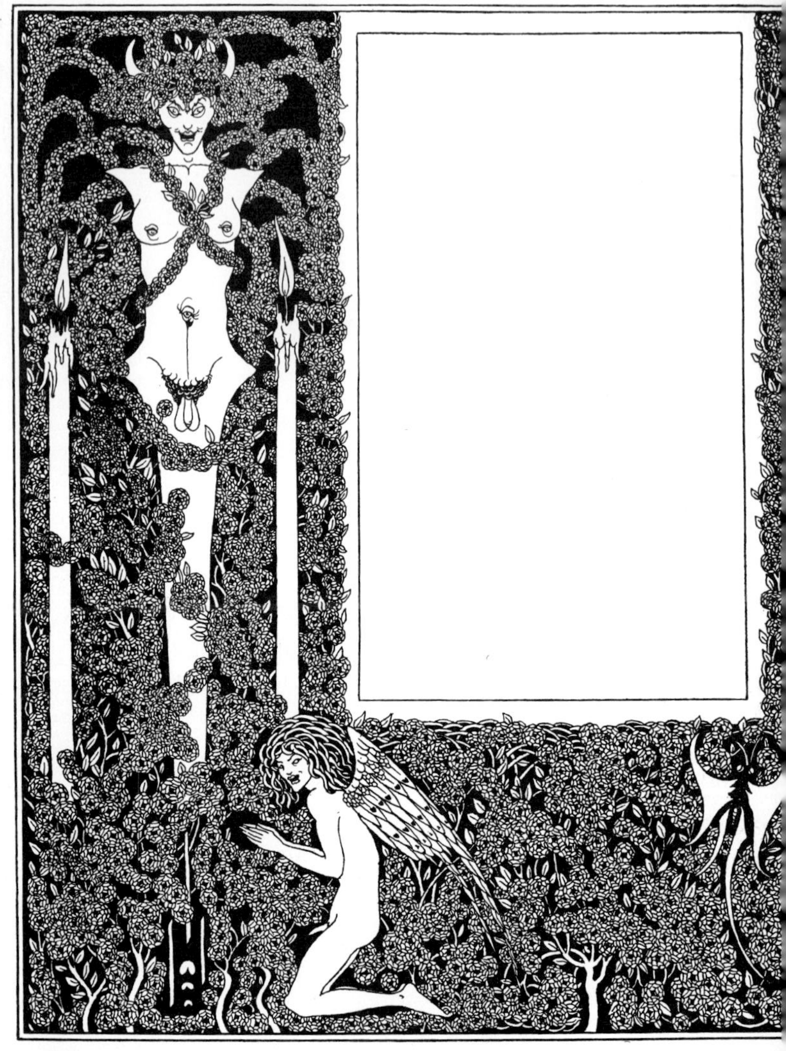

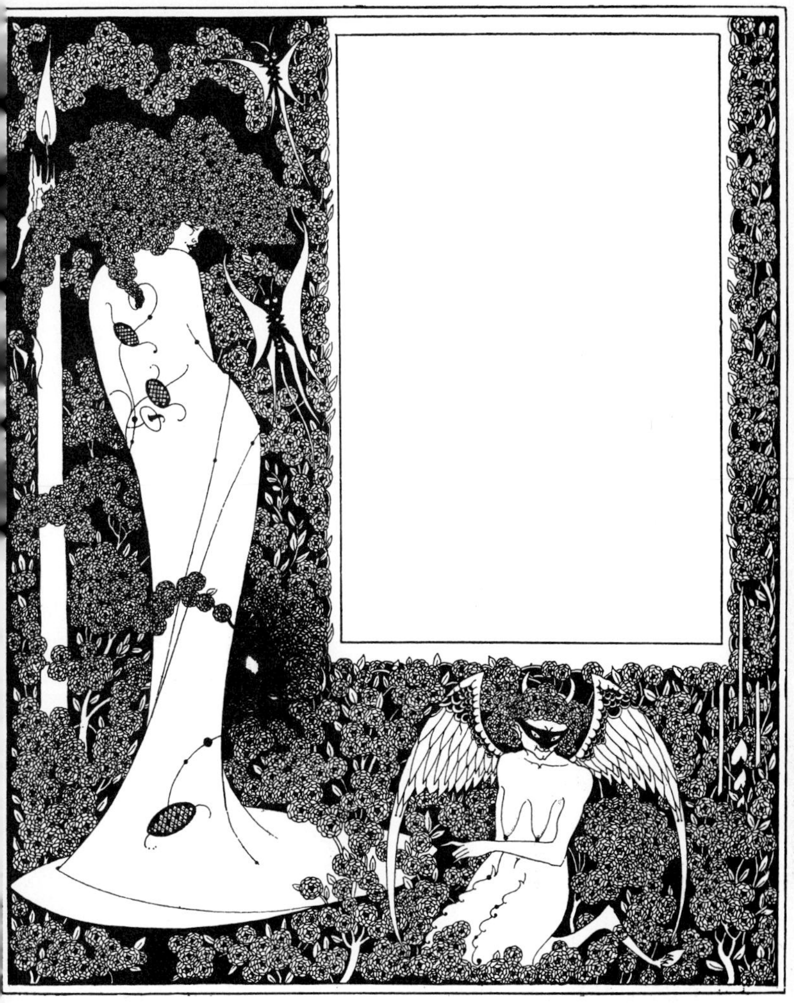

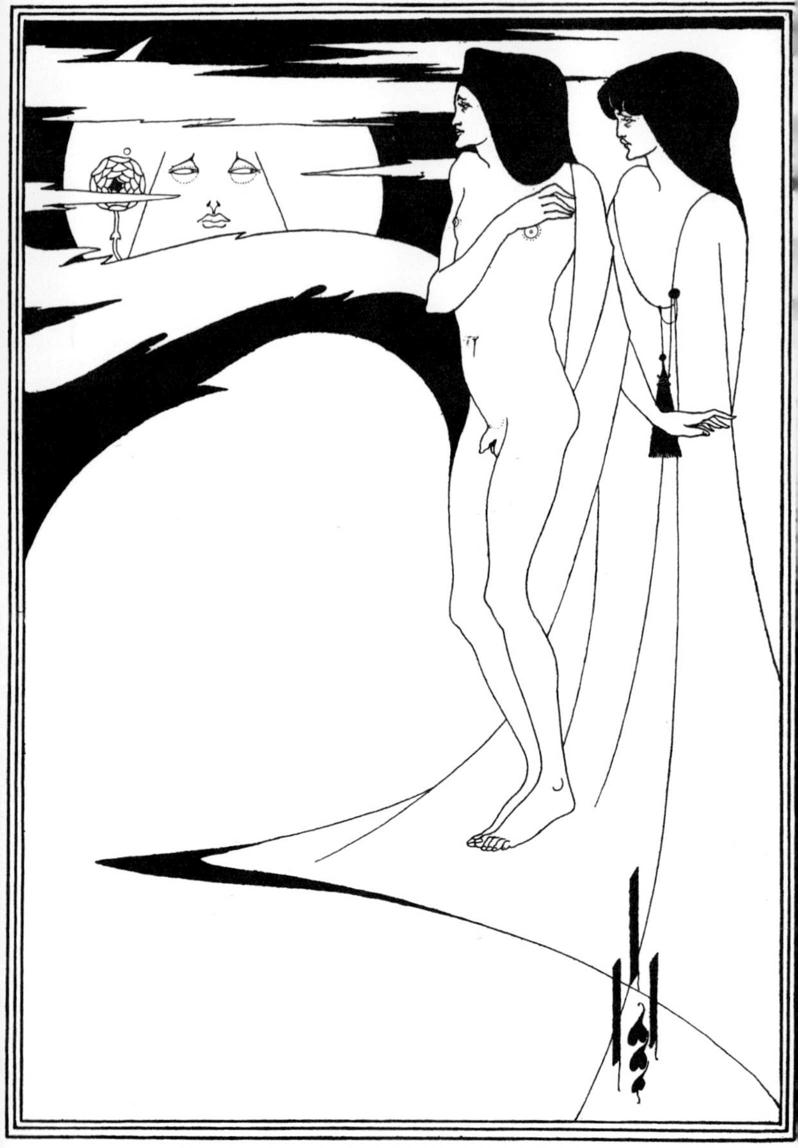

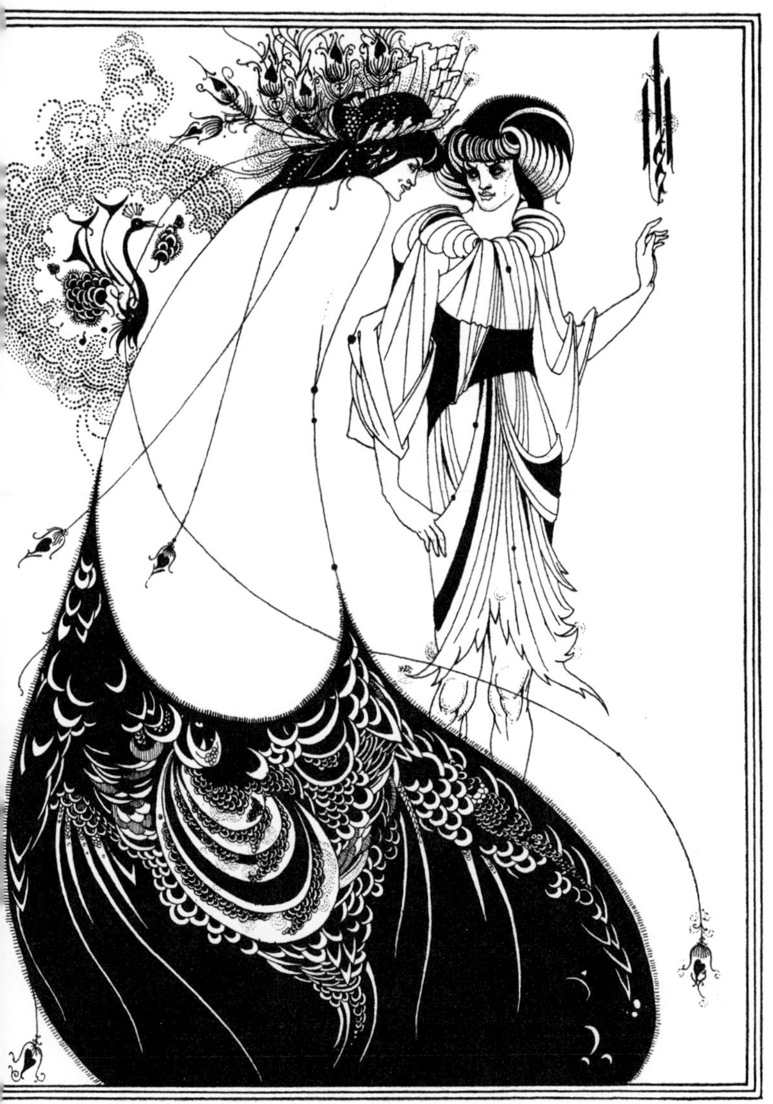

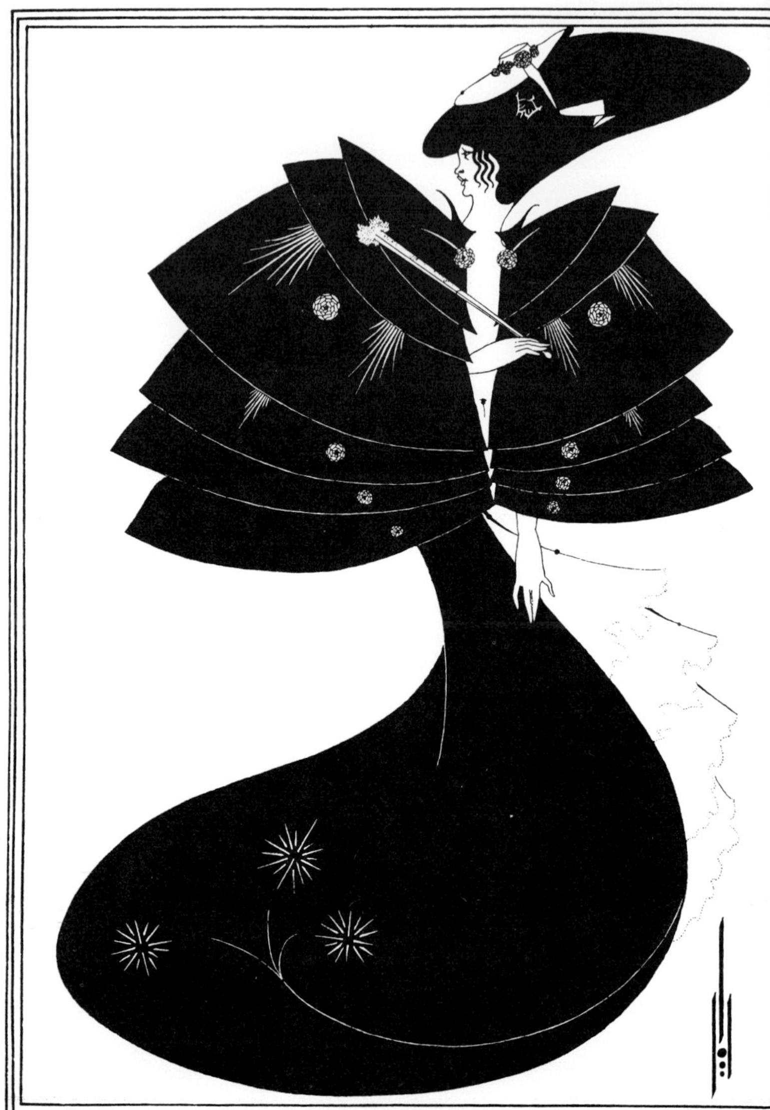

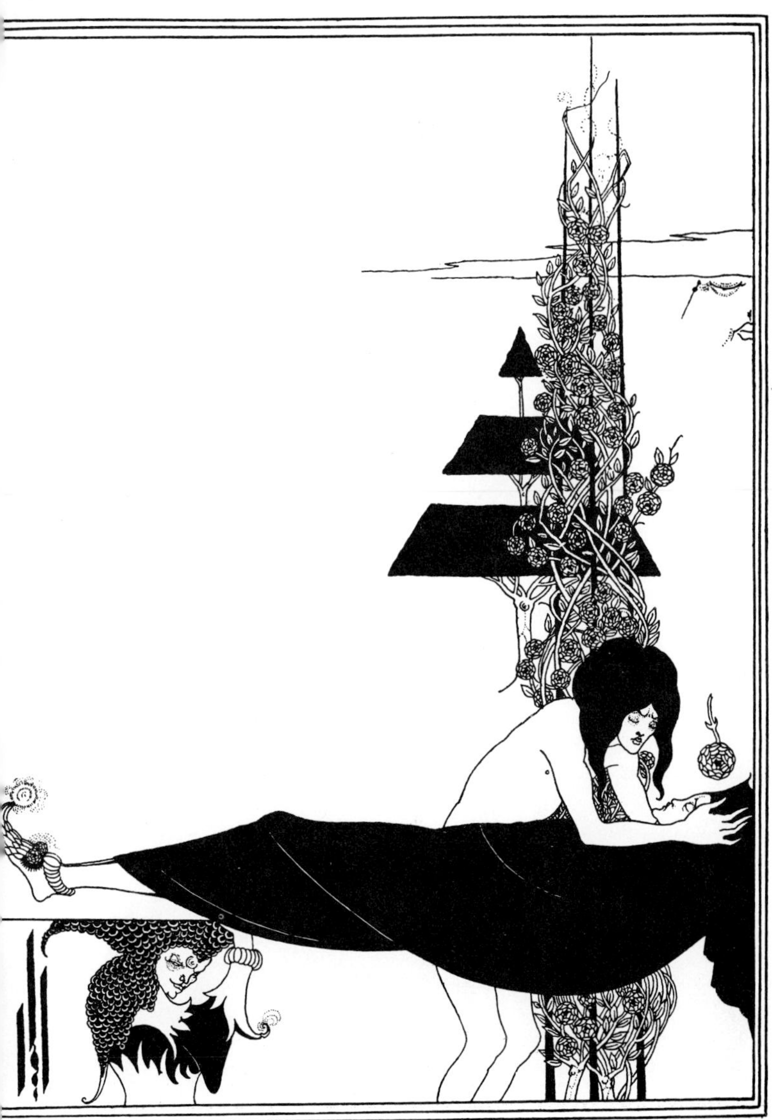

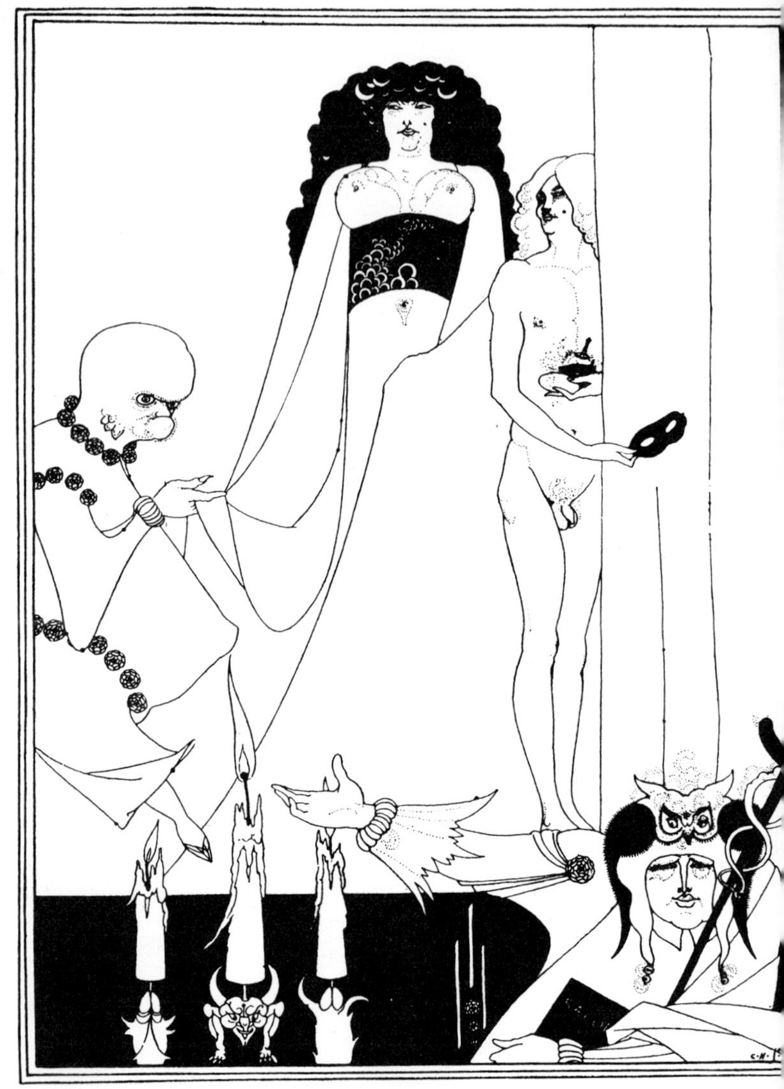

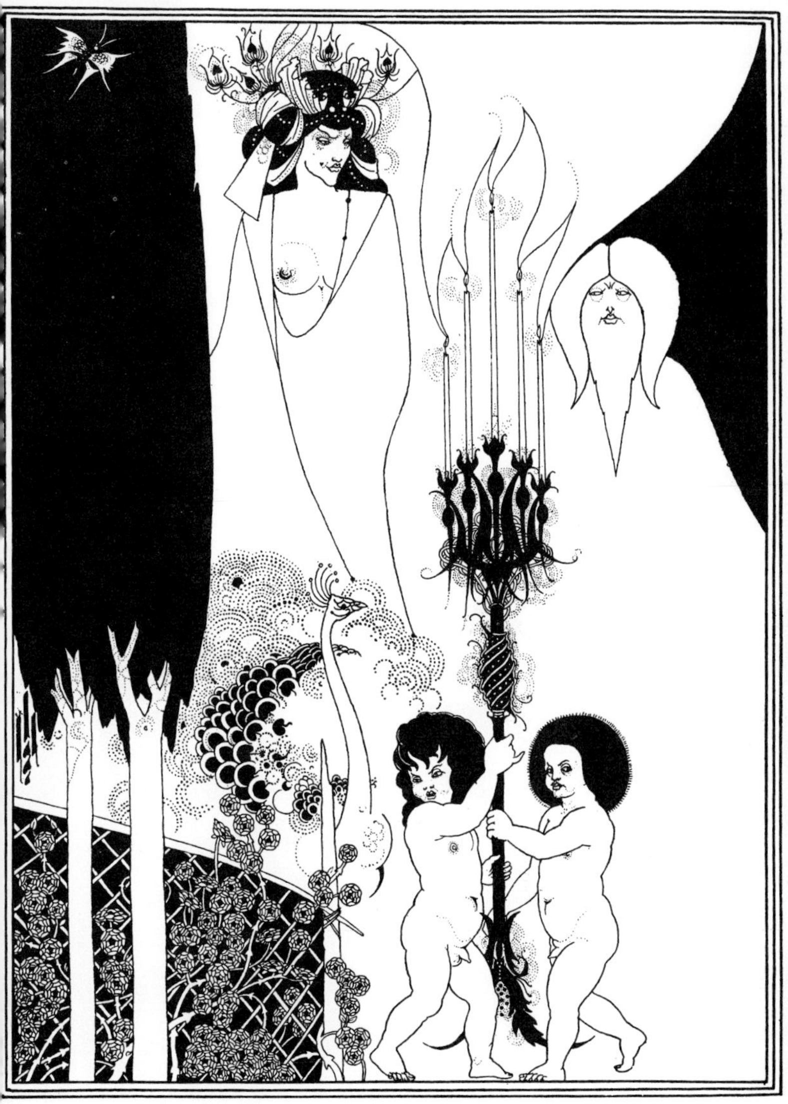

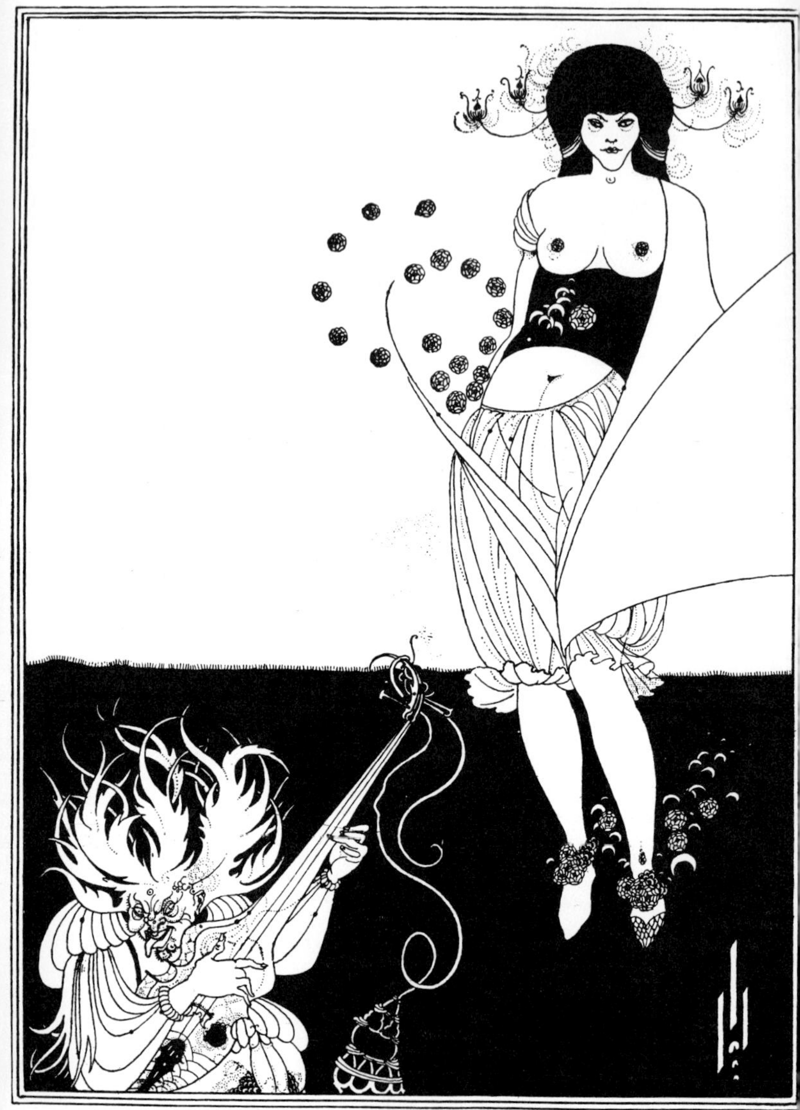

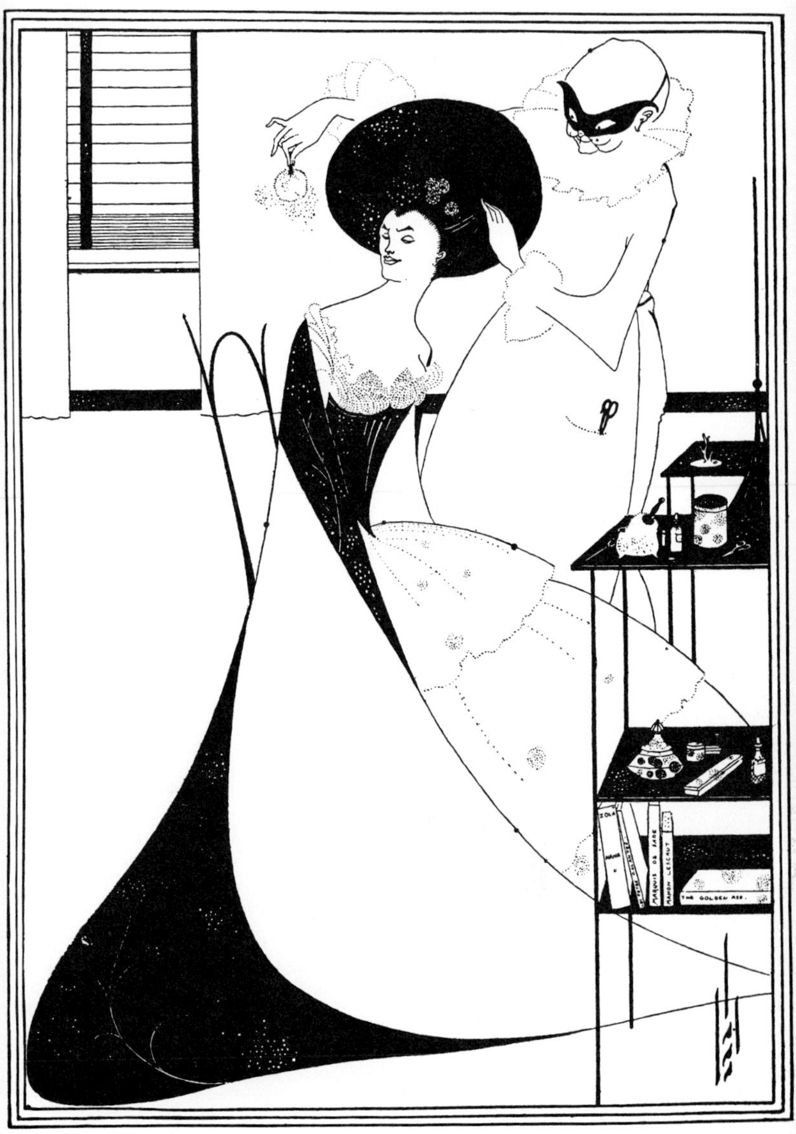
ZOLA
NANA
MARQUIS DE SADE
MANON LESCAUT
THE GOLDEN ASS.

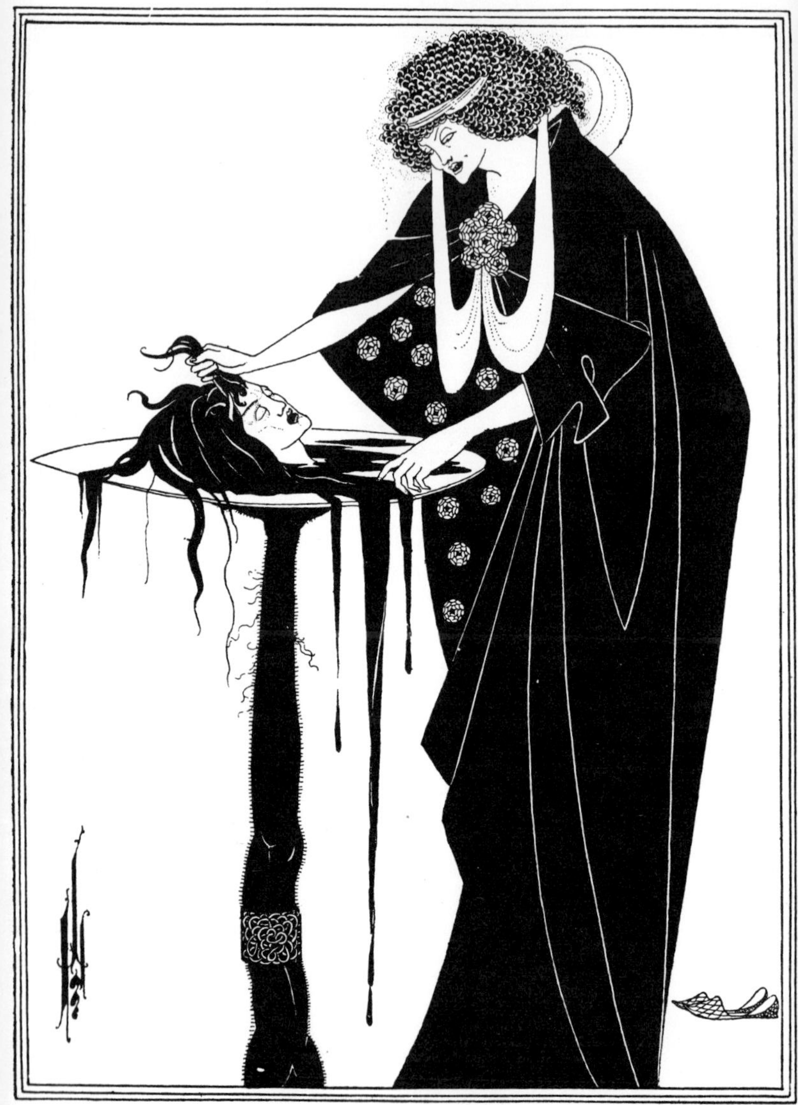

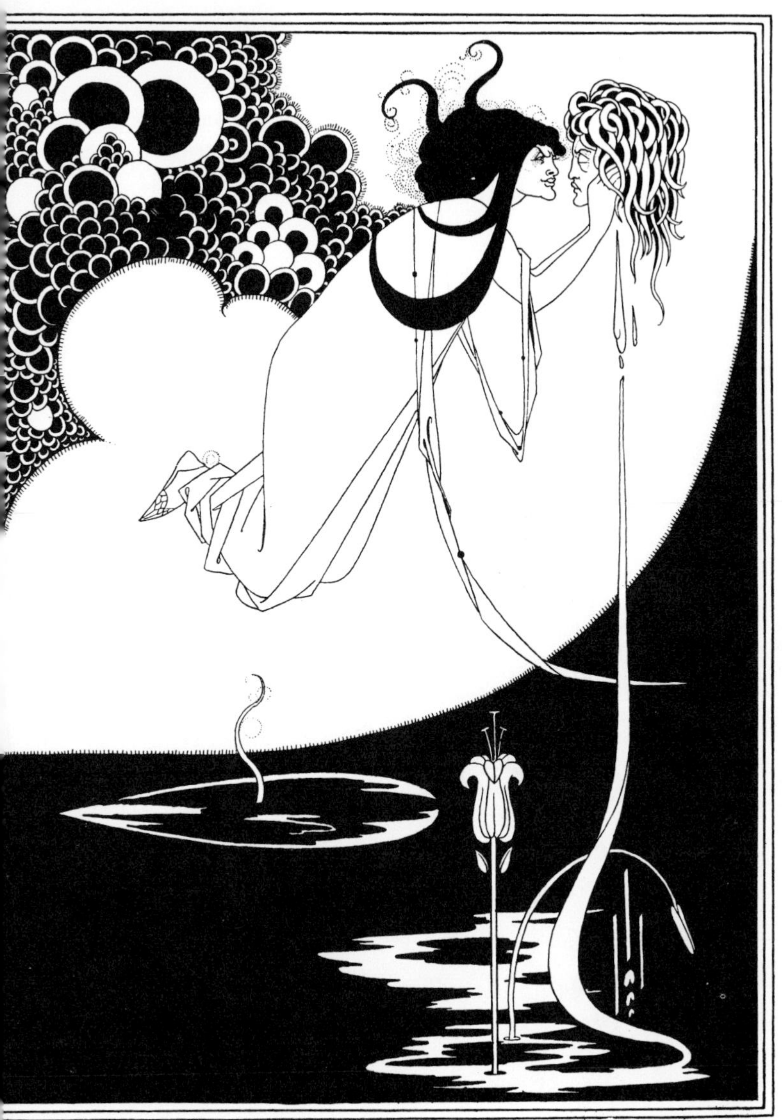

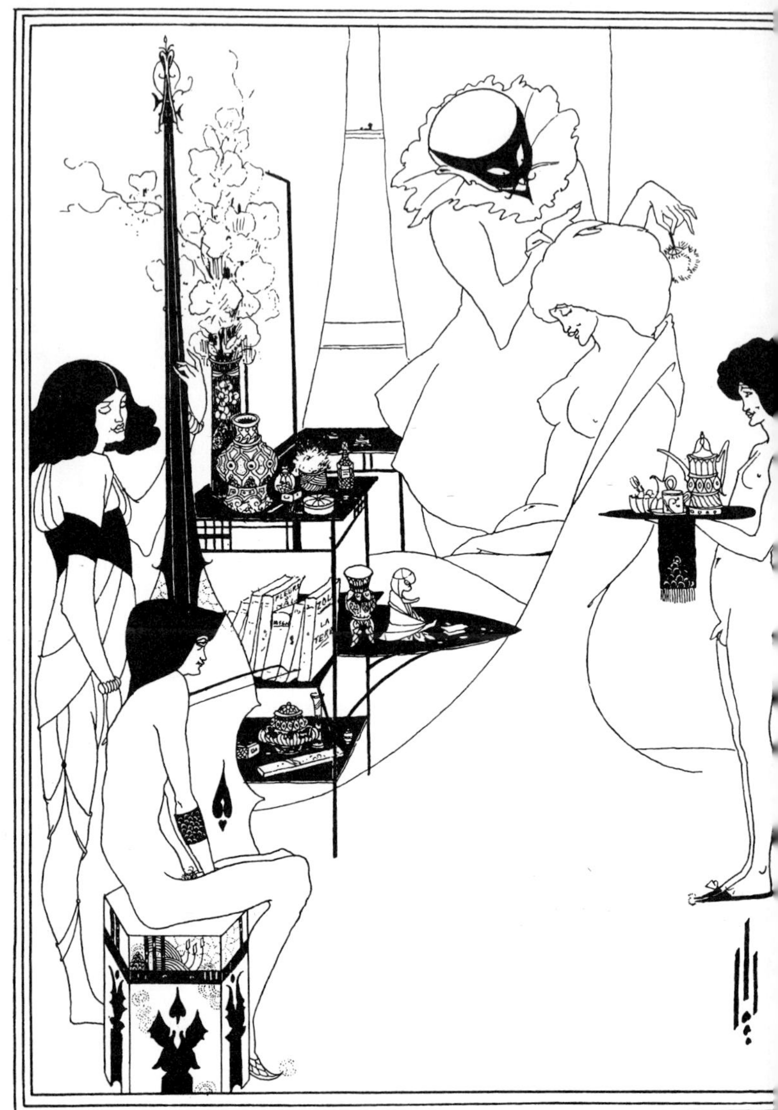
FLEURS
LA

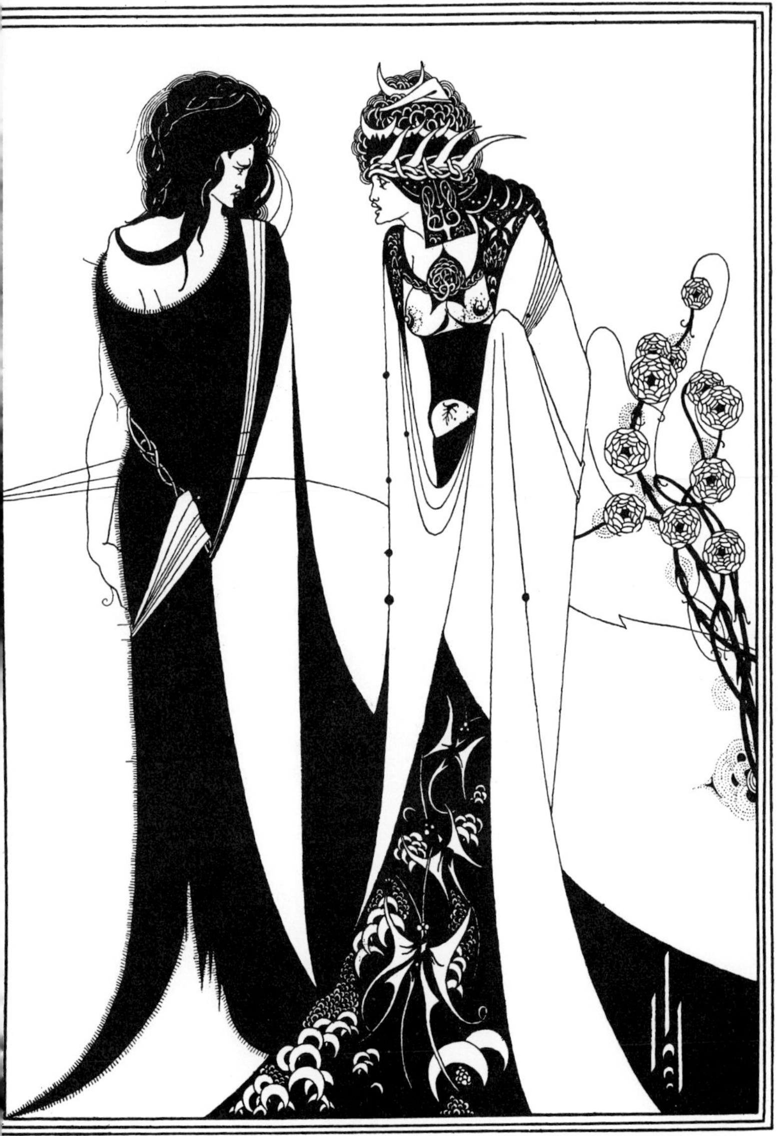

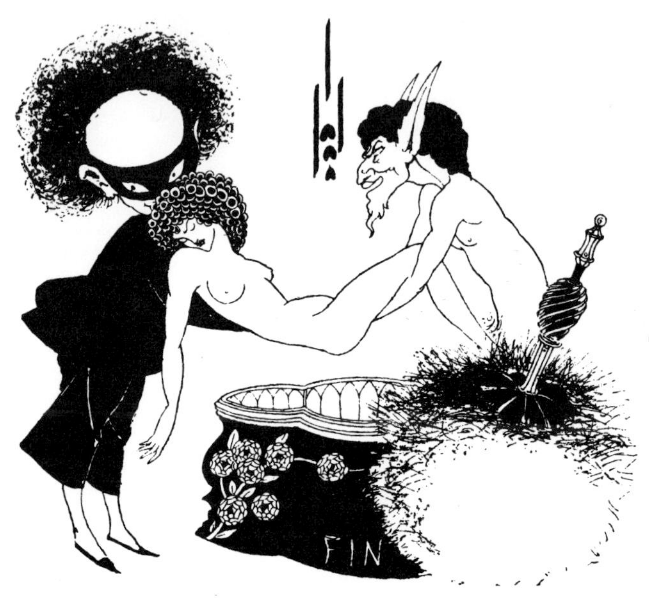
FIN

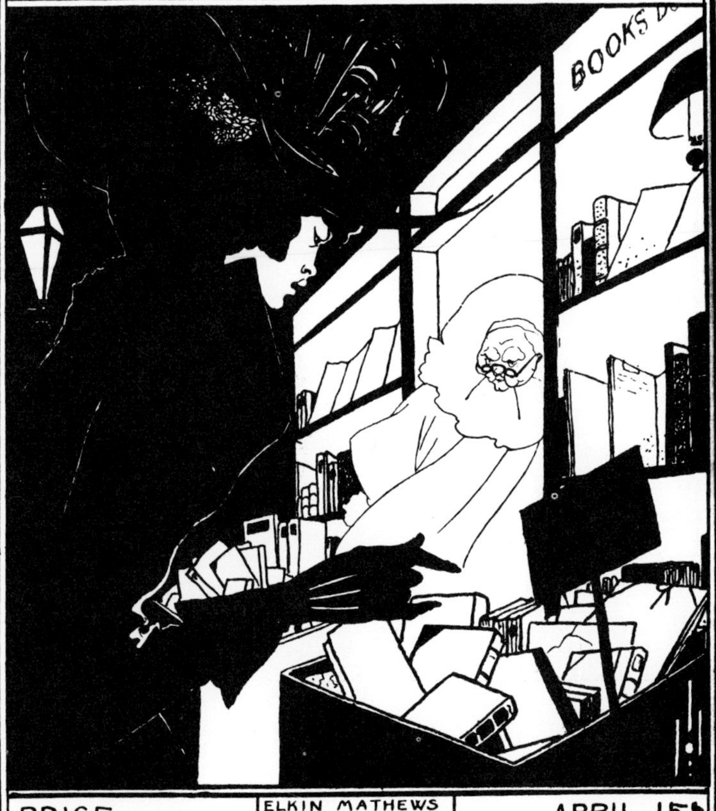
THE YELLOW BOOK
AN ILLVSTRATED QVARTERLY.
BOOKS
PRICE
FIVE SHILLINGS
ELKIN MATHEWS
AND JOHN LANE.
THE BODLEY HEAD
VIGO ST. LONDON.
APRIL 15th
MDCCCXCIV.

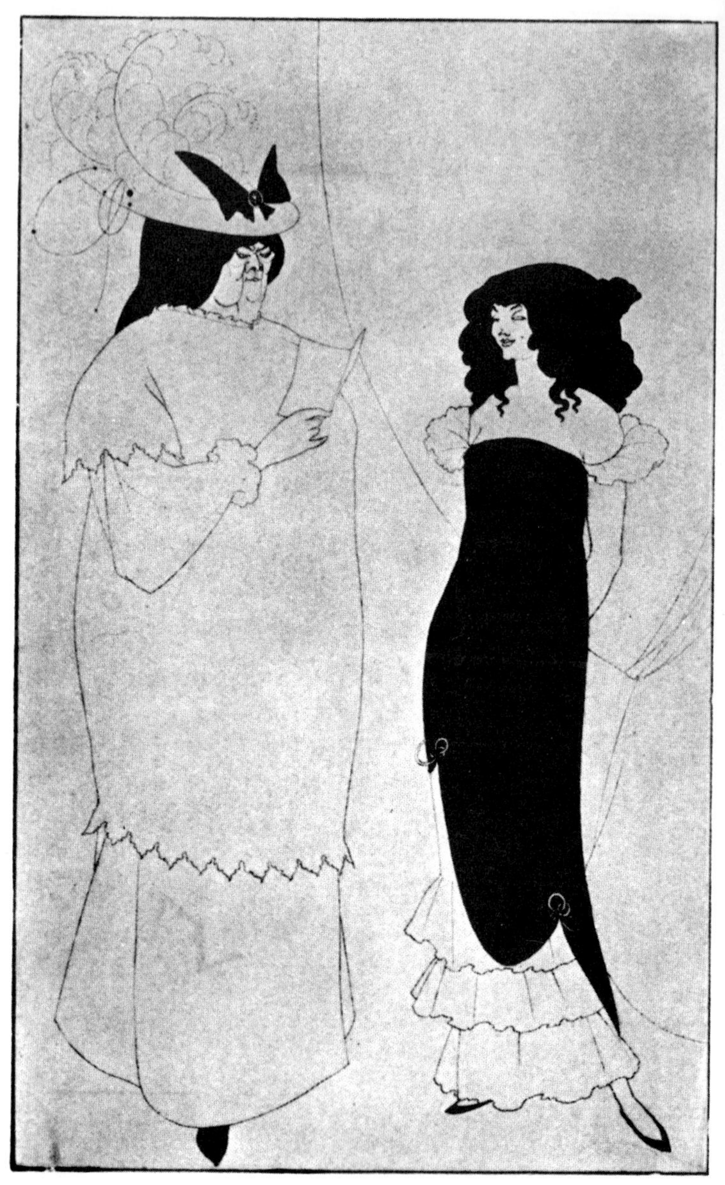

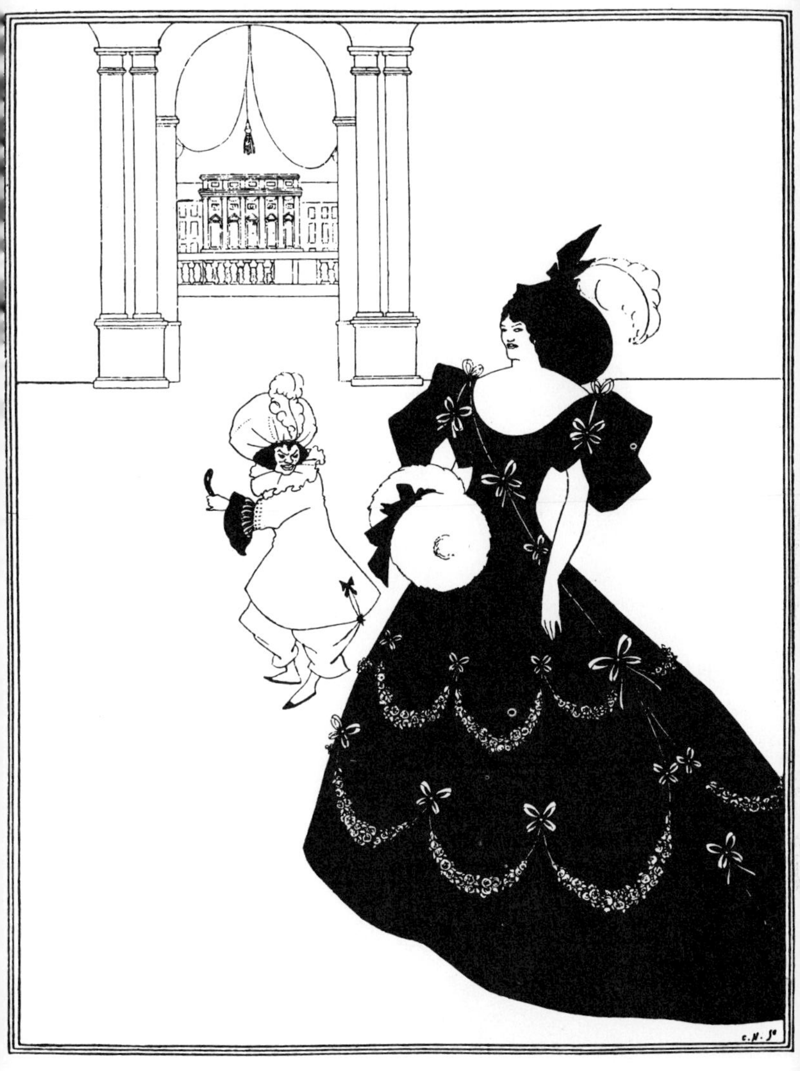

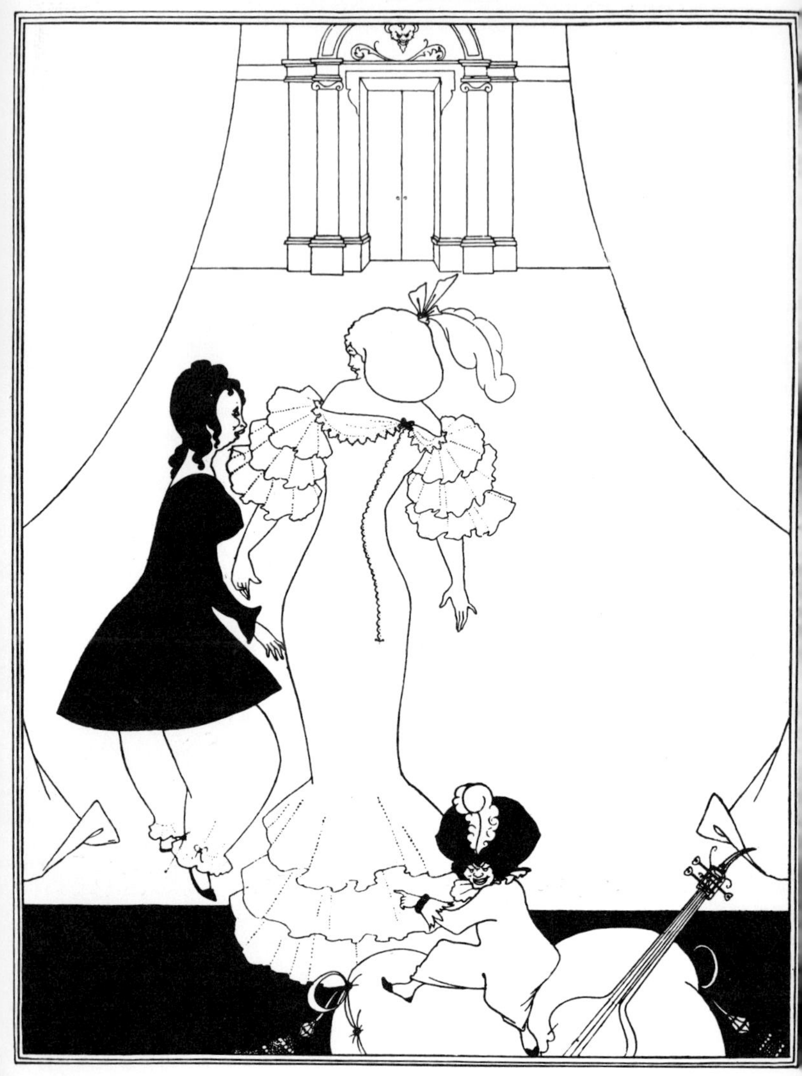

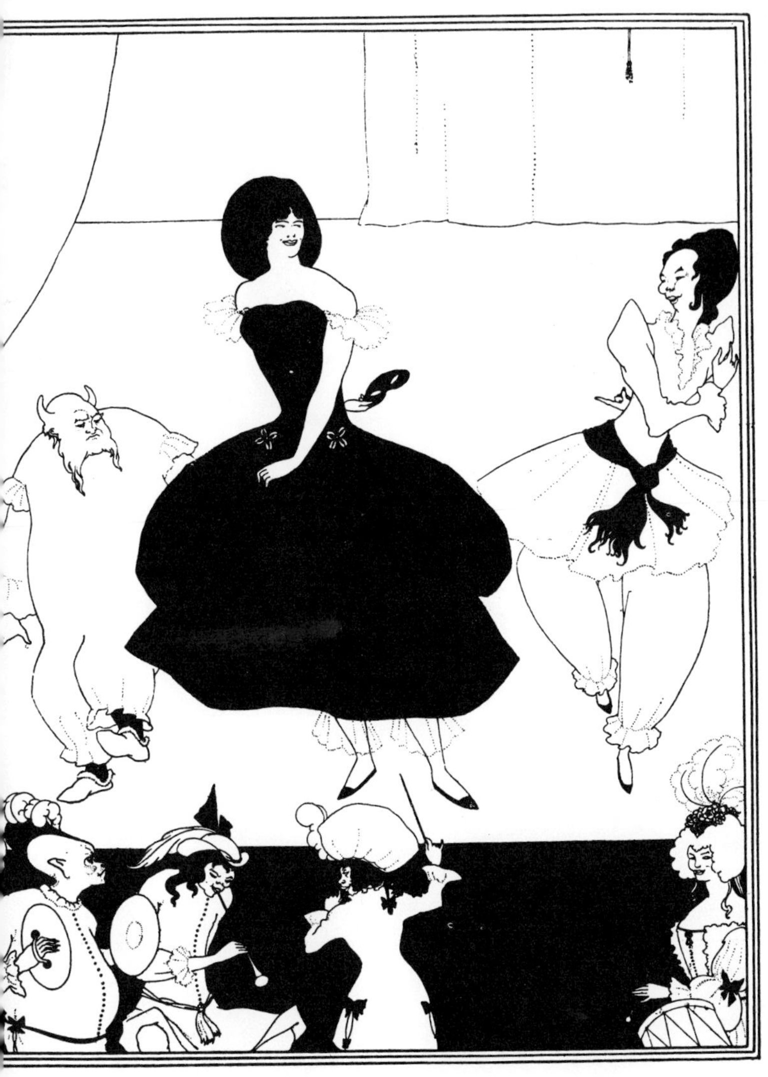

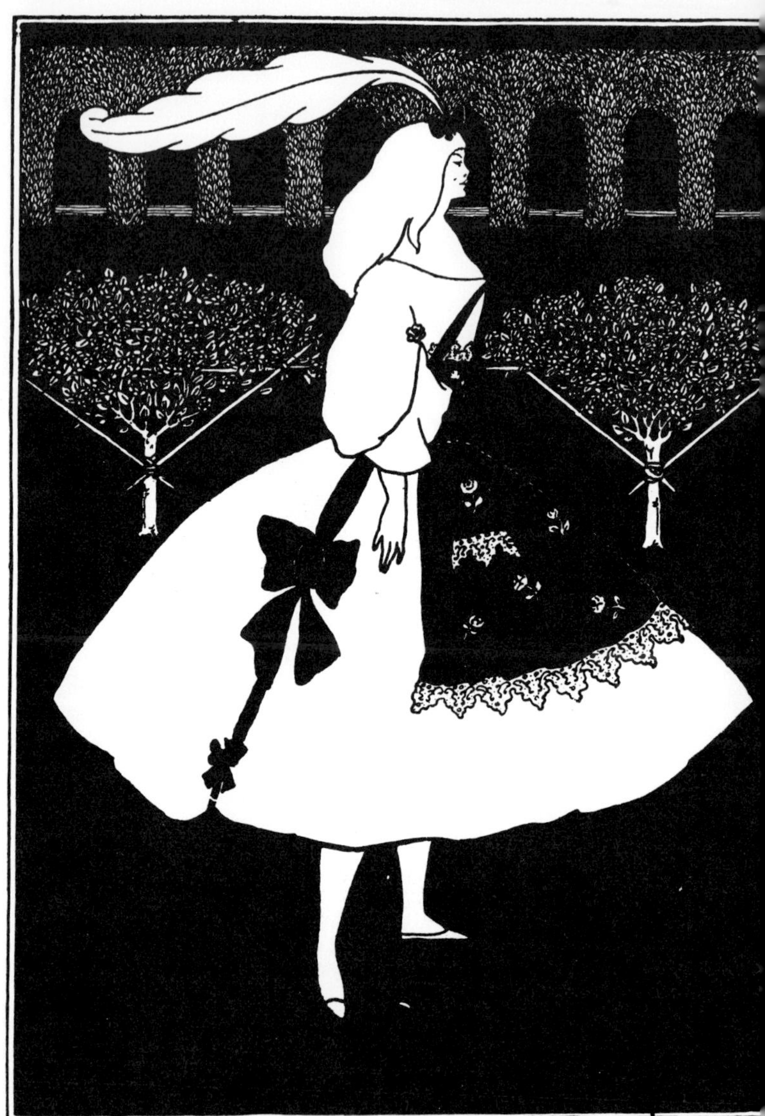

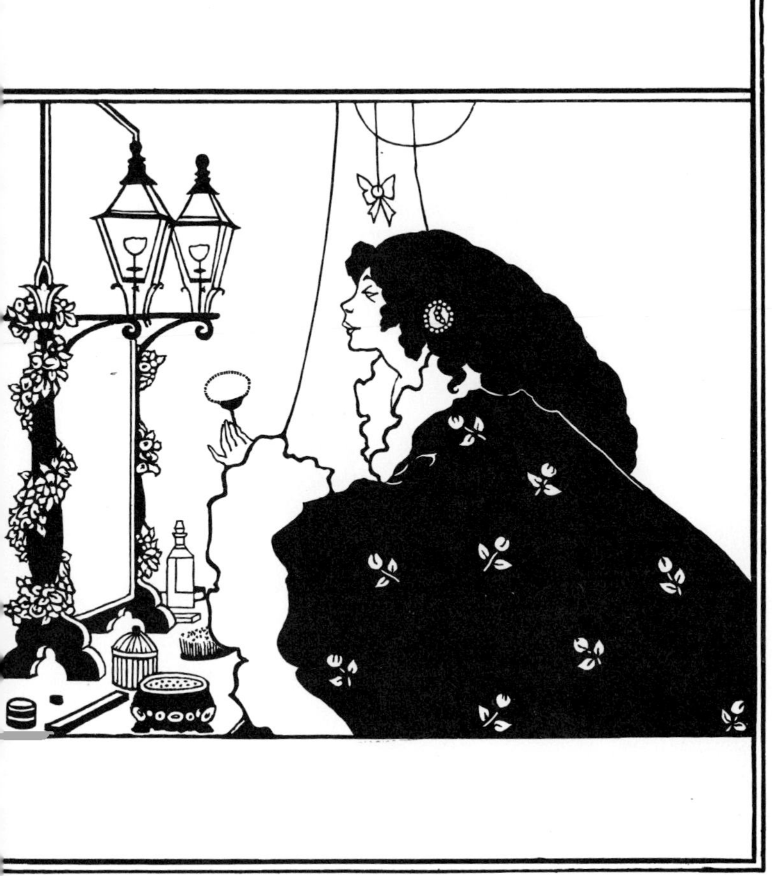

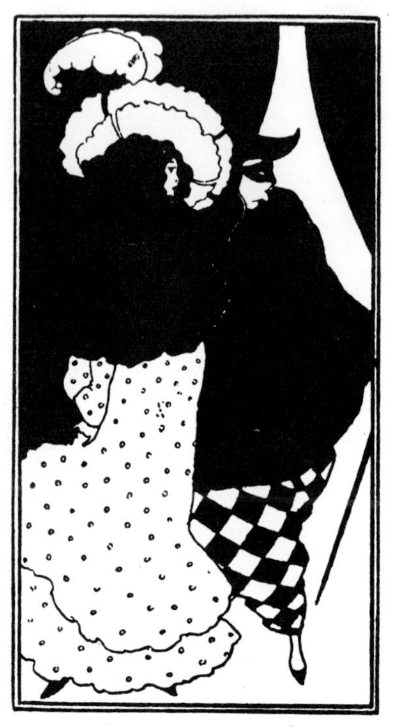

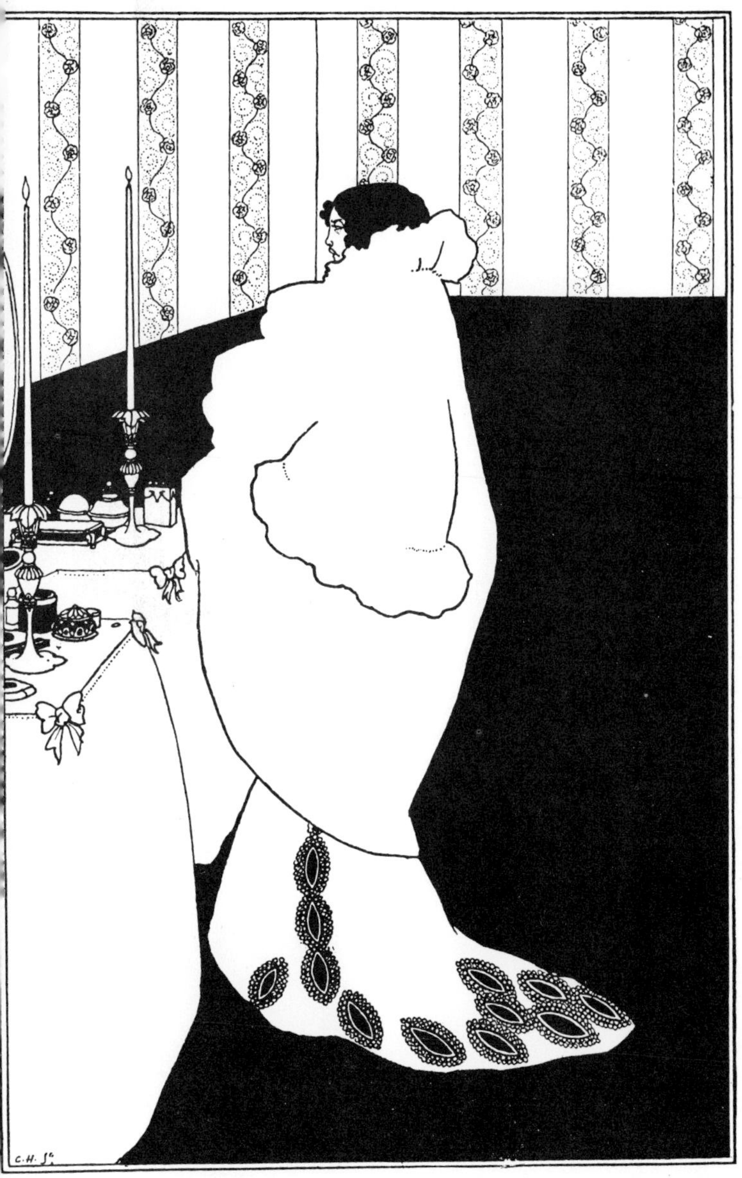

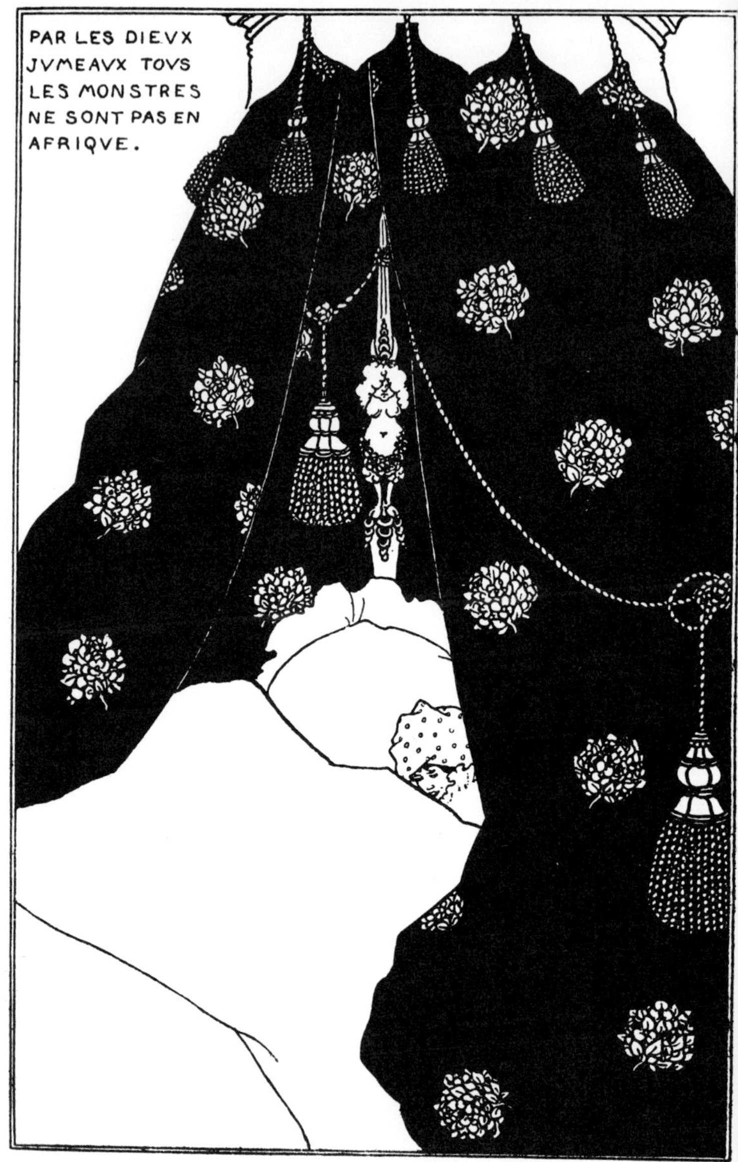
PAR LES DIEVX
JVMEAVX TOVS
LES MONSTRES
NE SONT PAS EN
AFRIQVE.

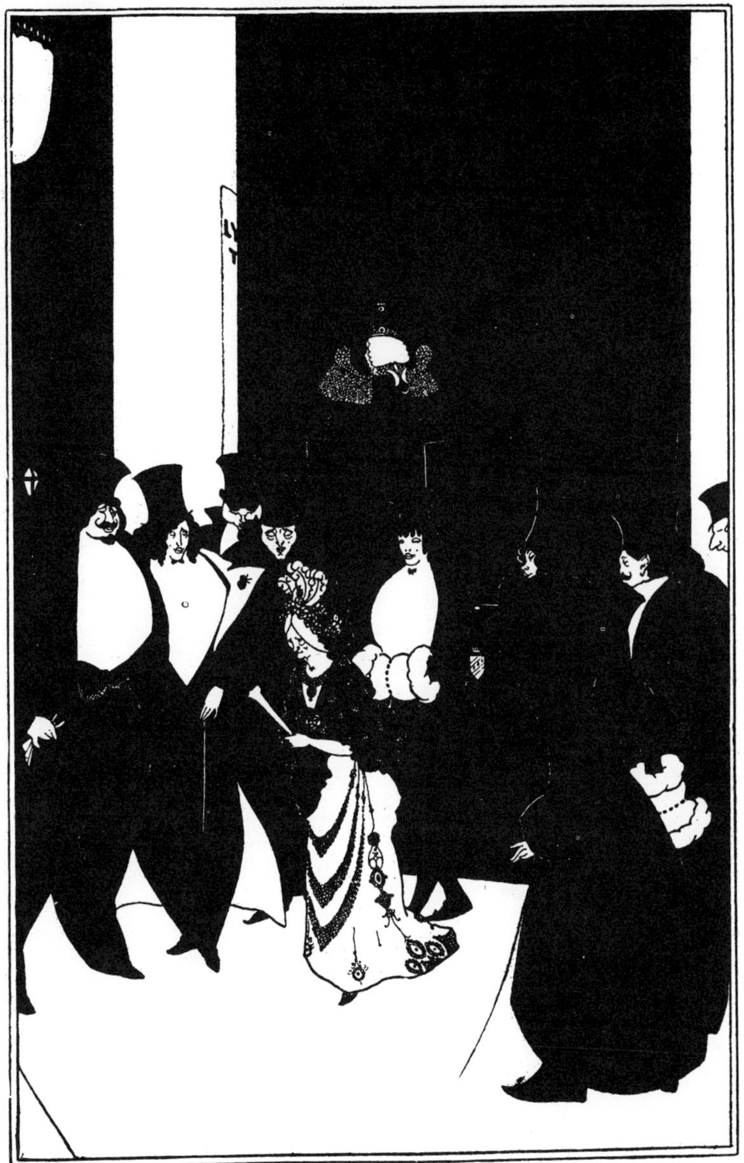

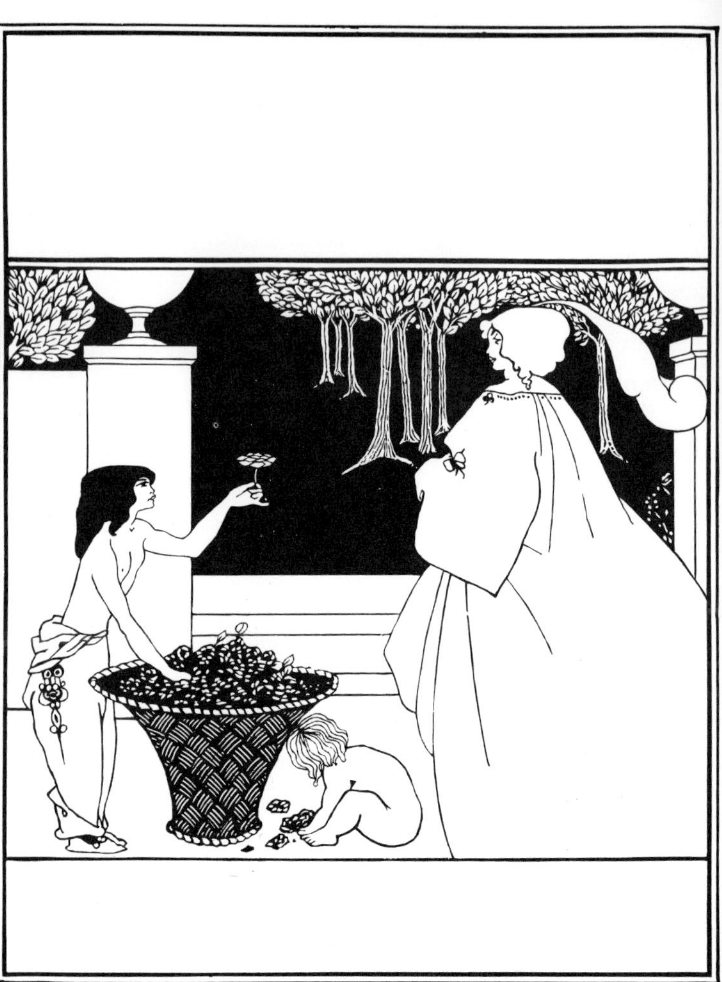

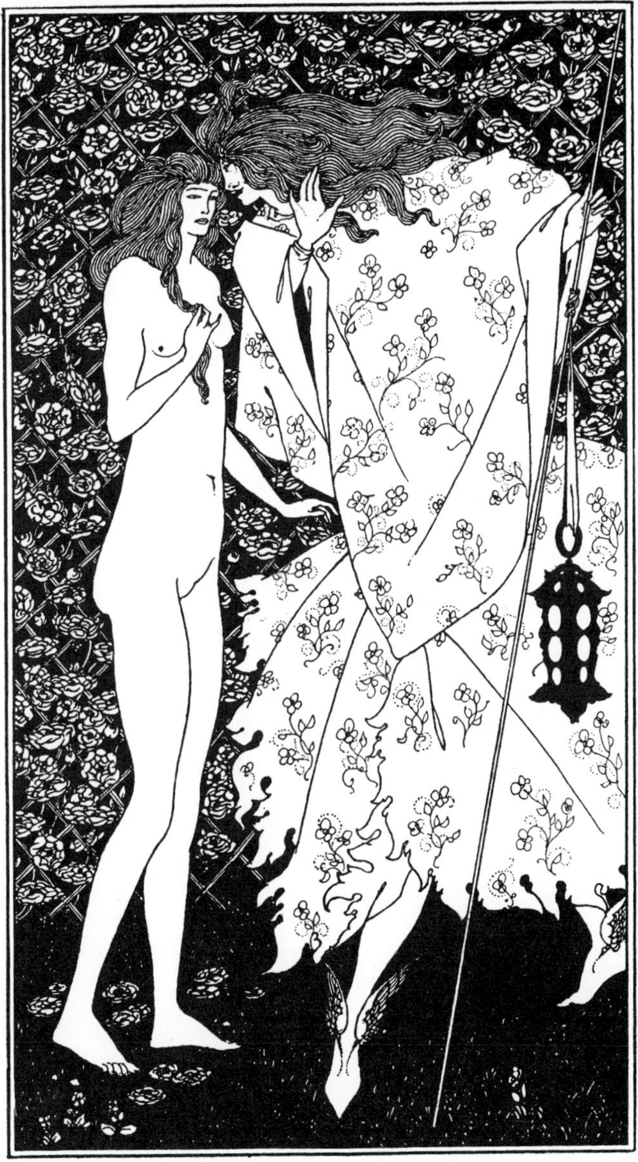

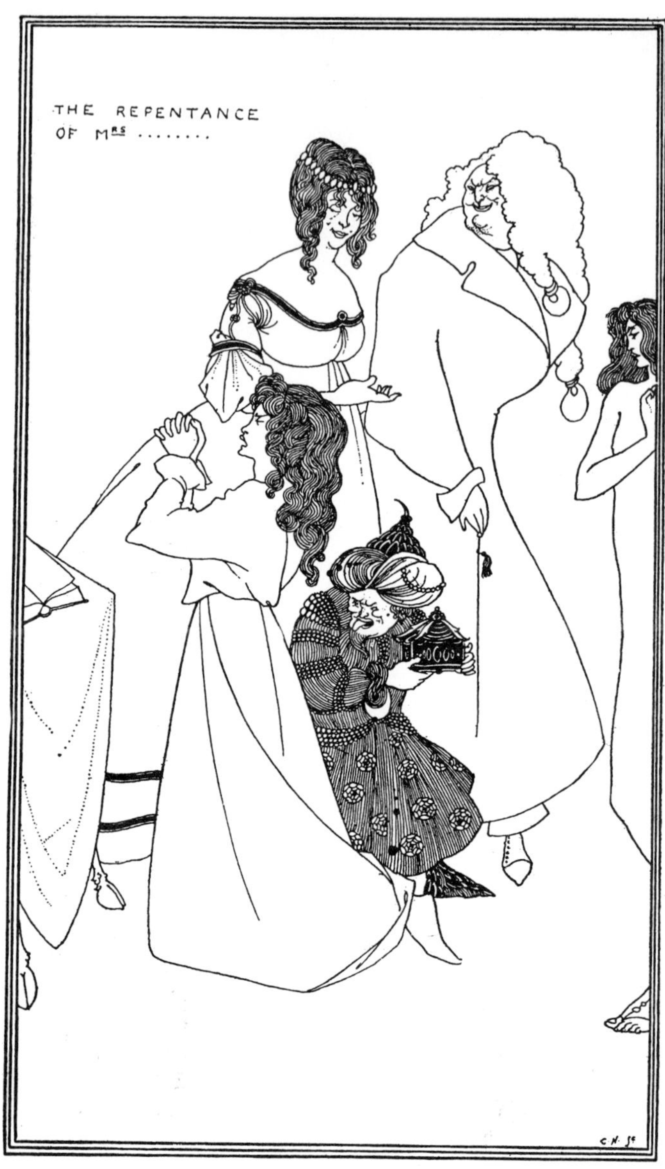
THE REPENTANCE
OF Mrs ....
C.N. Sc

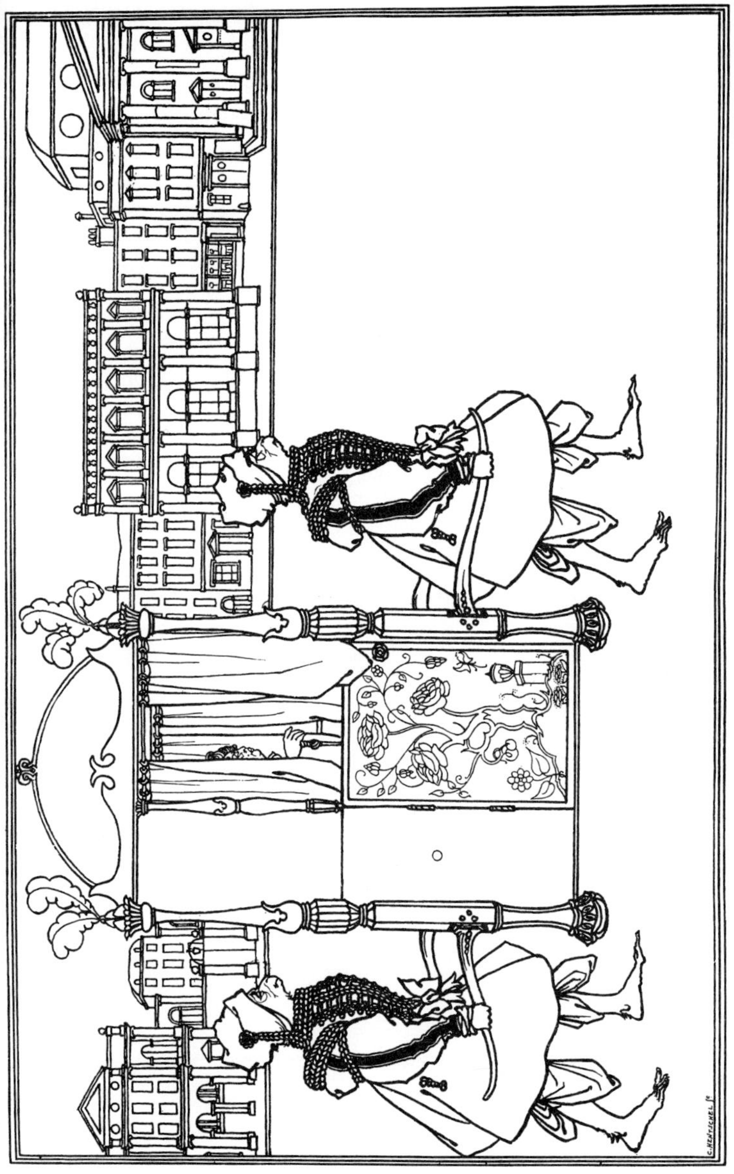

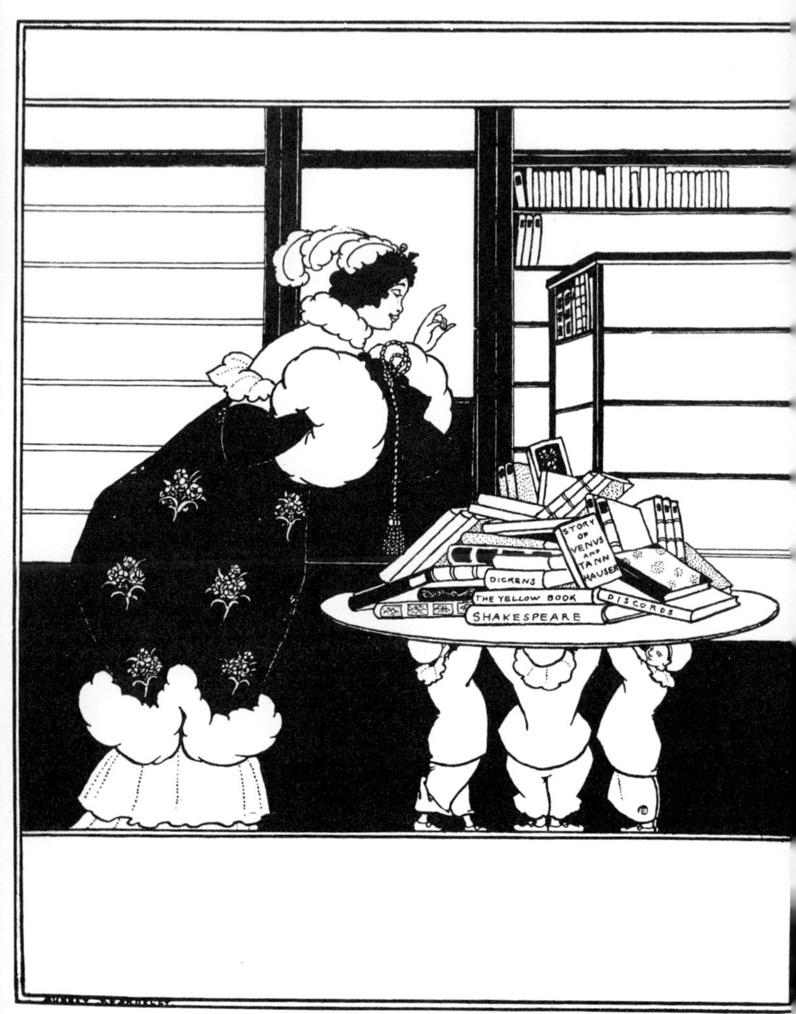
STORY OF VENUS AND TANN HAUSER
DICKENS
THE YELLOW BOOK
DISCORDS
SHAKESPEARE

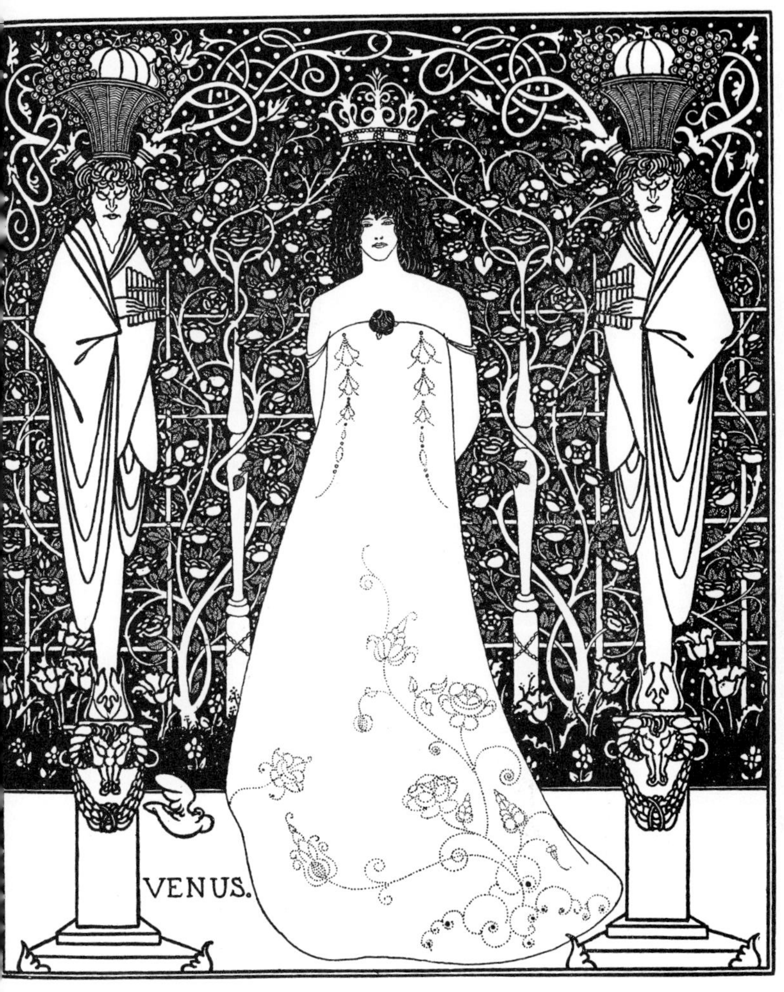
VENUS.

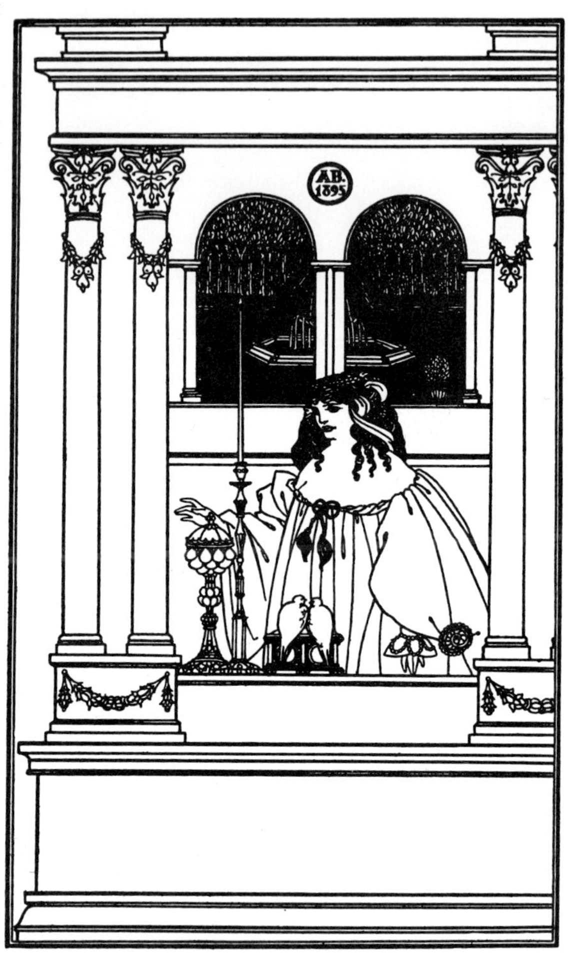
AB.
1895

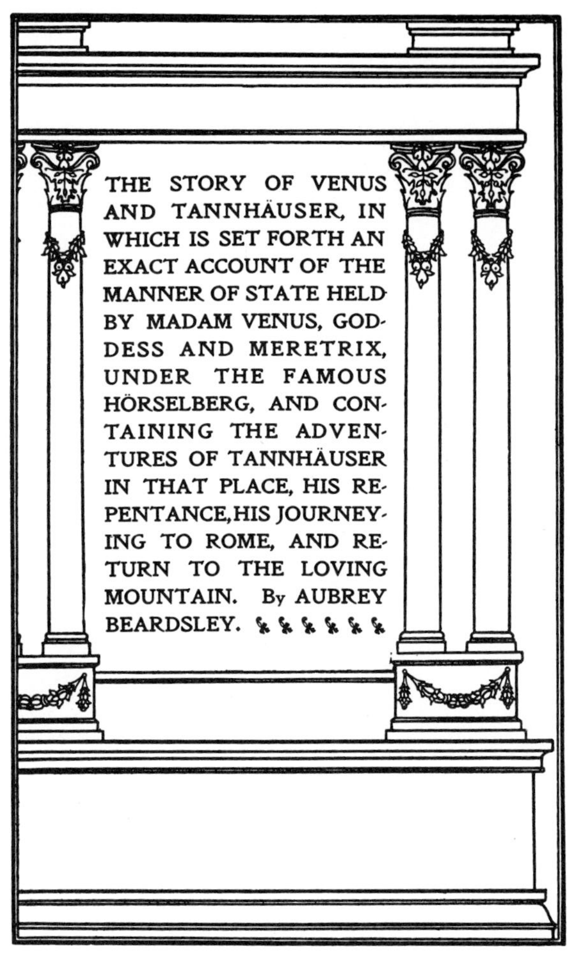

THE STORY OF VENUS AND TANNHÄUSER, IN WHICH IS SET FORTH AN EXACT ACCOUNT OF THE MANNER OF STATE HELD BY MADAM VENUS, GODDESS AND MERETRIX, UNDER THE FAMOUS HÖRSELBERG, AND CONTAINING THE ADVENTURES OF TANNHÄUSER IN THAT PLACE, HIS REPENTANCE, HIS JOURNEYING TO ROME, AND RETURN TO THE LOVING MOUNTAIN. By AUBREY BEARDSLEY.

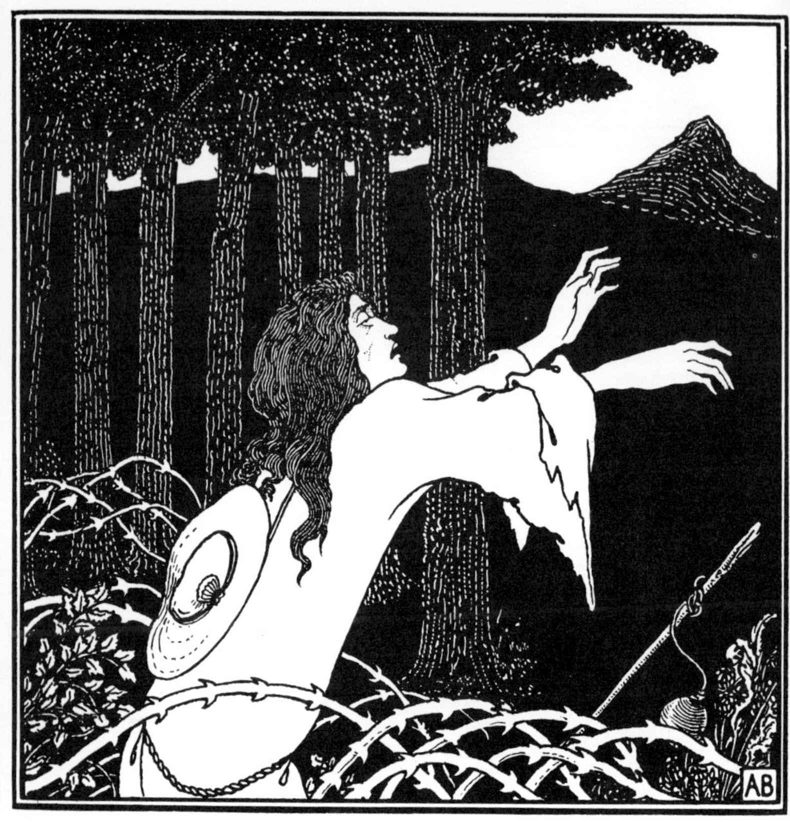
AB

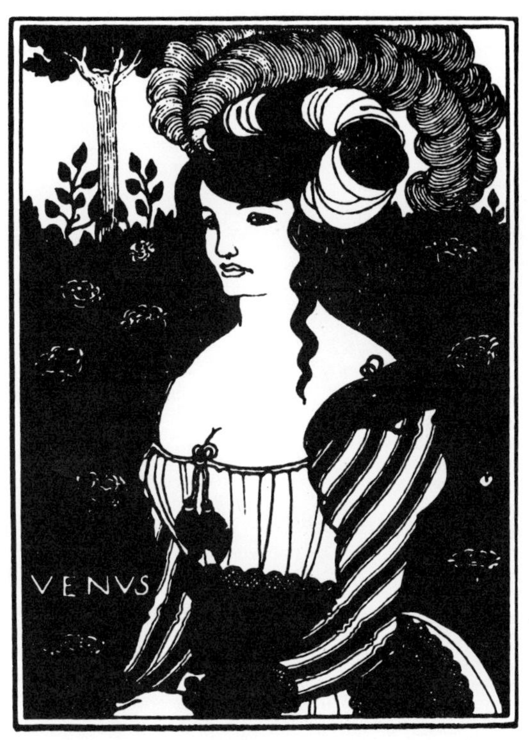
VENVS

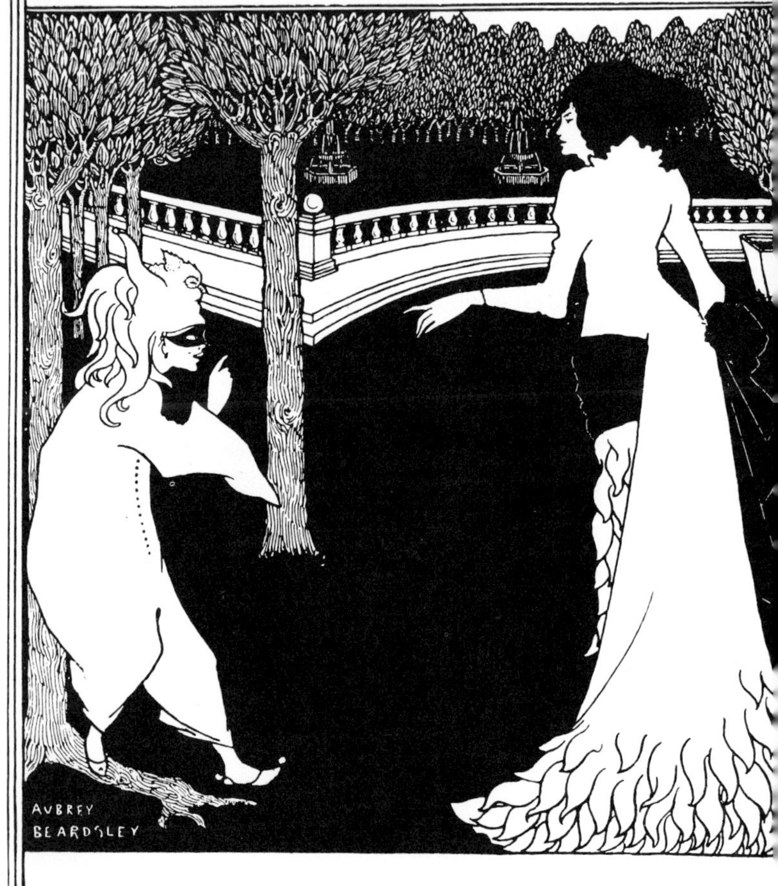
AUBREY
BEARDSLEY

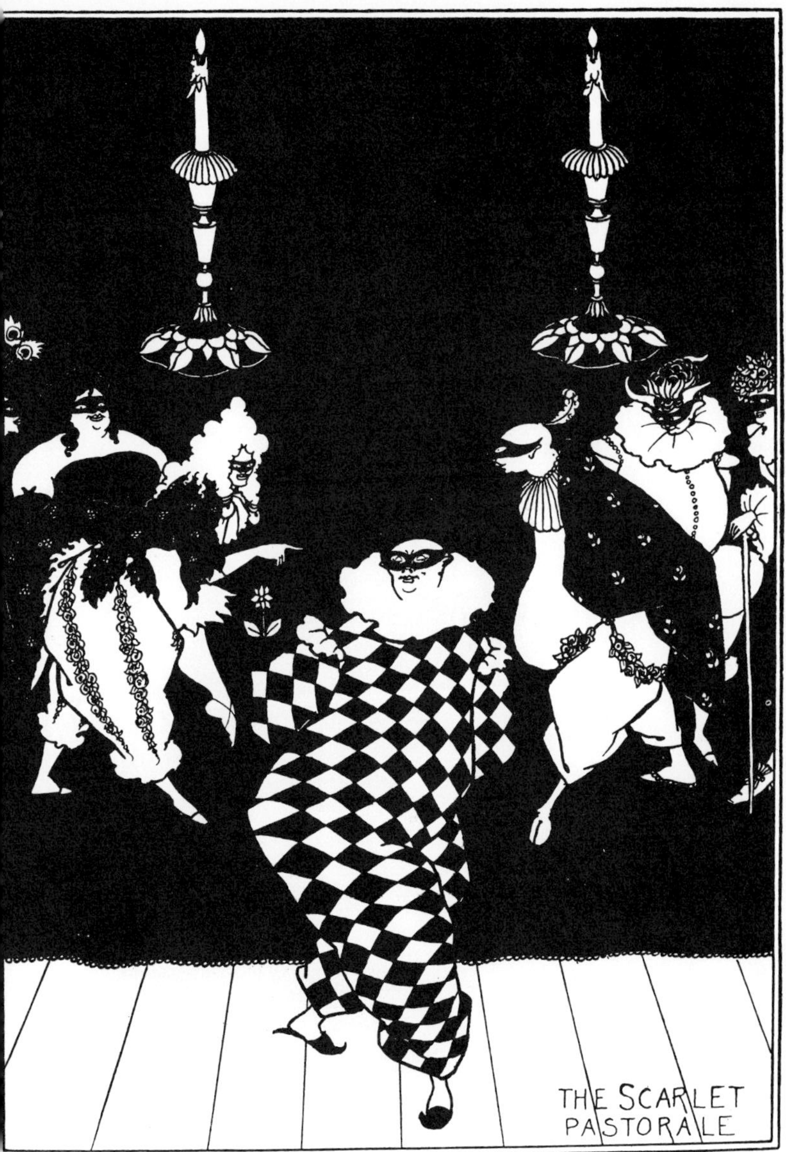
THE SCARLET
PASTORALE

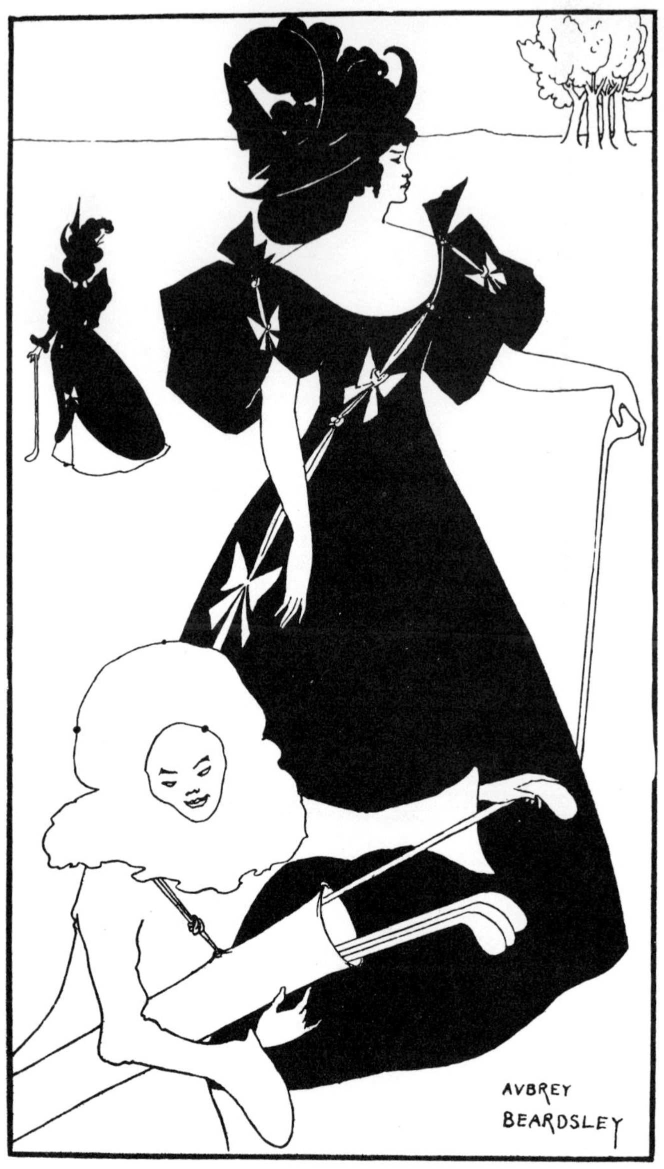
AVBREY
BEARDSLEY

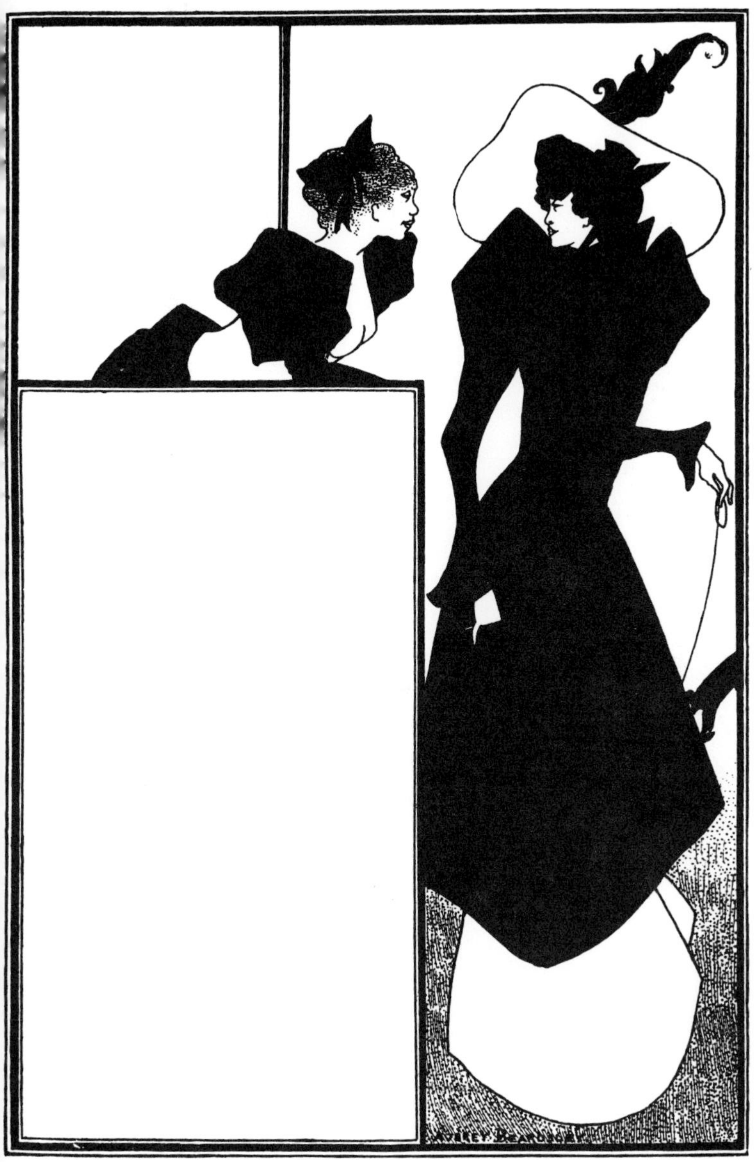

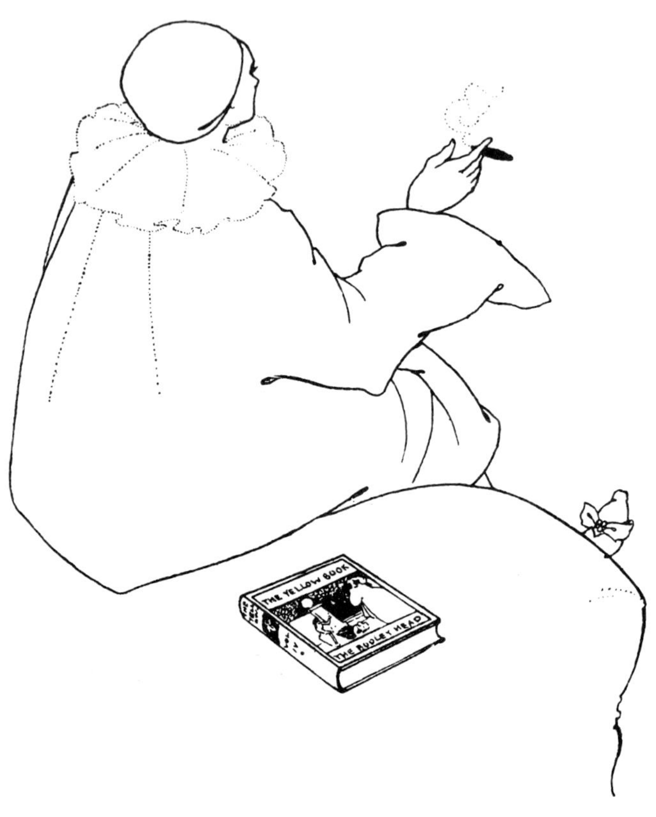
THE YELLOW BOOK
THE BODLEY HEAD

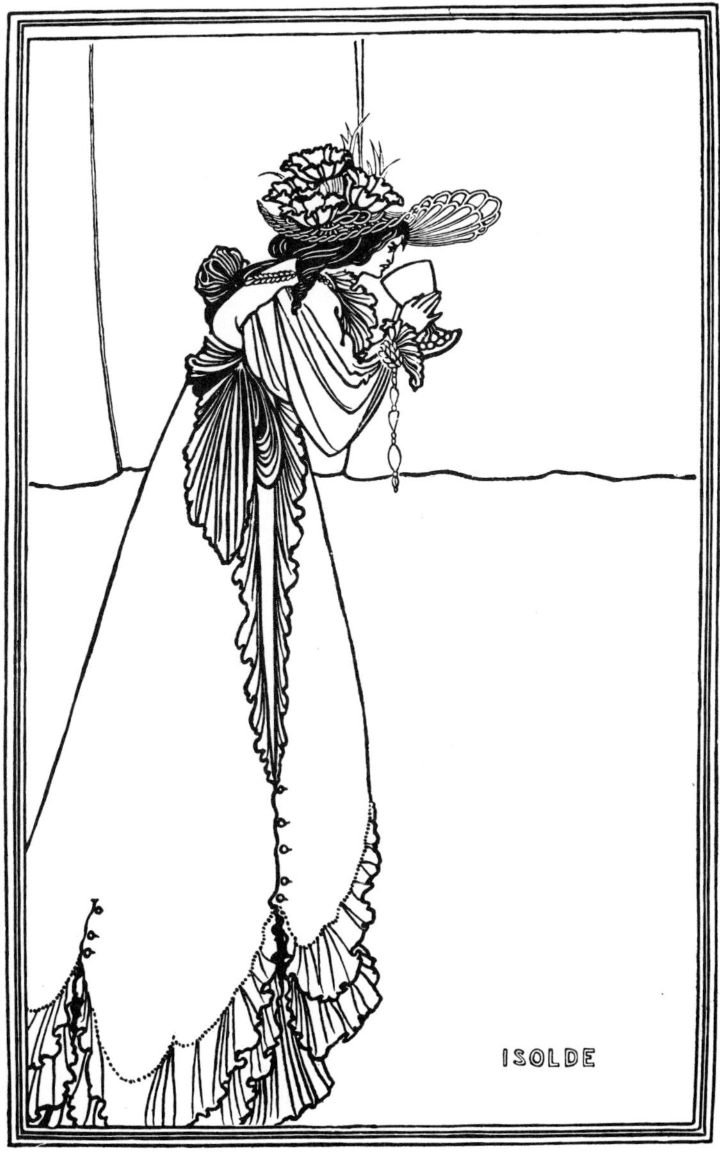
ISOLDE

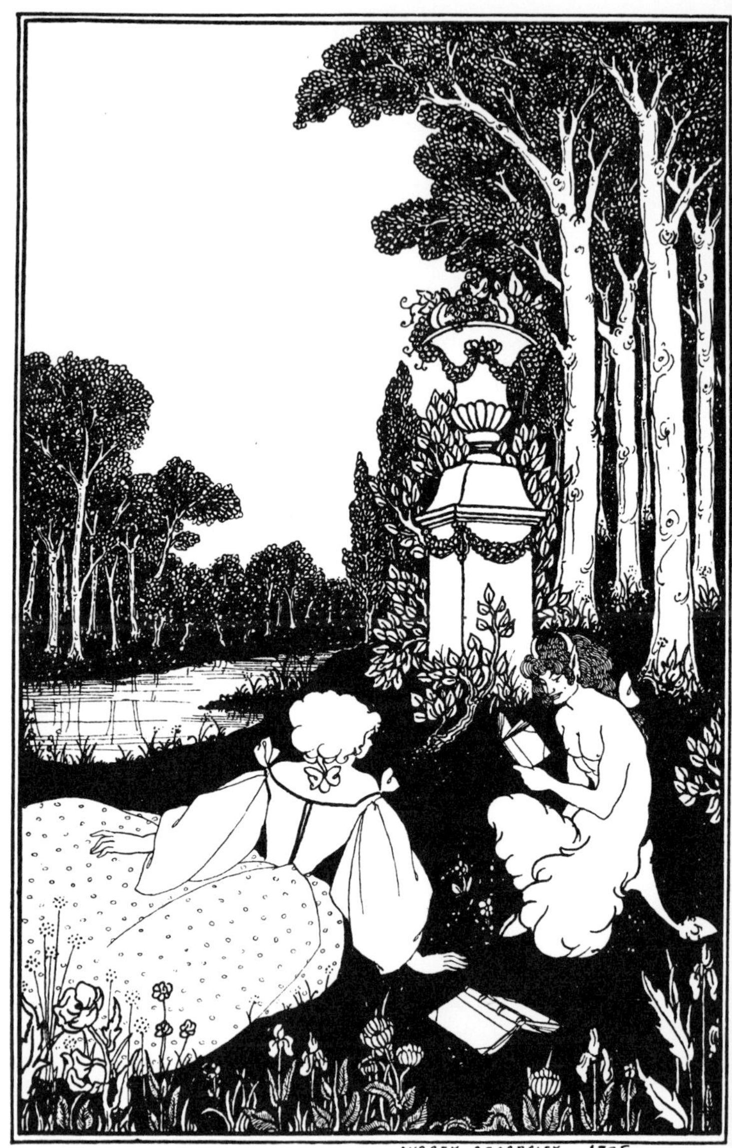
AVBREY BEARDSLEY. 1895.

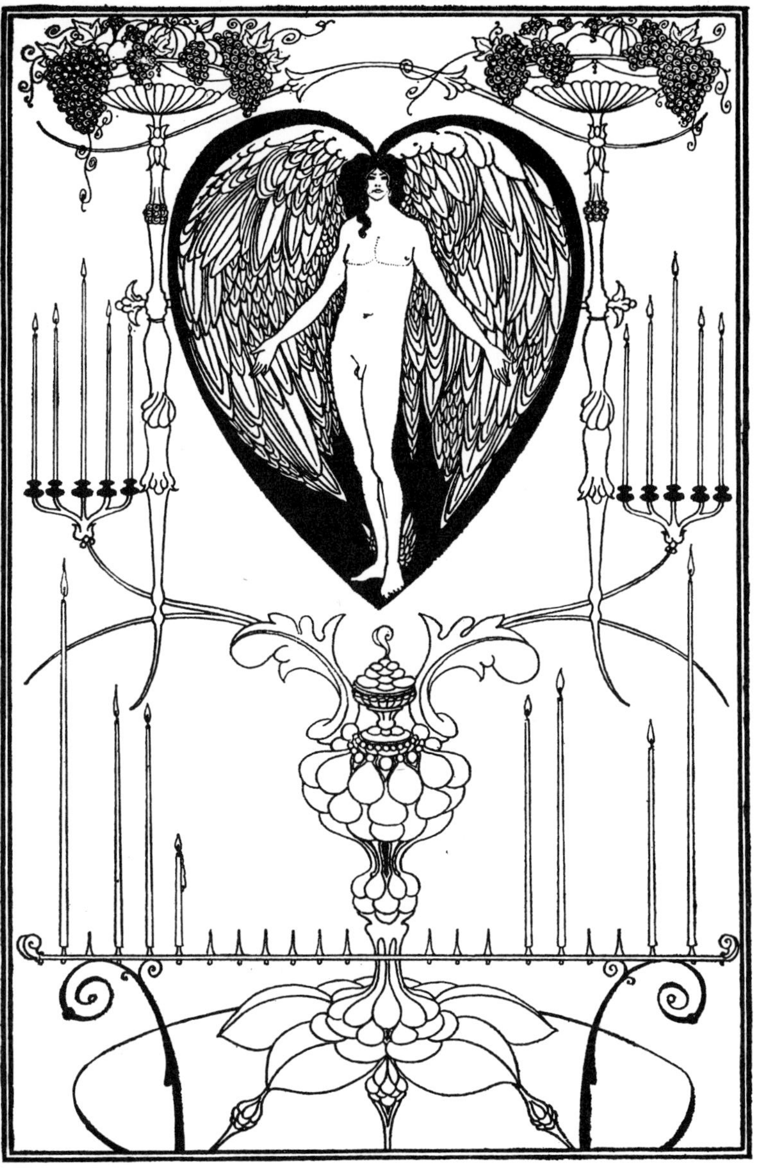

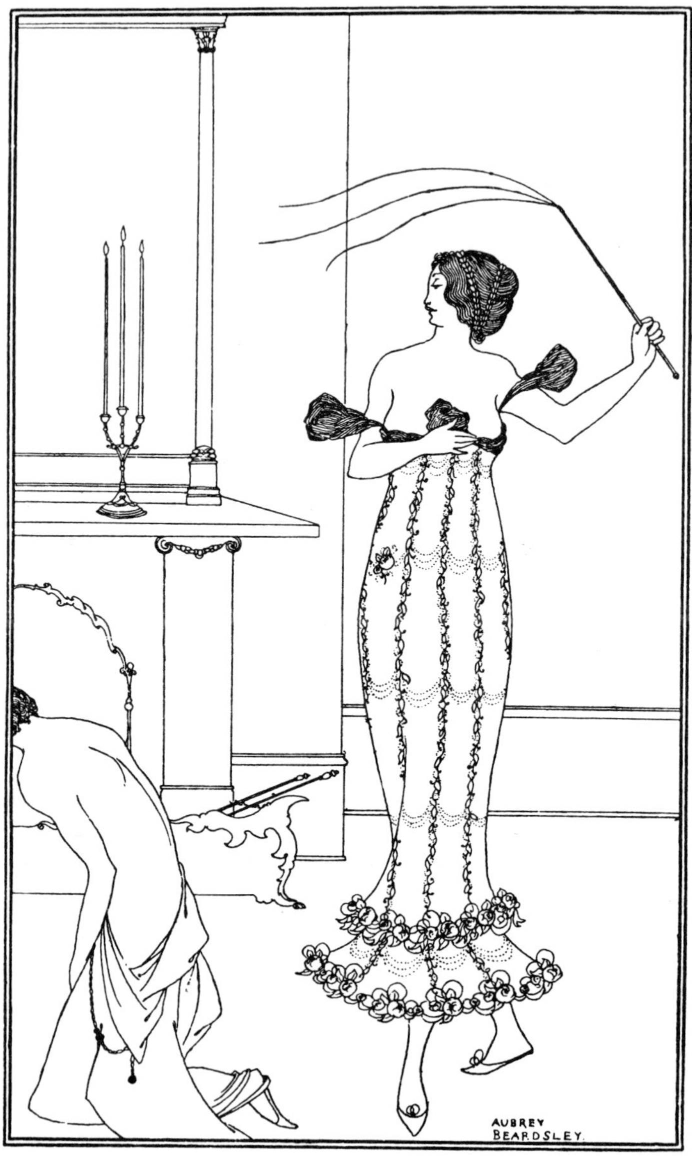
AUBREY
BEARDSLEY.

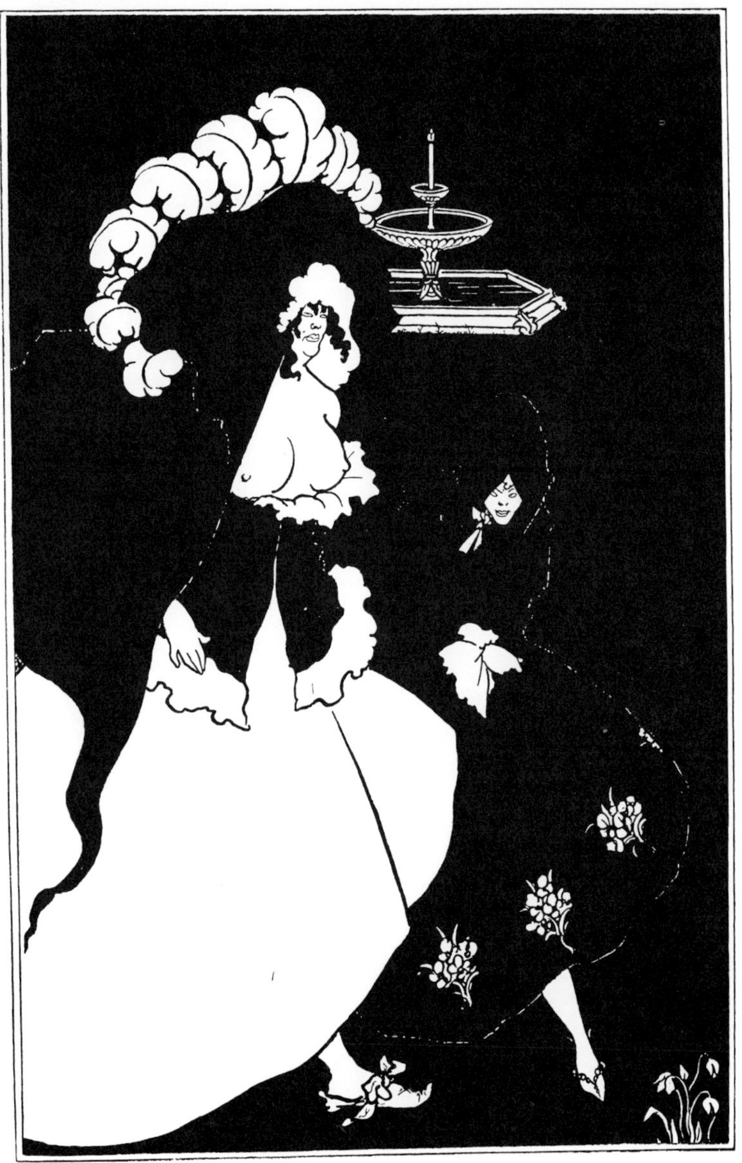

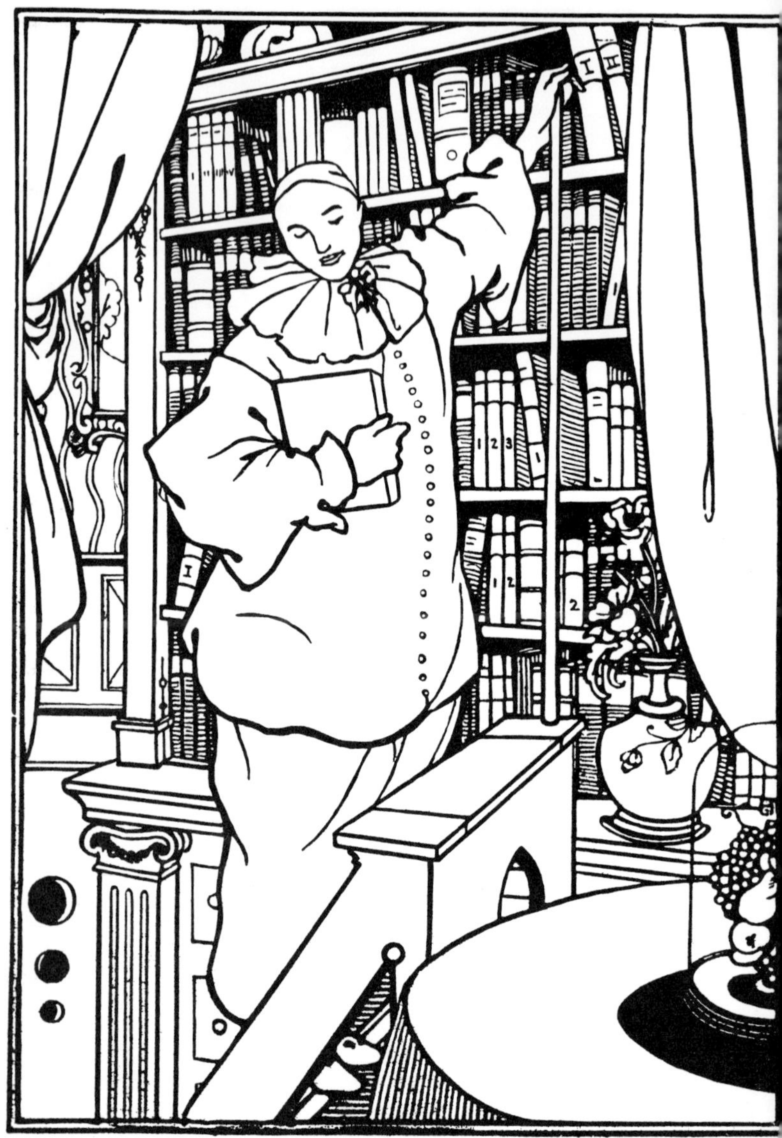

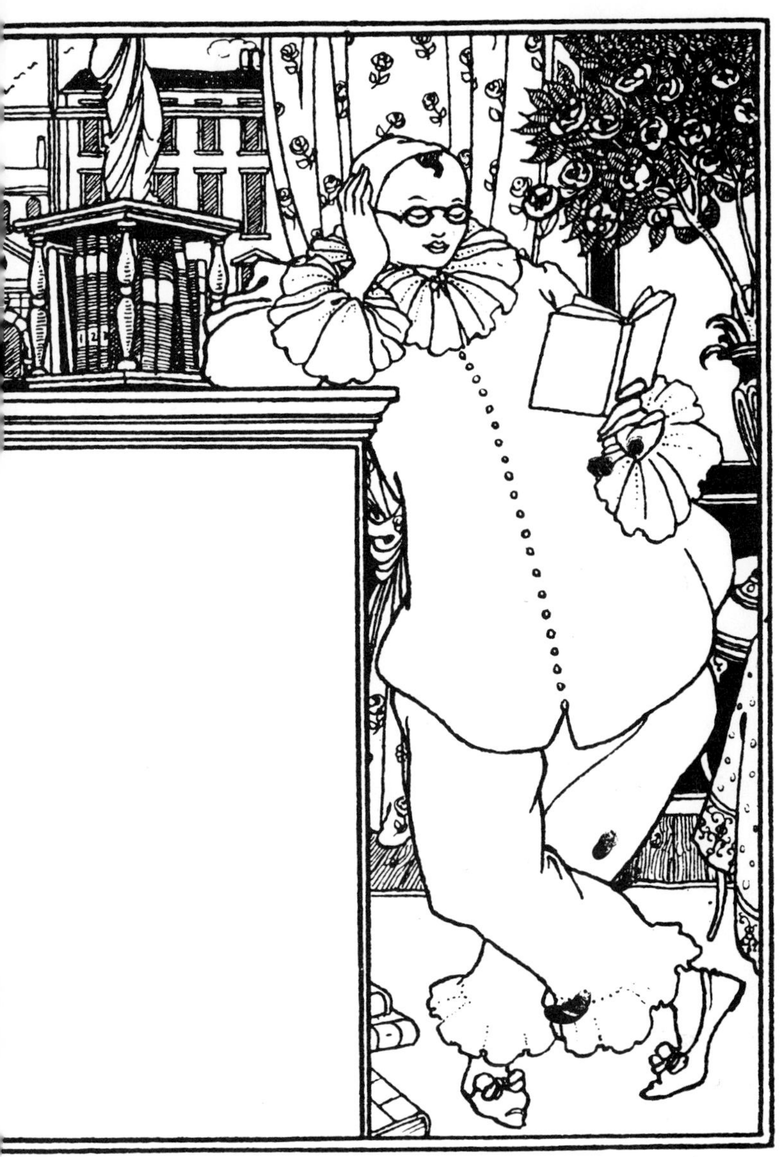

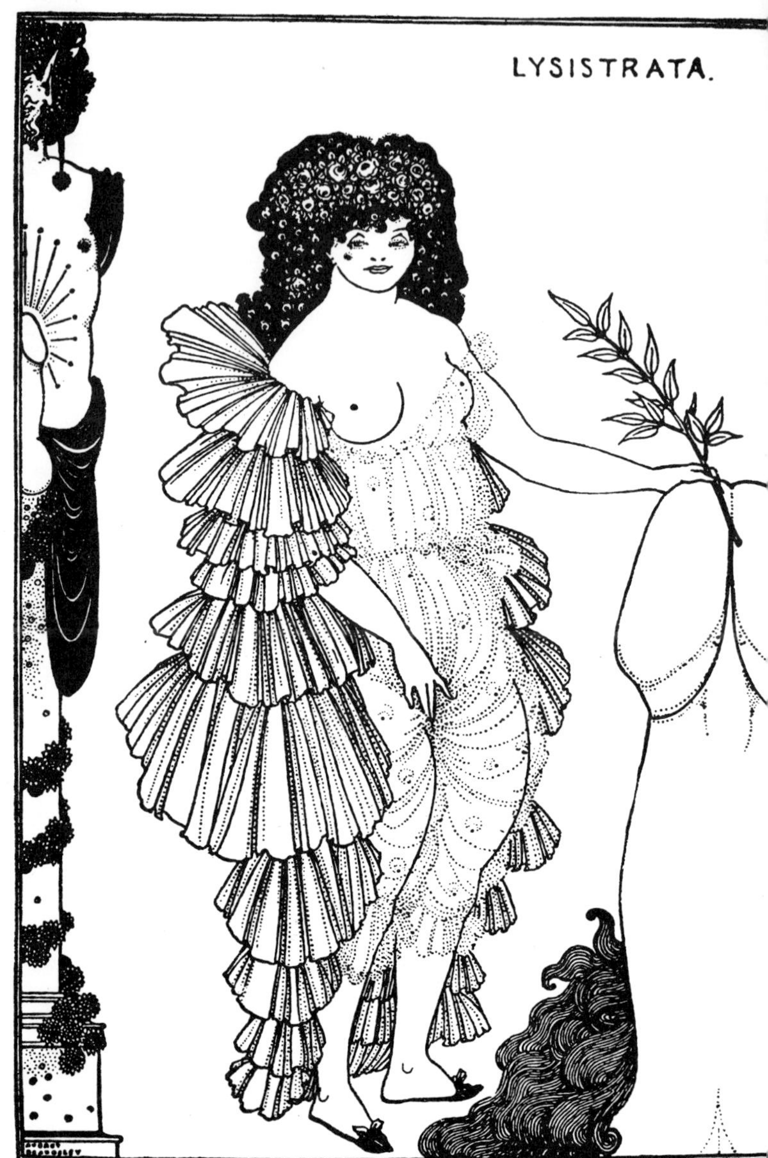
LYSISTRATA.

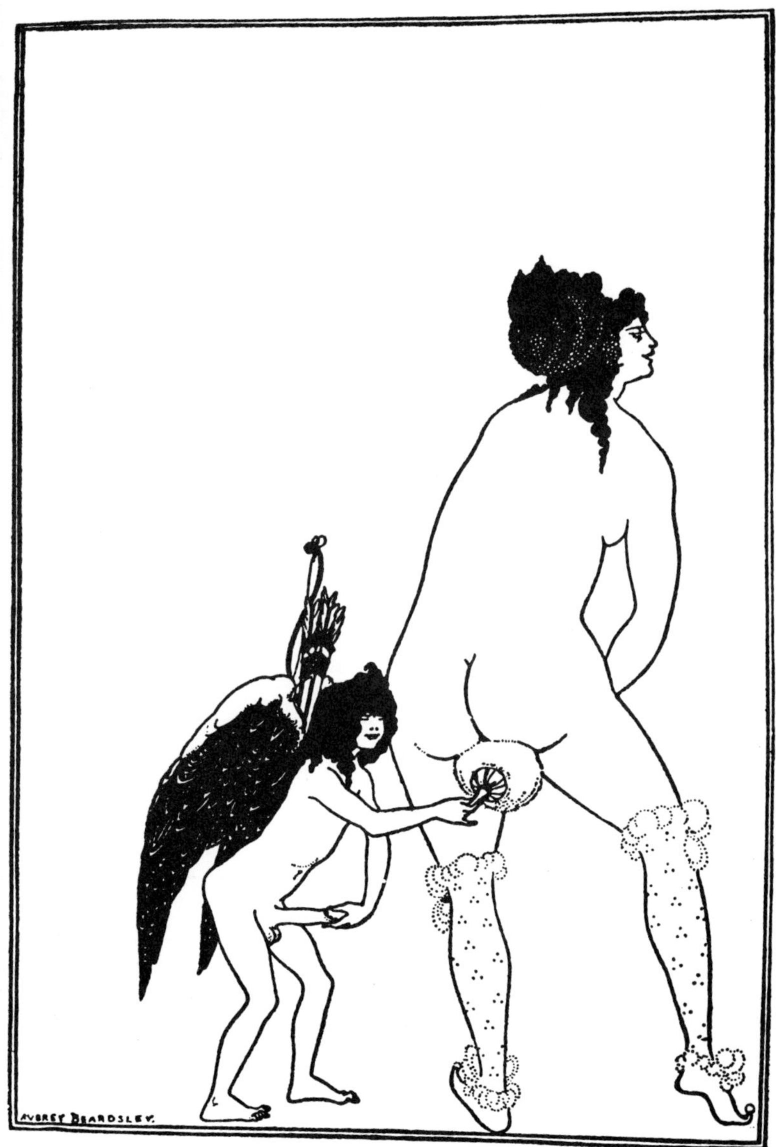
AVBREY BEARDSLEY.

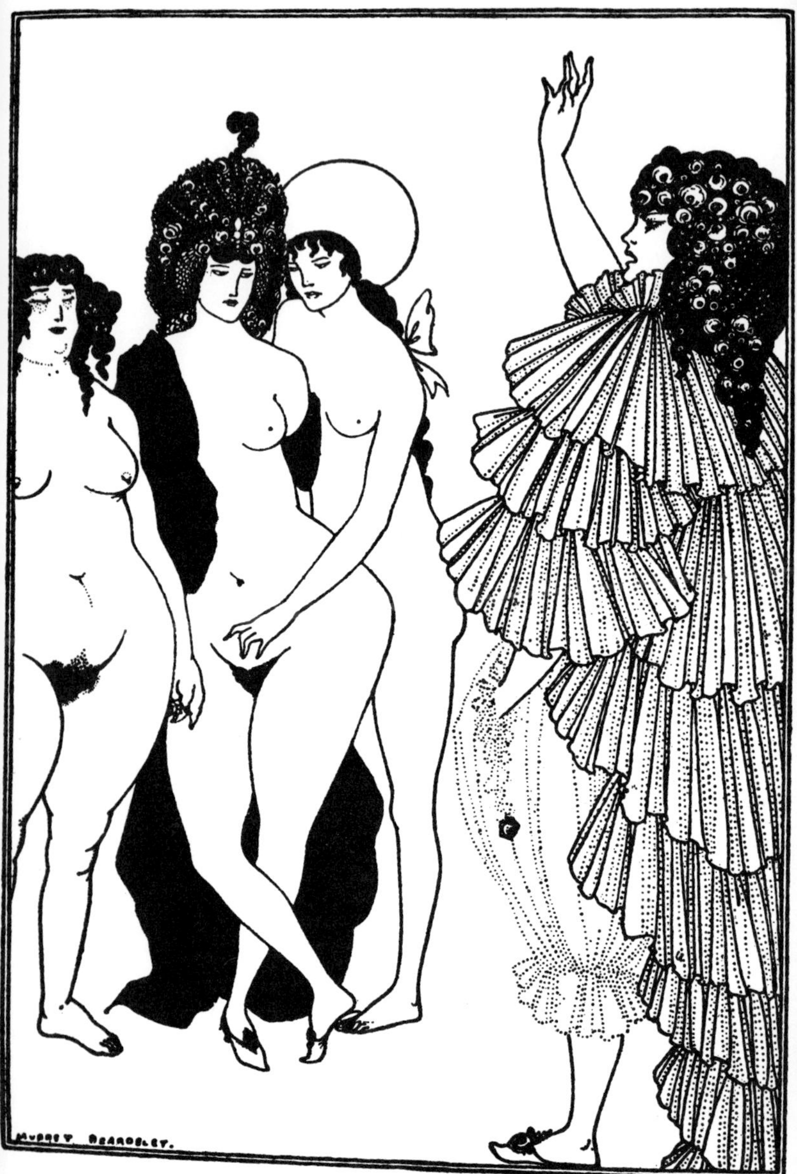
AUBREY BEARDSLEY.

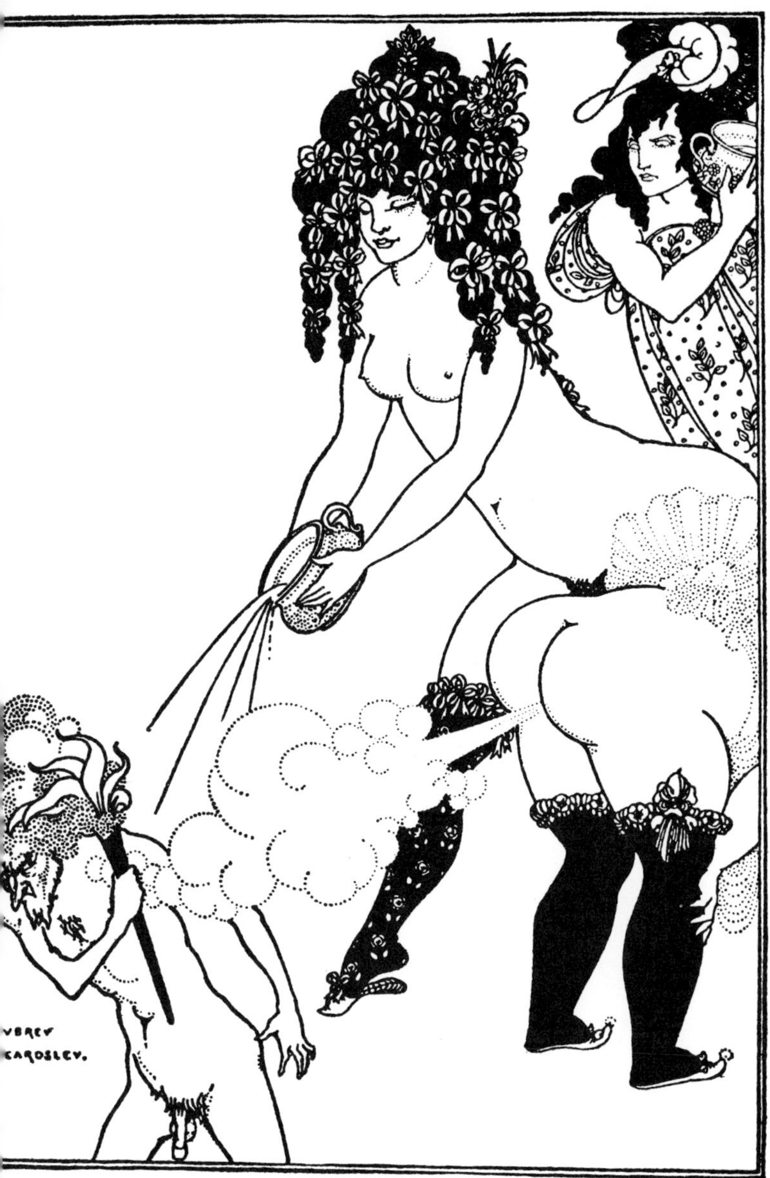

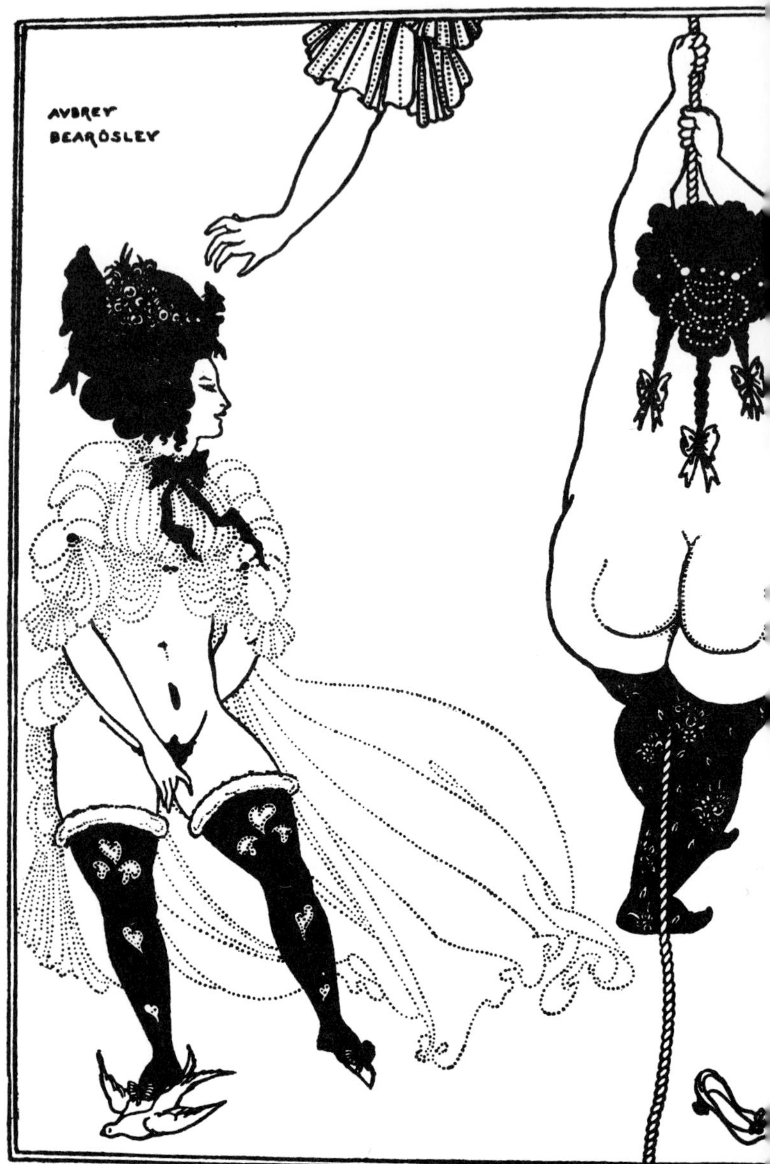
AVBREY
BEARDSLEY

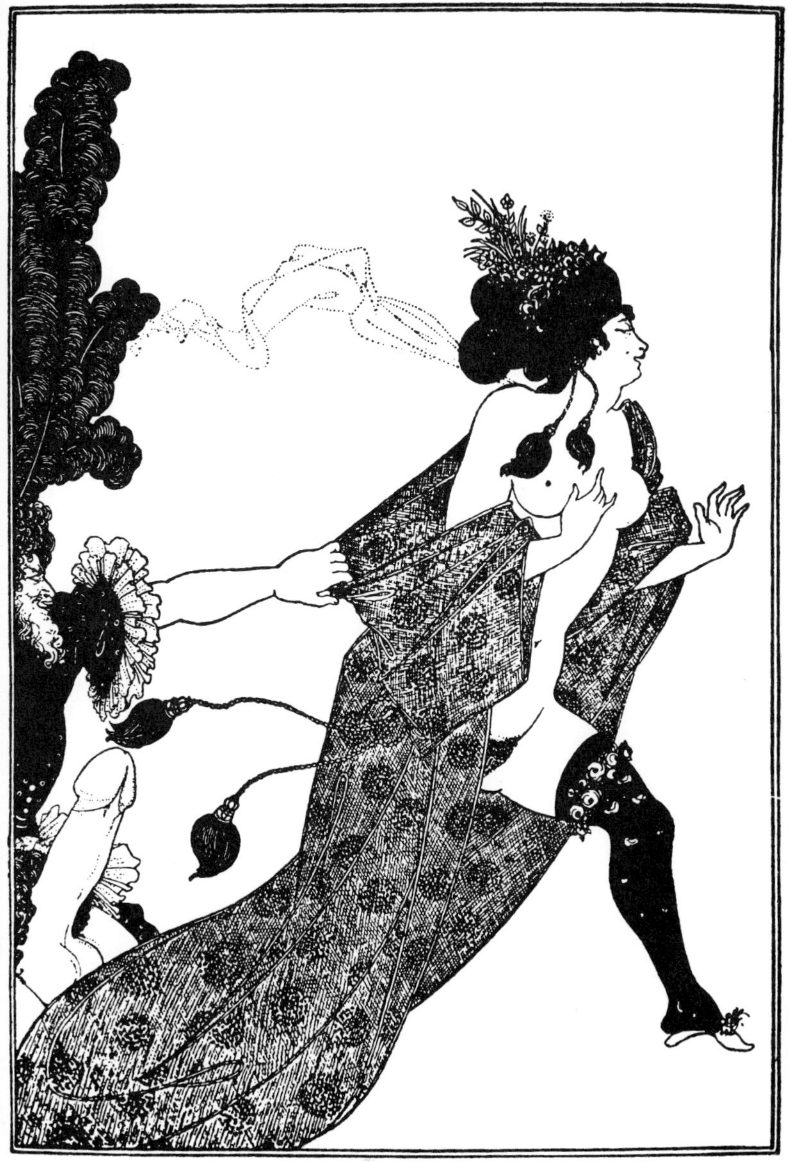

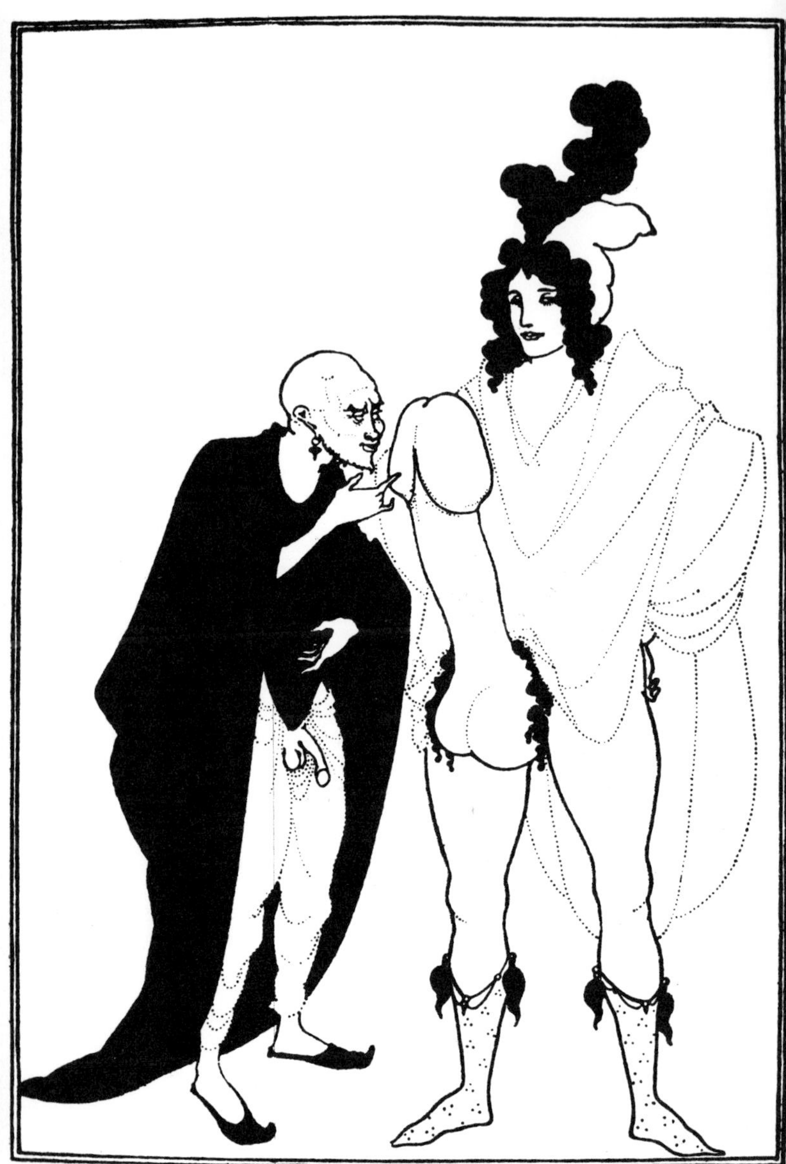

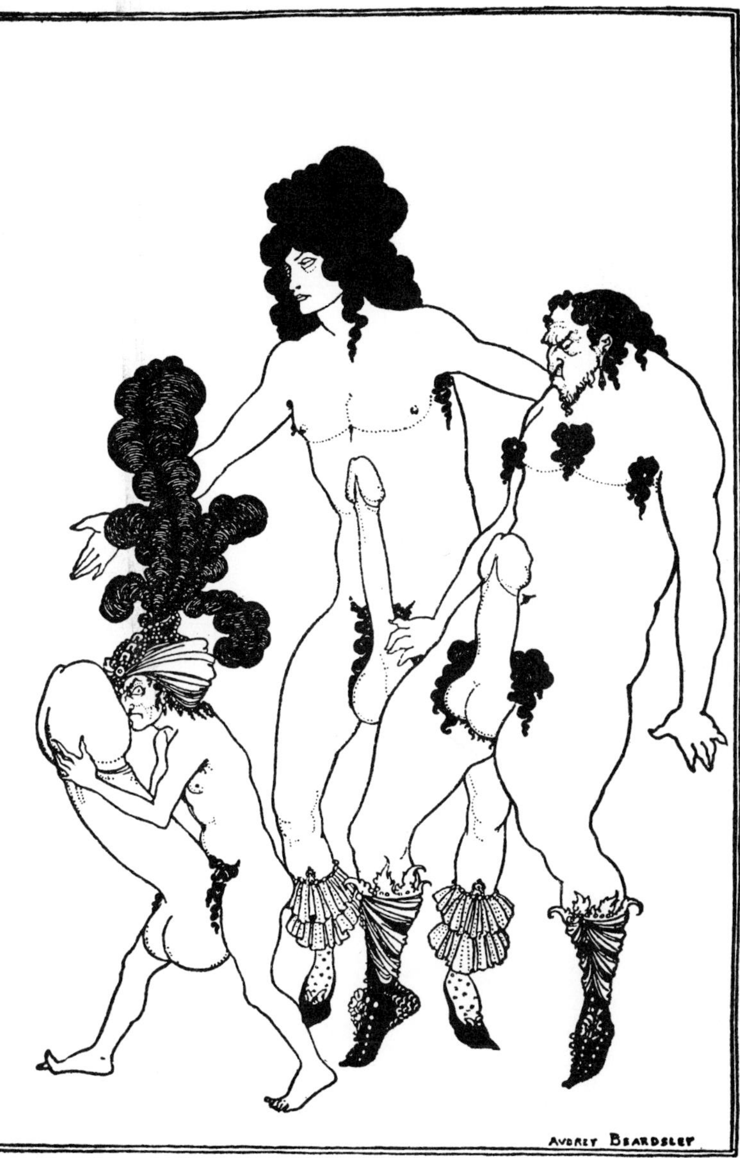
AUBREY BEARDSLEY

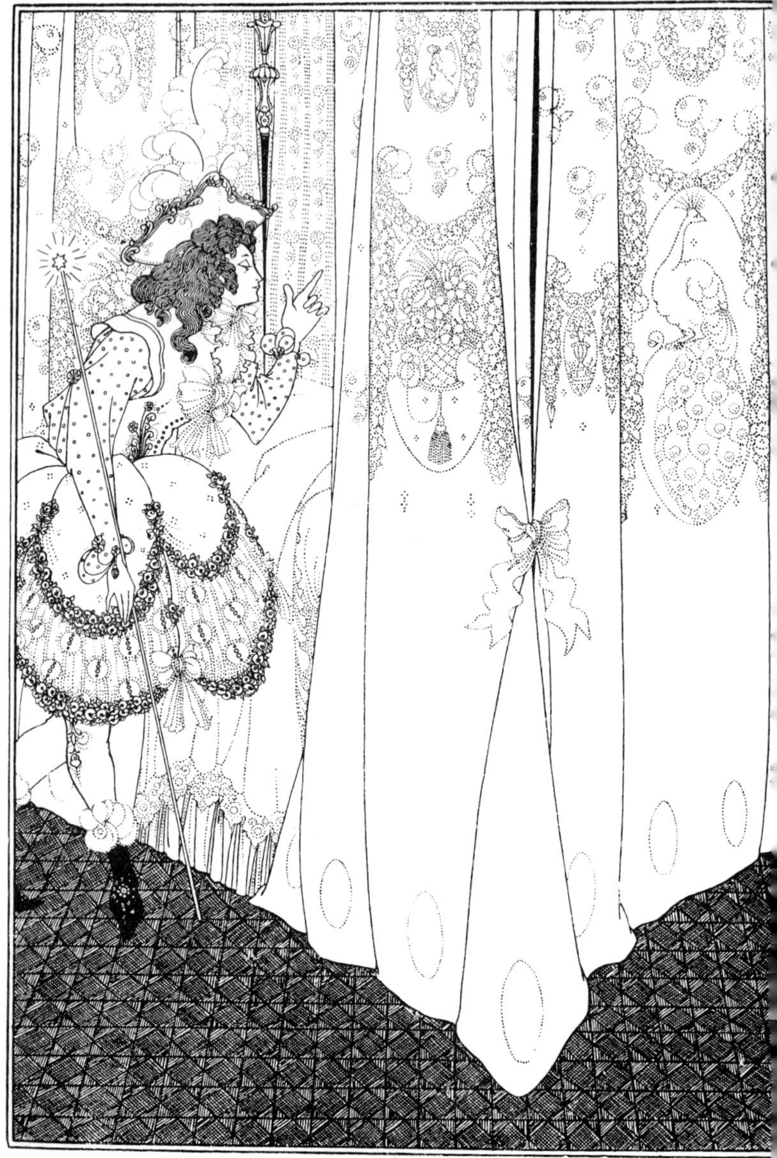

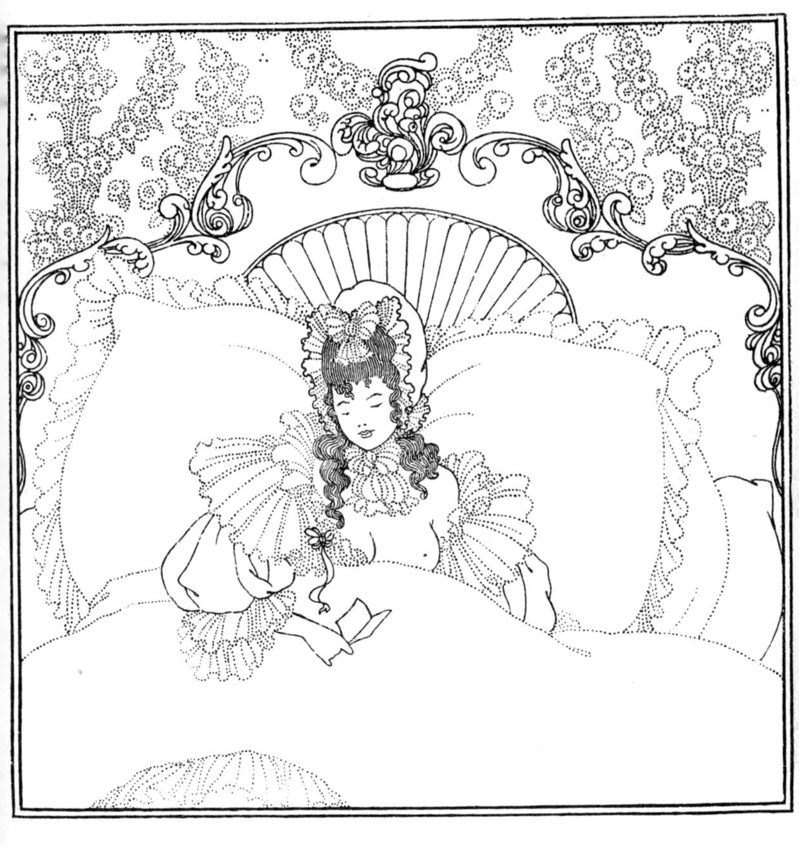

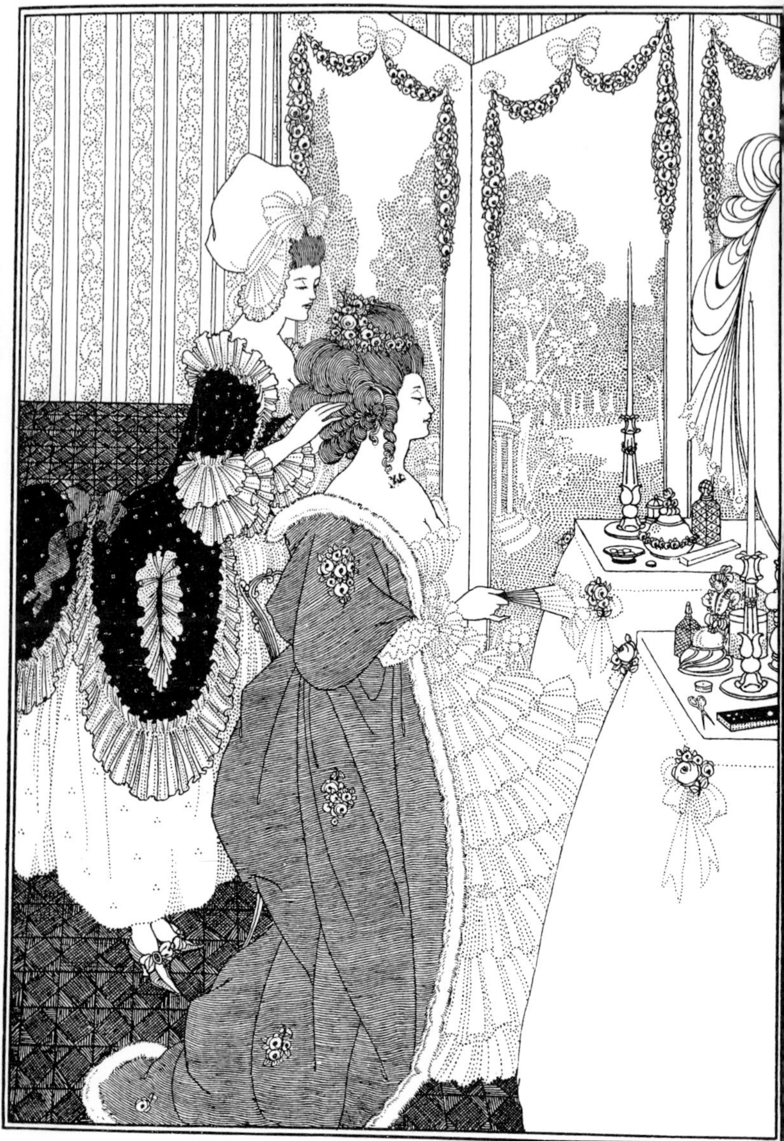

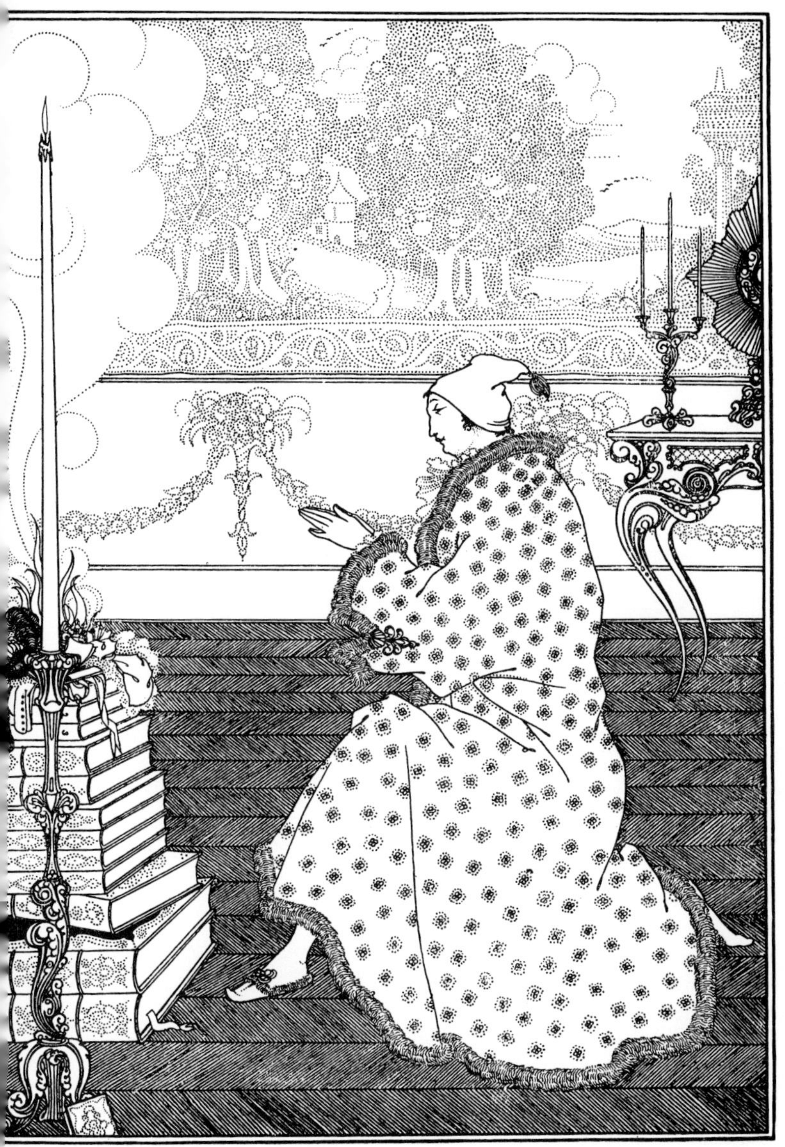

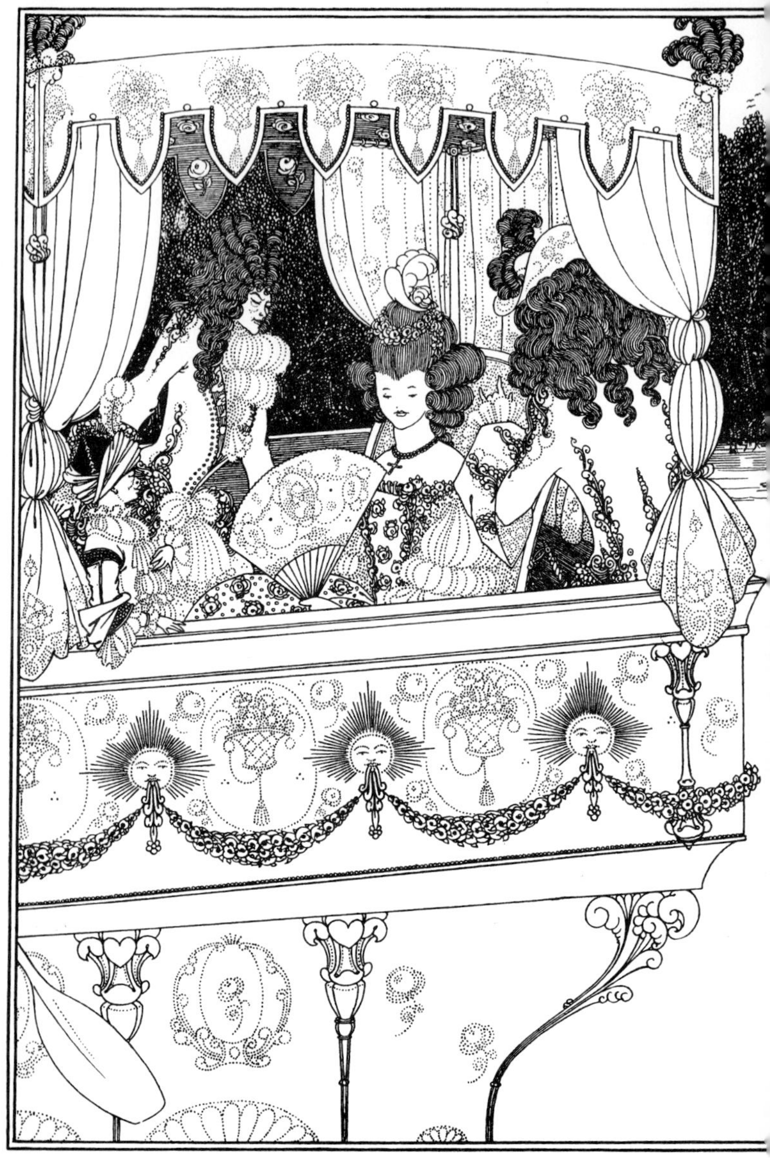

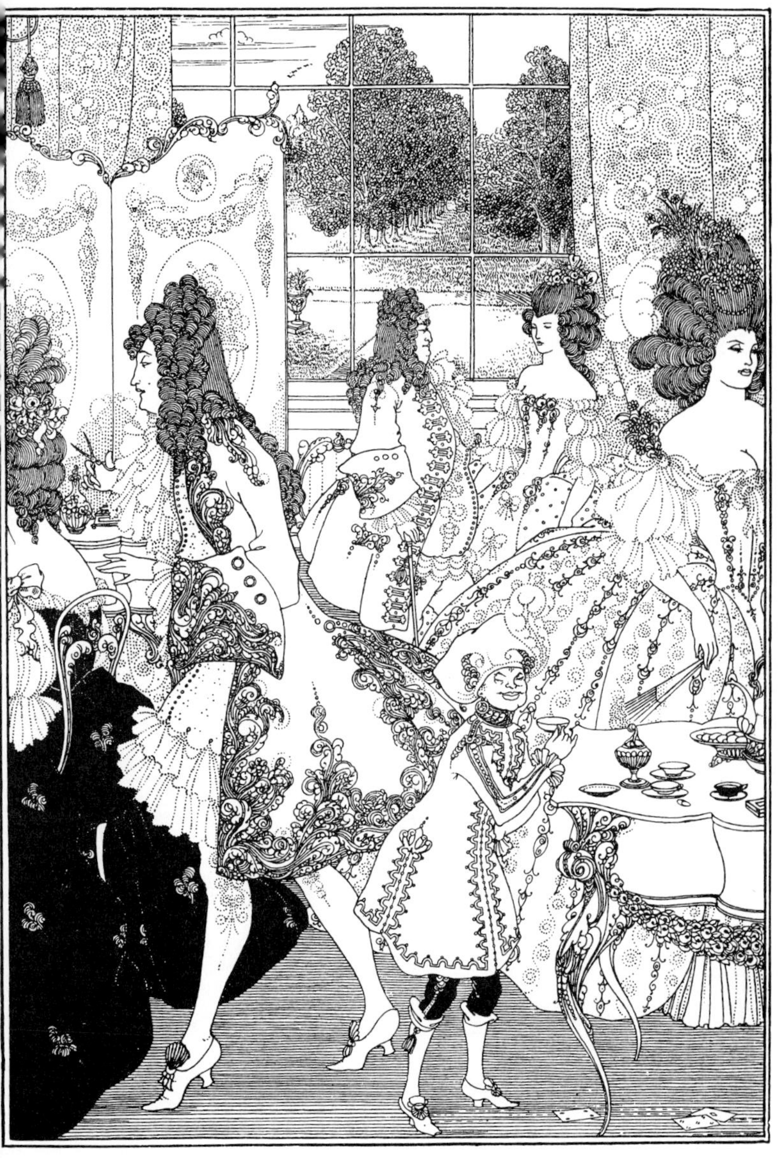

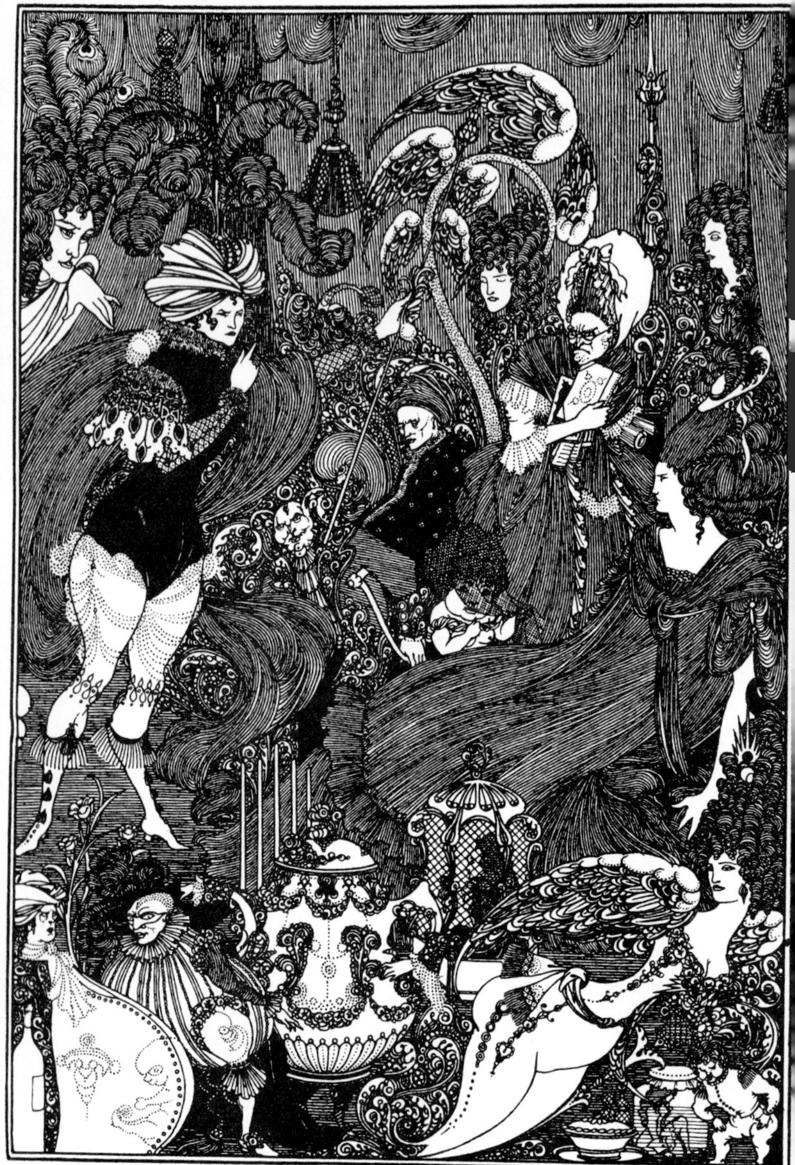

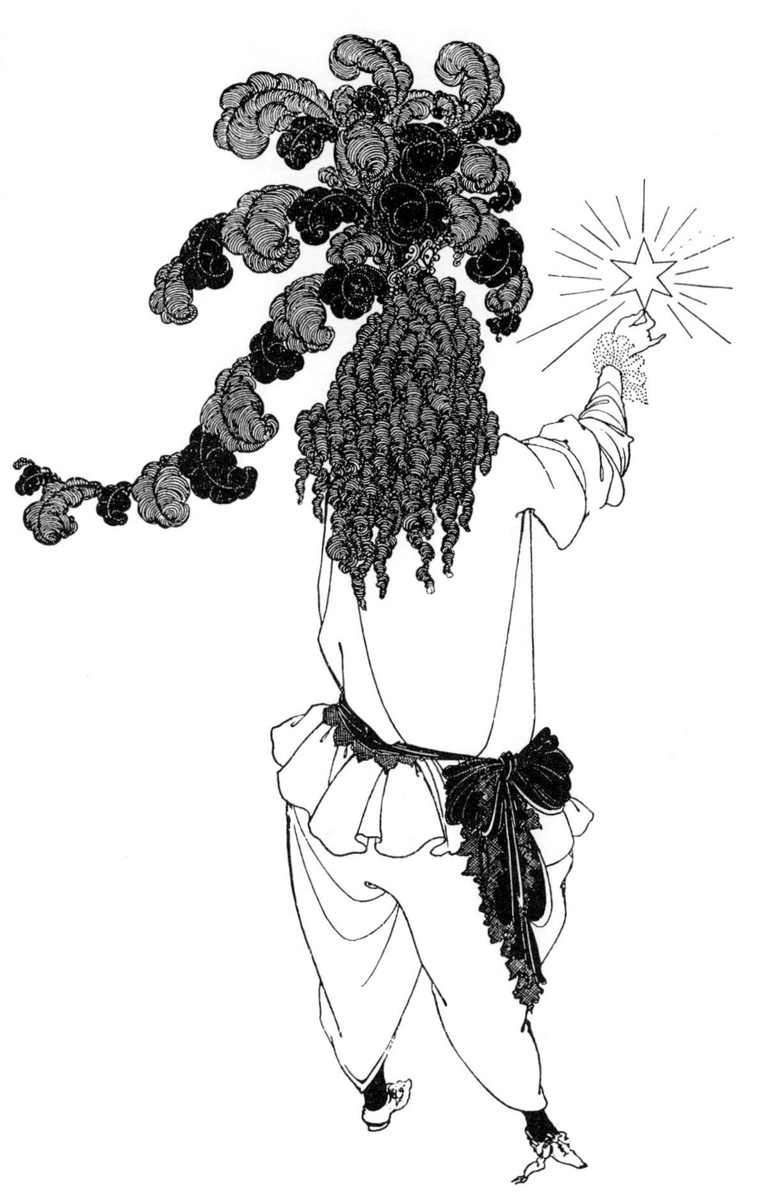

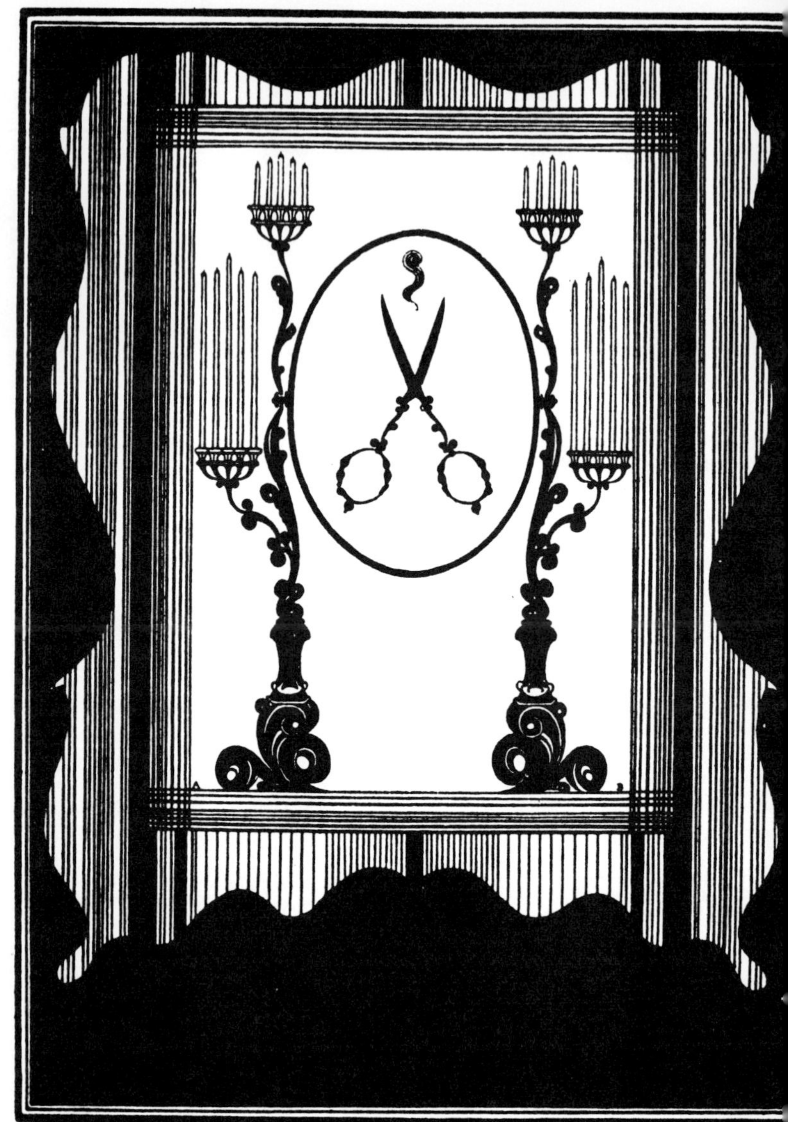

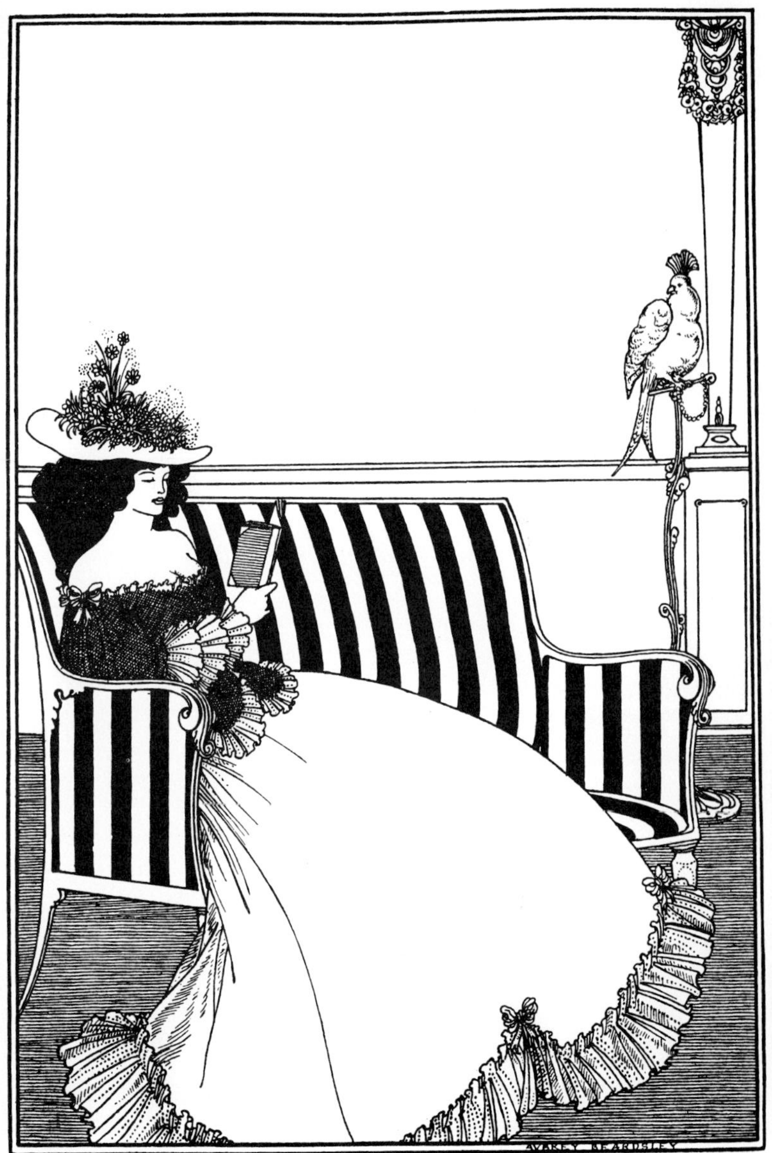

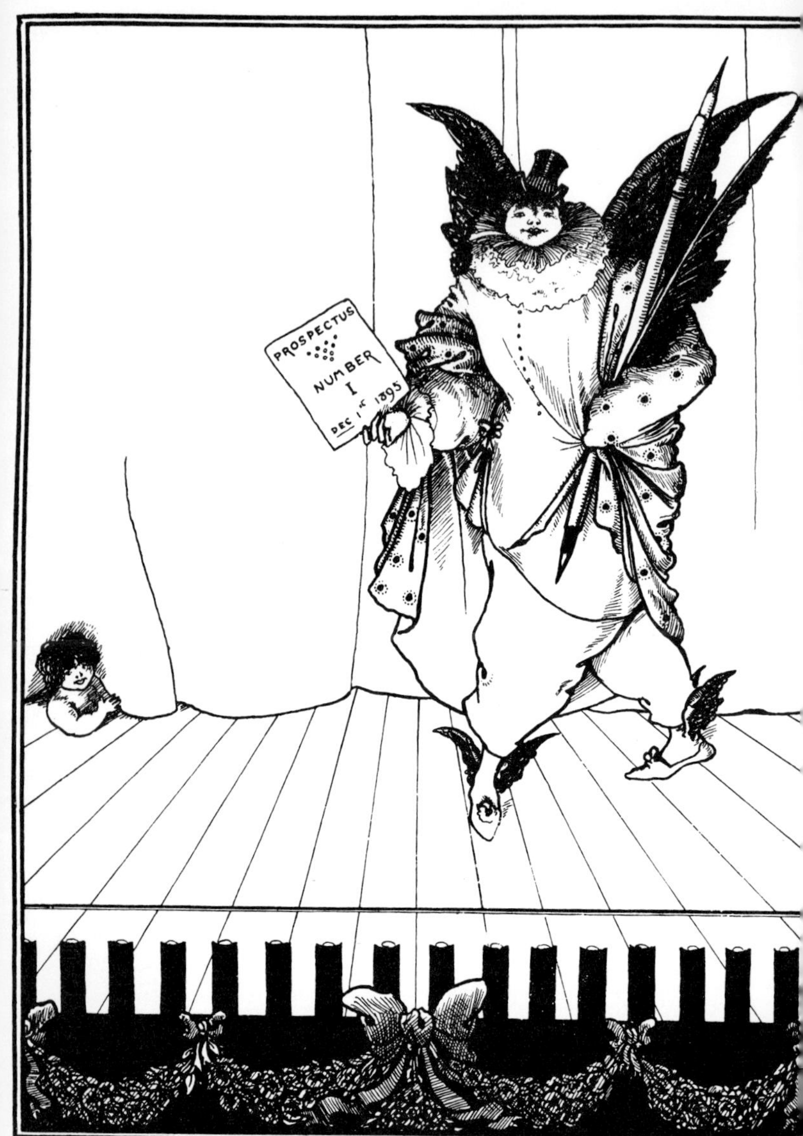
PROSPECTUS
NUMBER
I
DEC 1st 1893
AVBREY BEARDSLEY

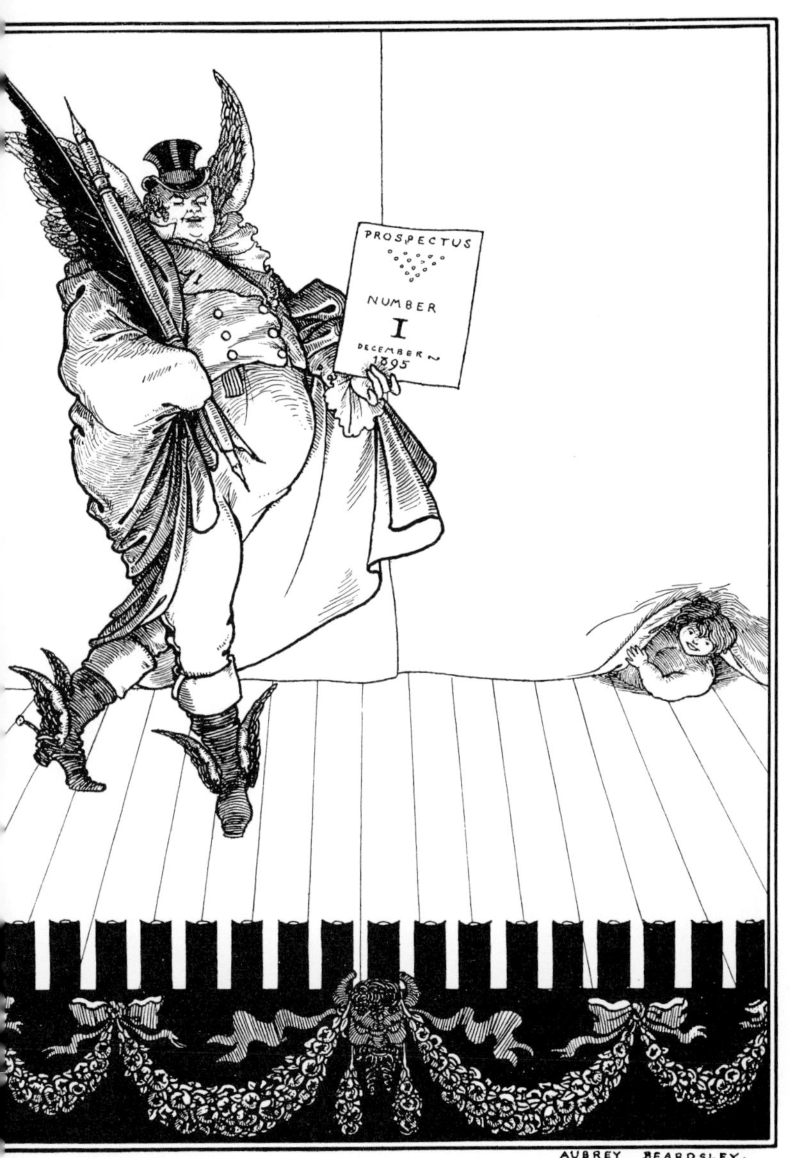
PROSPECTUS
NUMBER
I
DECEMBER
1895
AUBREY BEARDSLEY.

THE SAVOY

AUBREY BEARDSLEY. 189

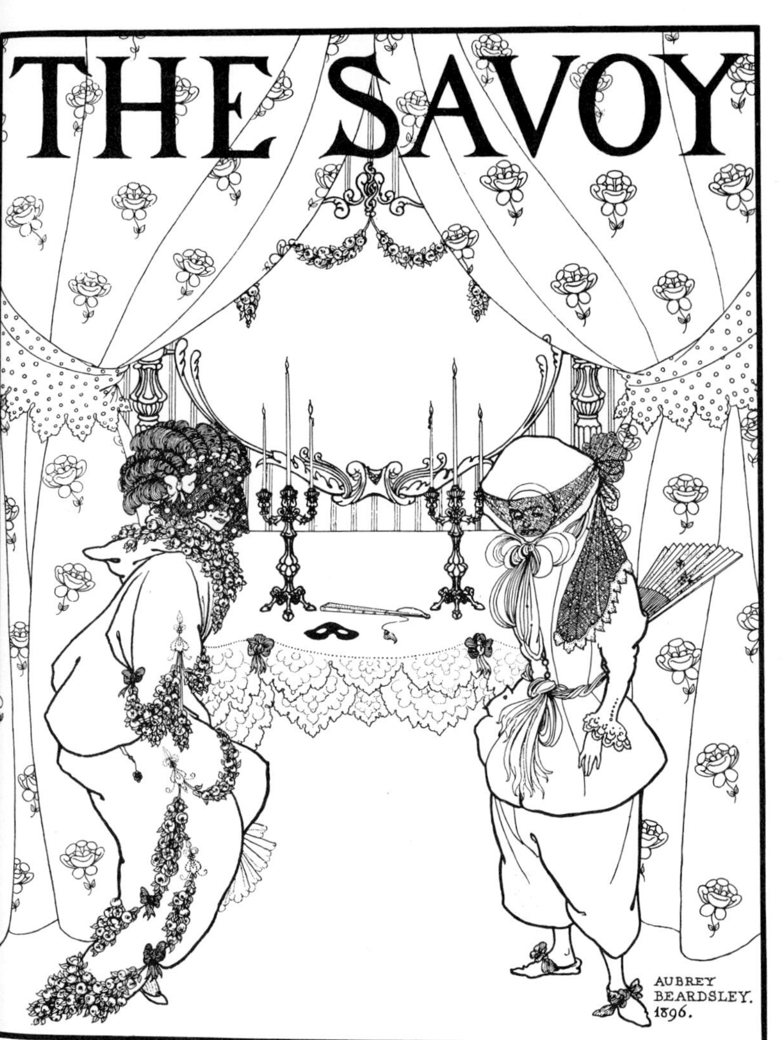
THE SAVOY
AUBREY
BEARDSLEY.
1896.

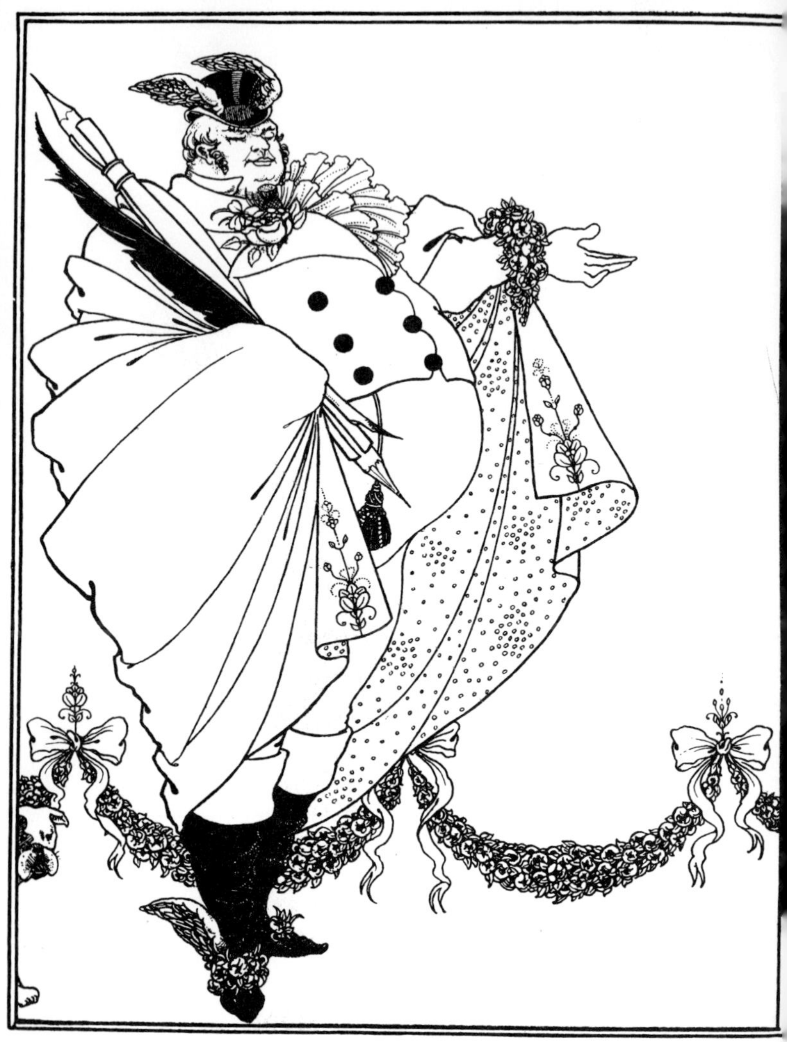

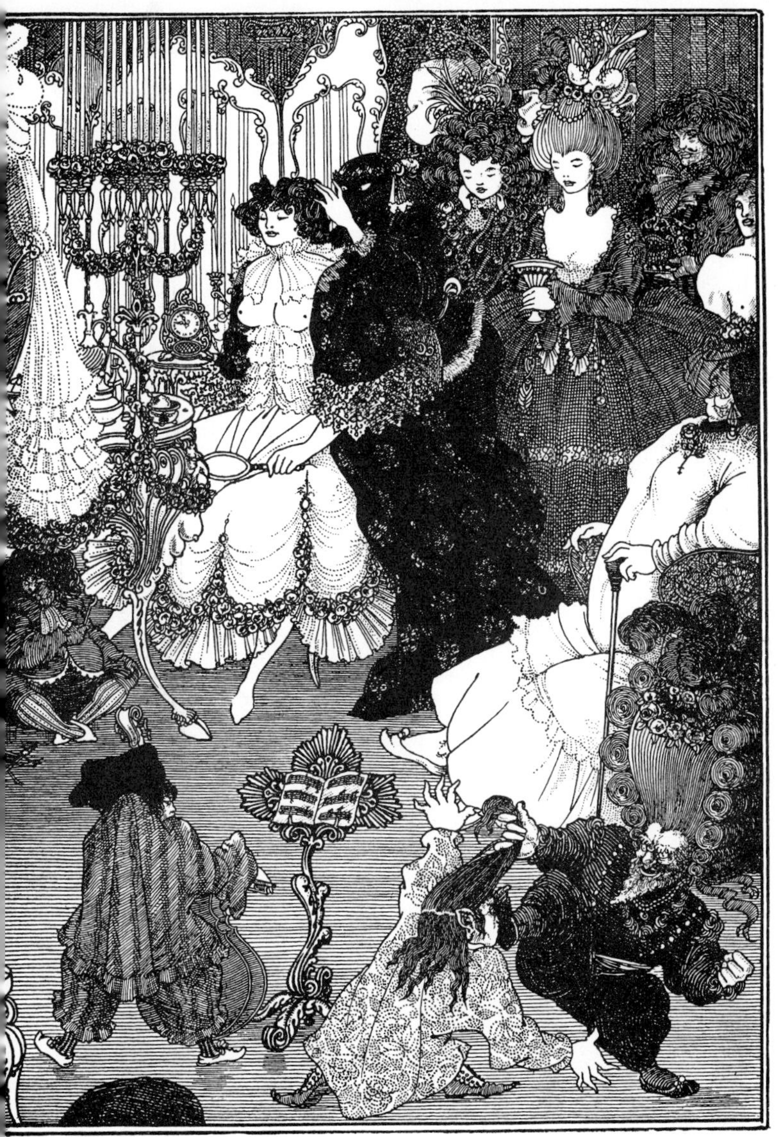

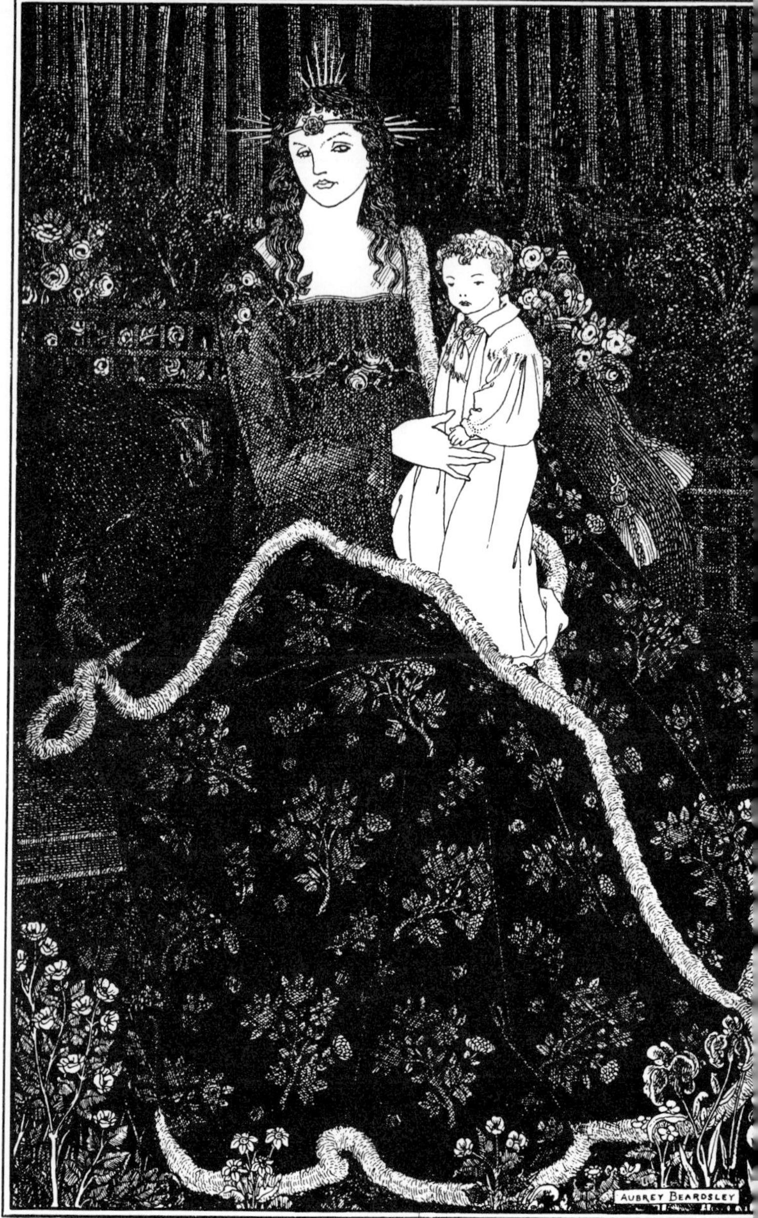
AUBREY BEARDSLEY

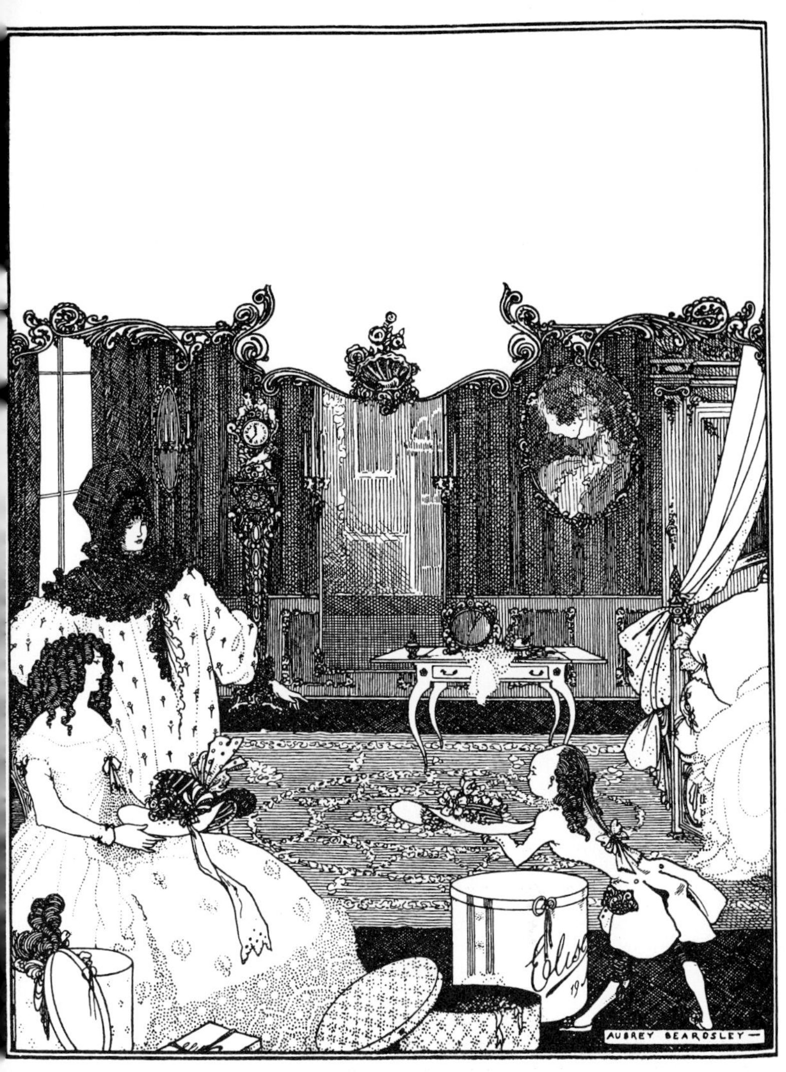
AUBREY BEARDSLEY

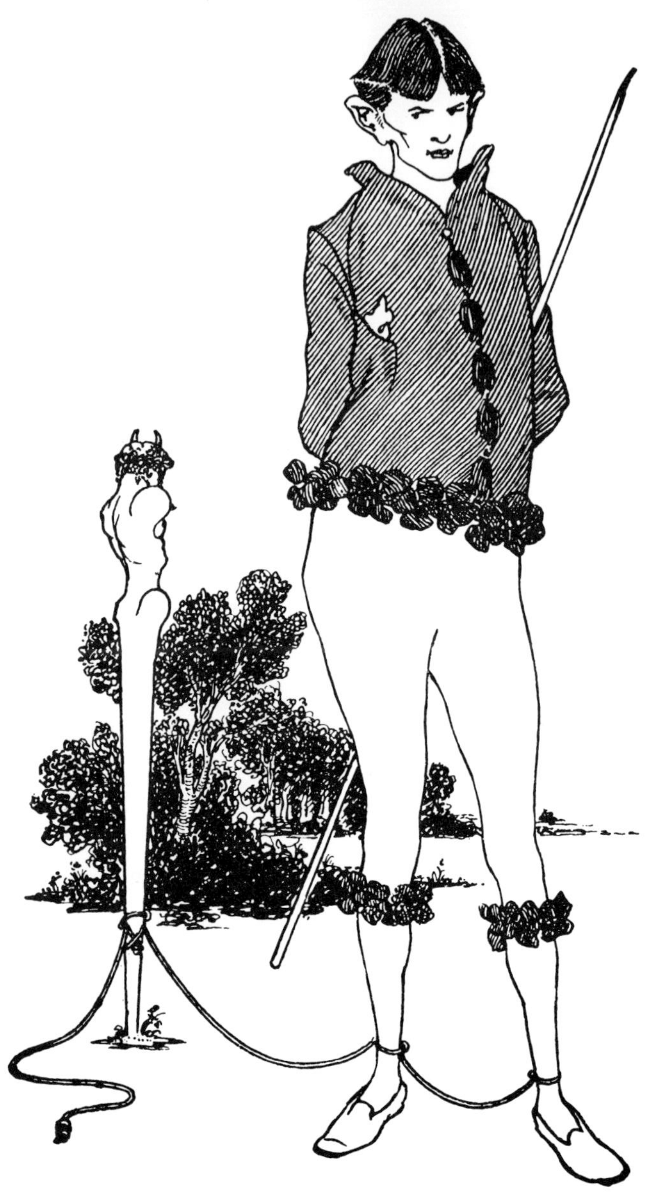

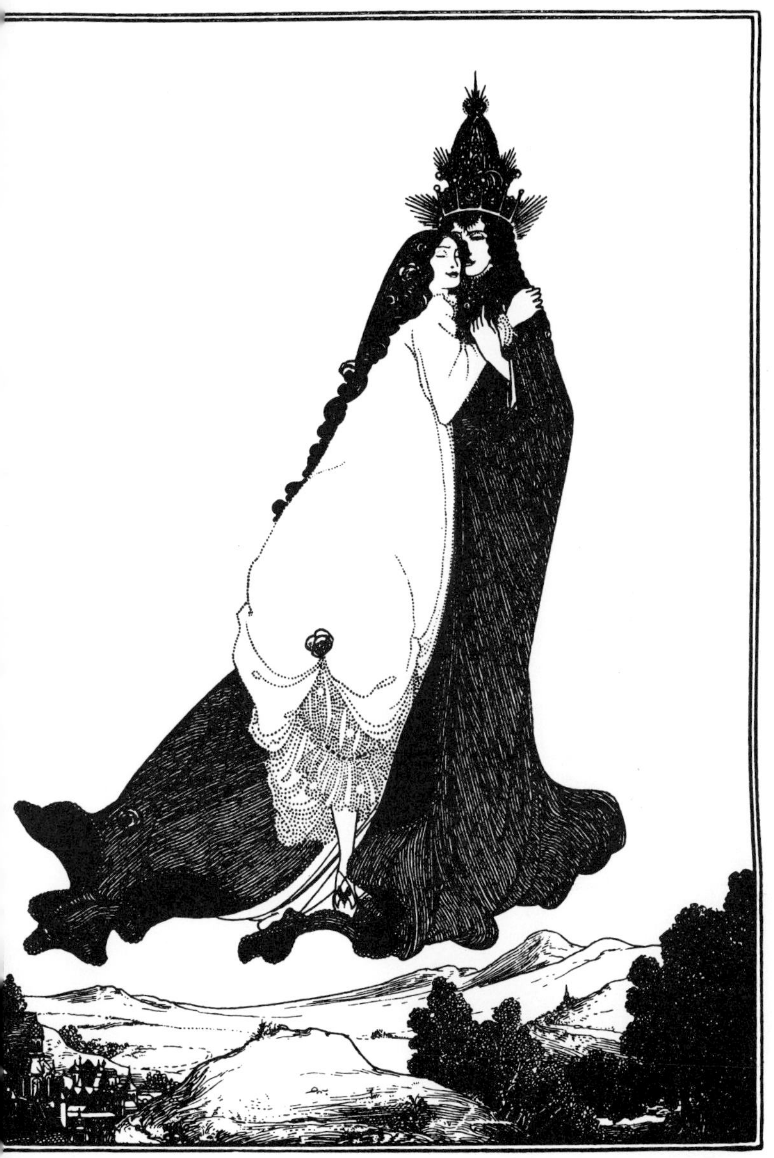

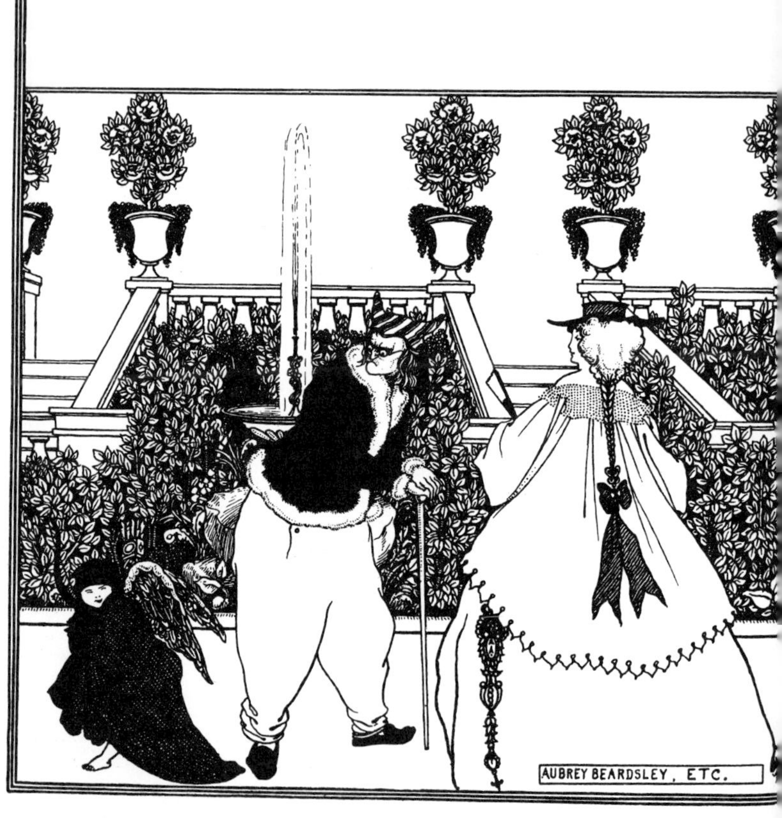
AUBREY BEARDSLEY, ETC.

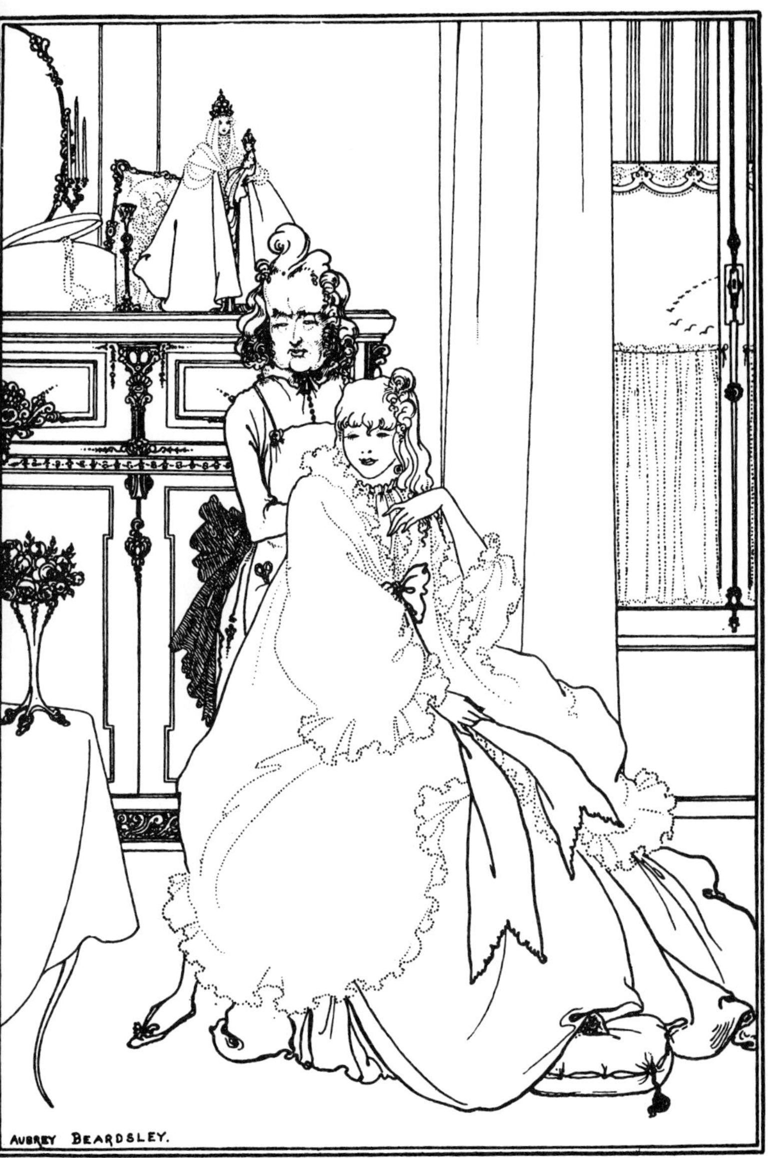
AUBREY BEARDSLEY.

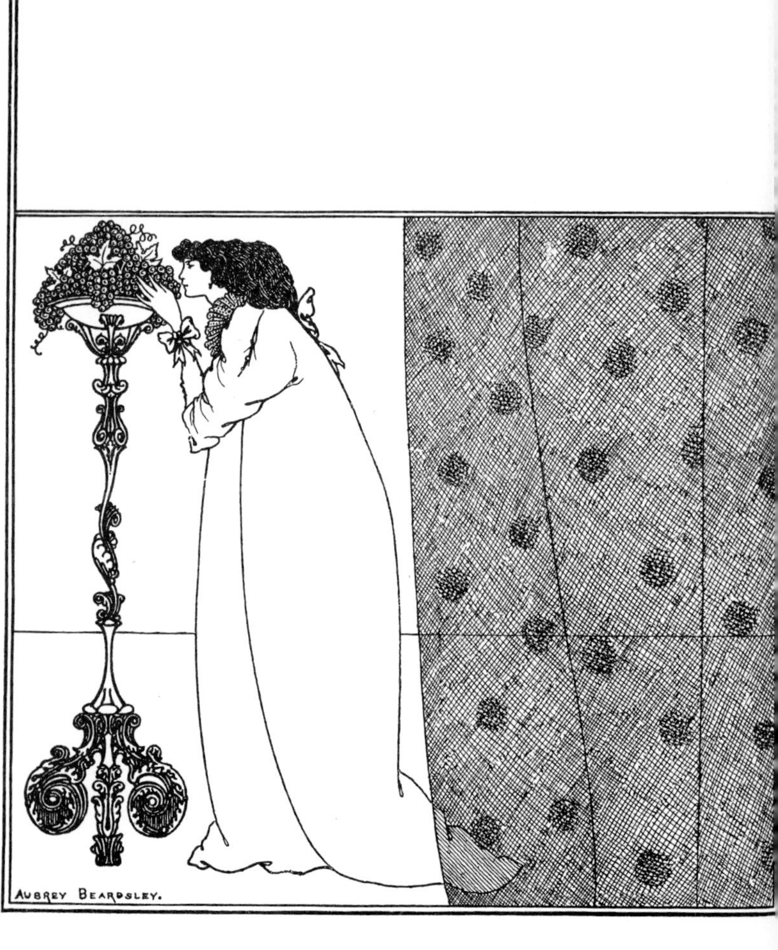
AUBREY BEARDSLEY.

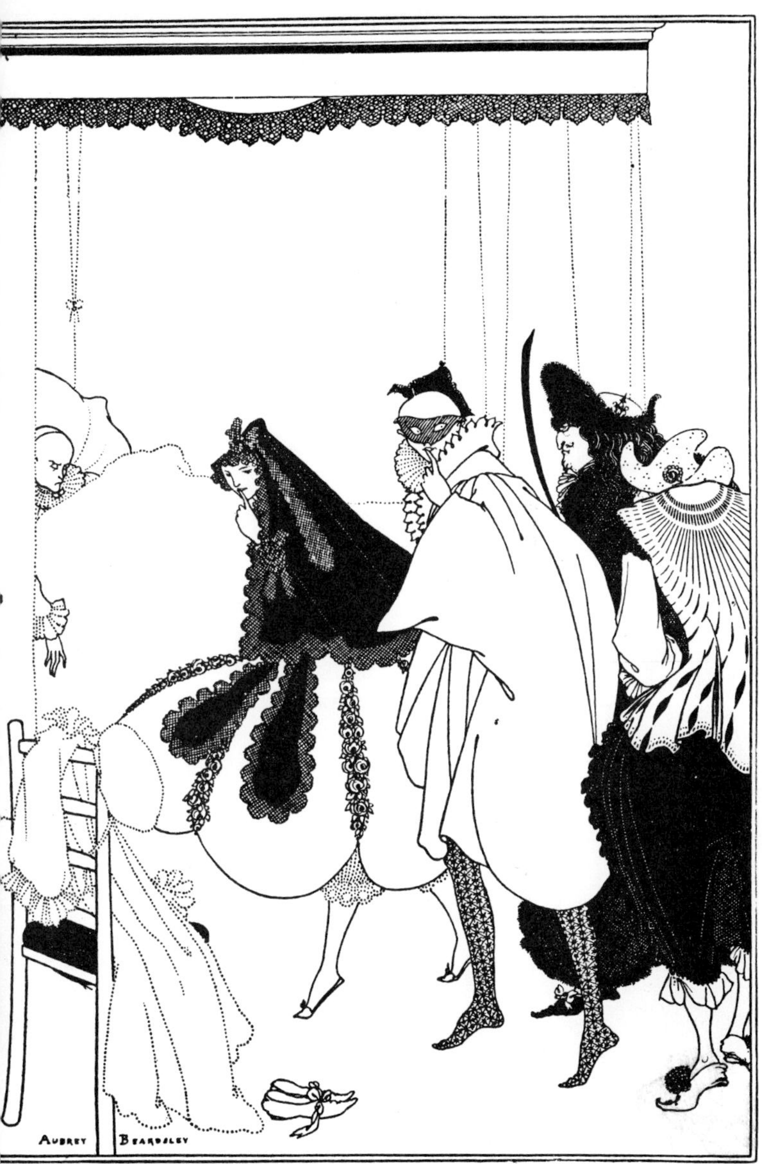
AUBREY BEARDSLEY

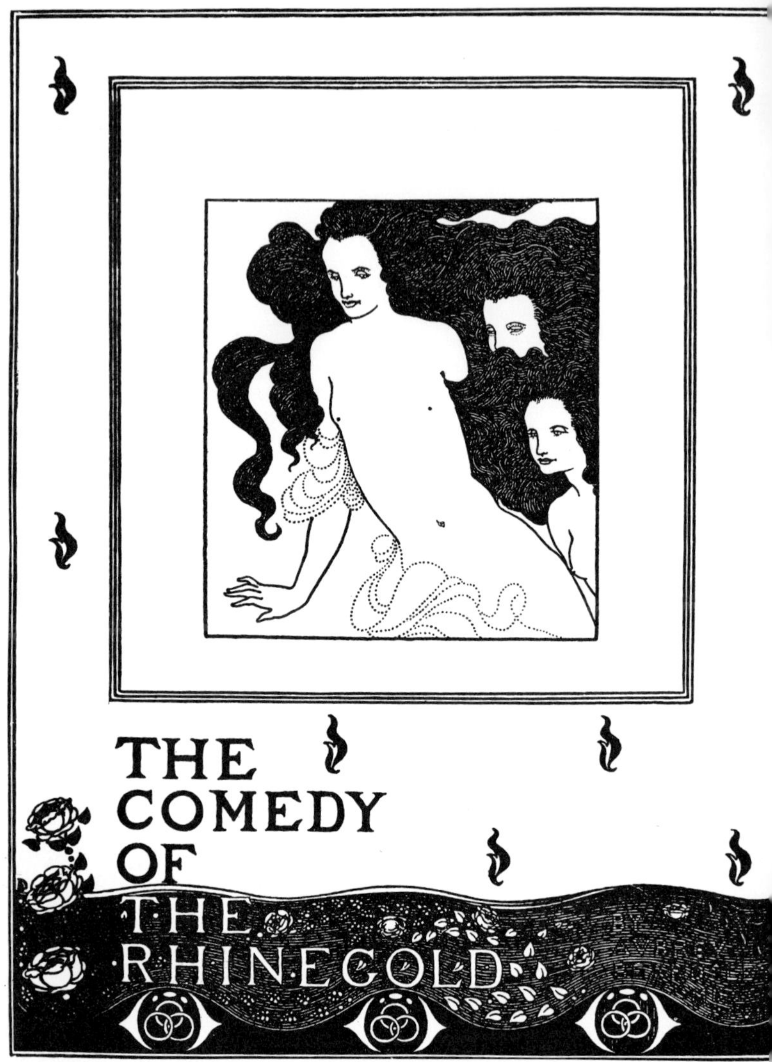
THE
COMEDY
OF
THE
RHINEGOLD

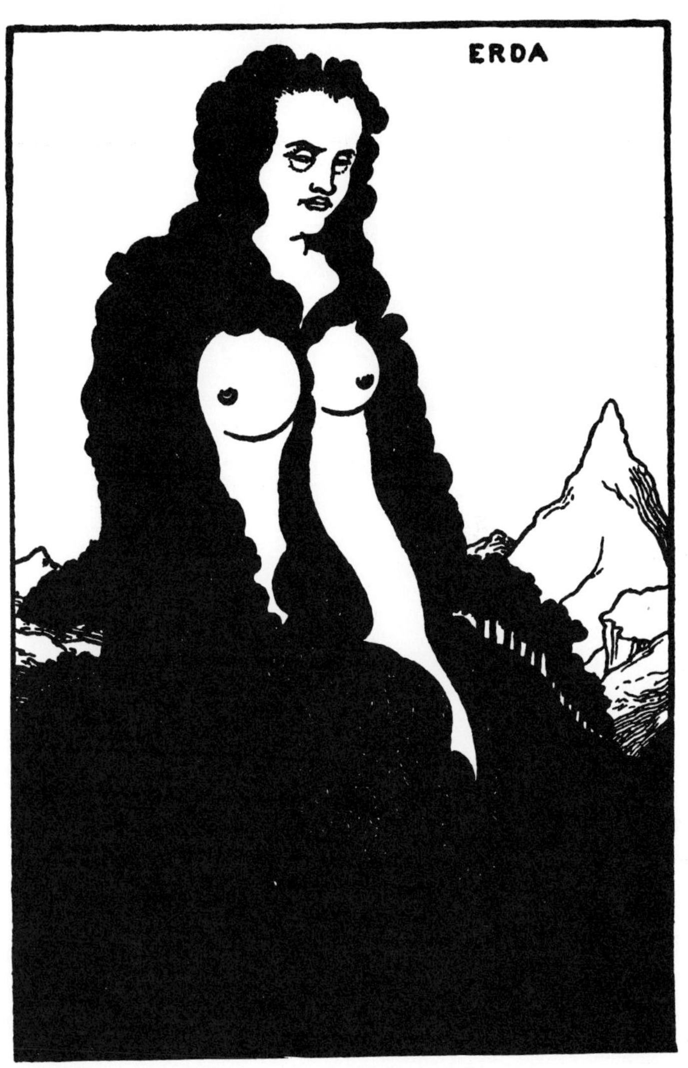
ERDA

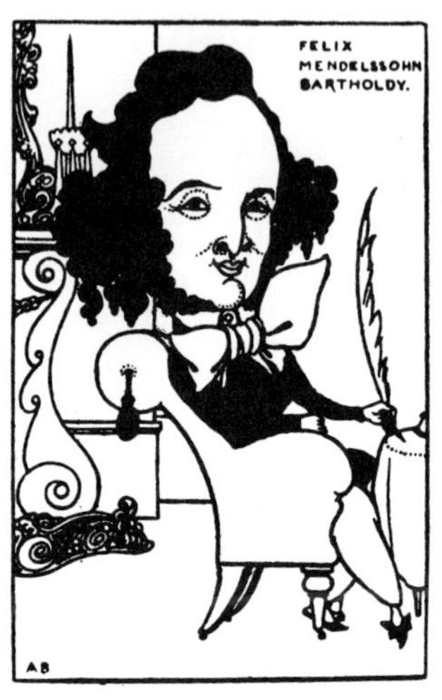
FELIX
MENDELSSOHN
BARTHOLDY.
AB

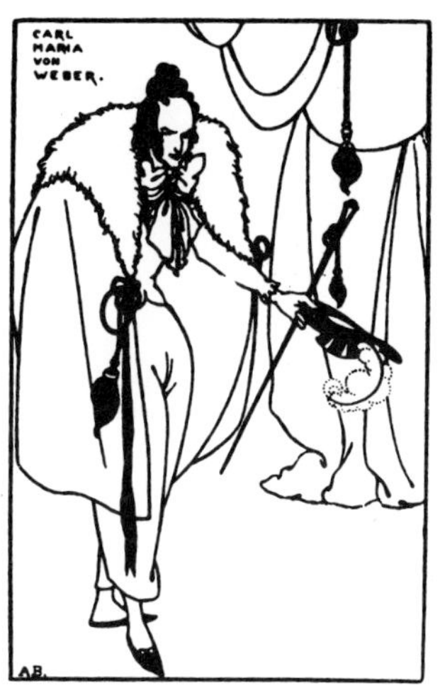
CARL
MARIA
VON
WEBER.
A.B.

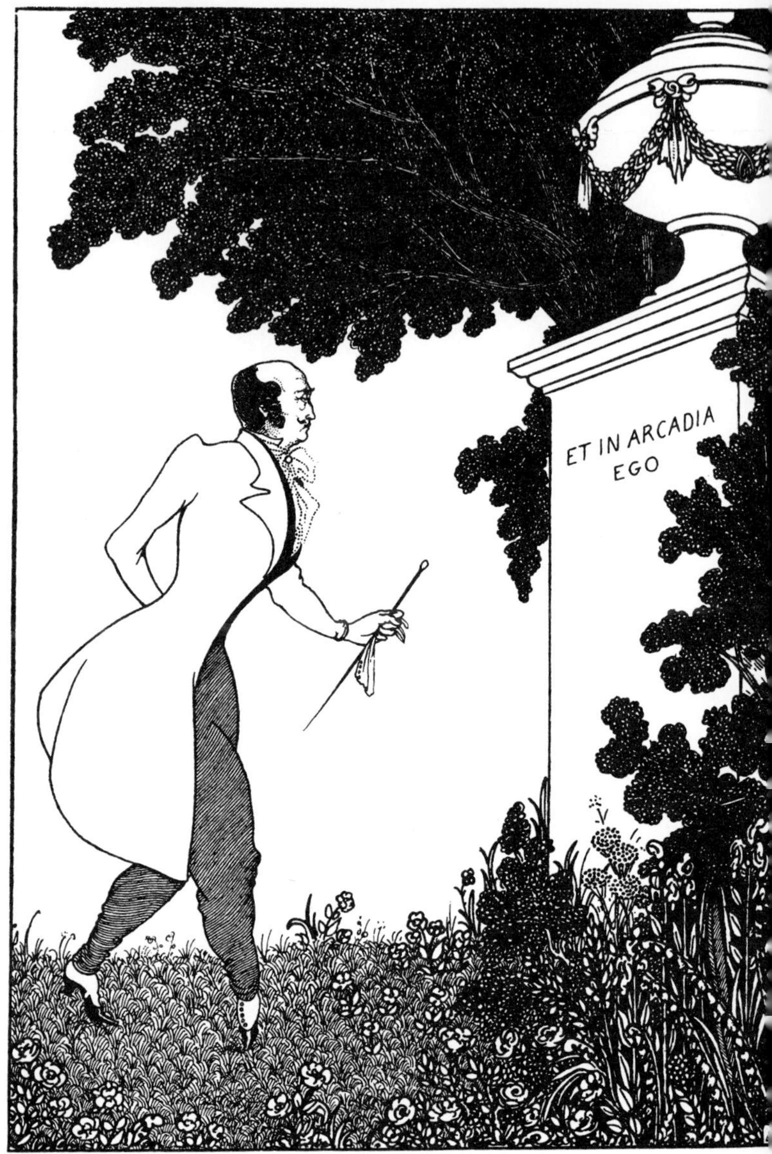
ET IN ARCADIA
EGO

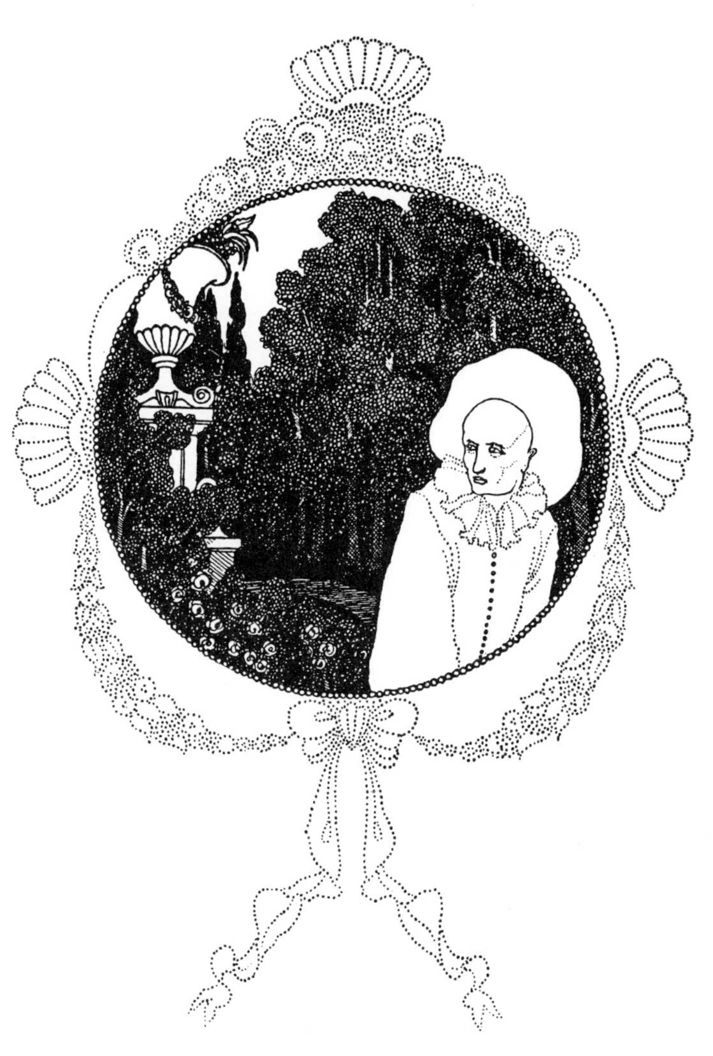

THE PIERROT OF THE MINVTE.

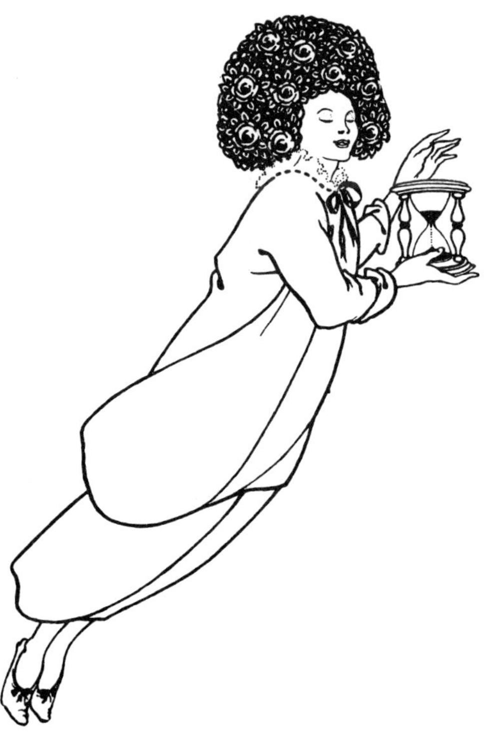

A BOOK OF FIFTY DRAWINGS

BY

AVBREY BEARDSLEY

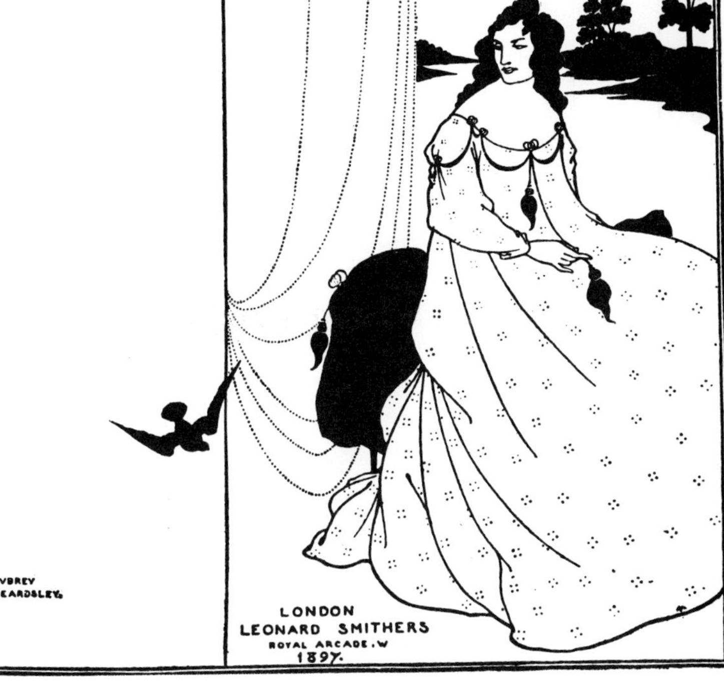

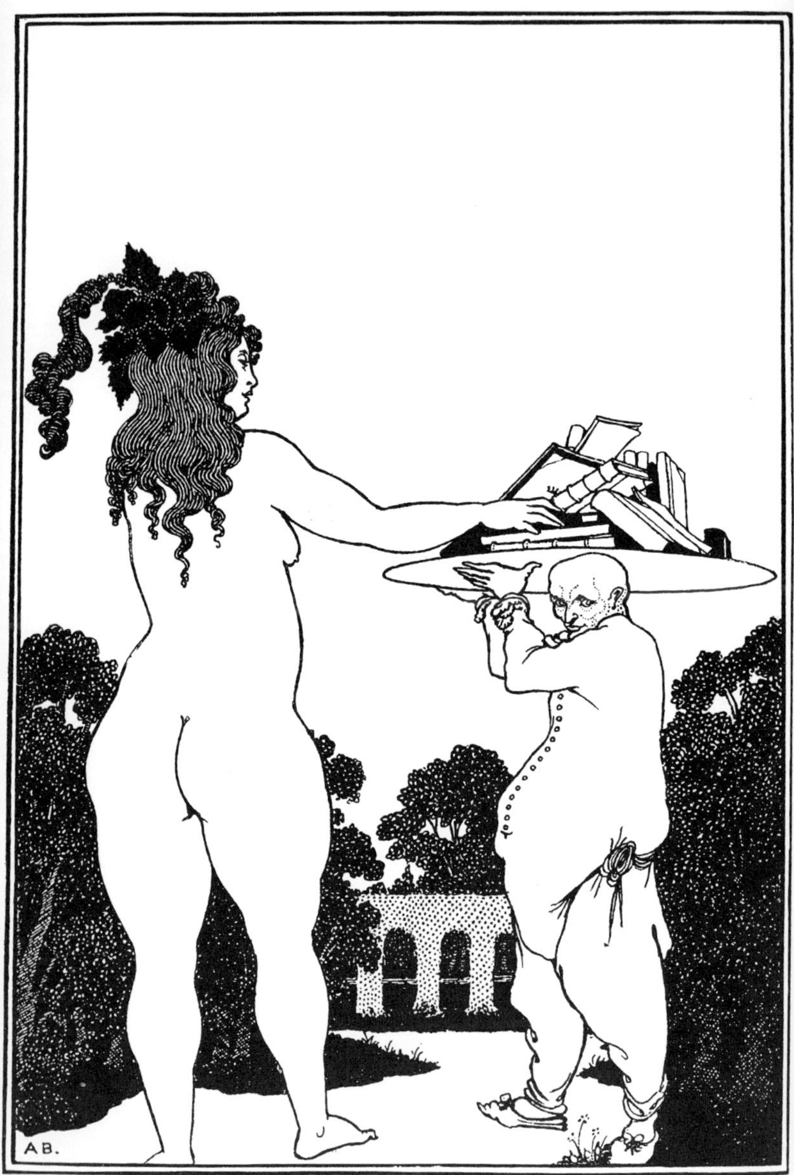
AB.

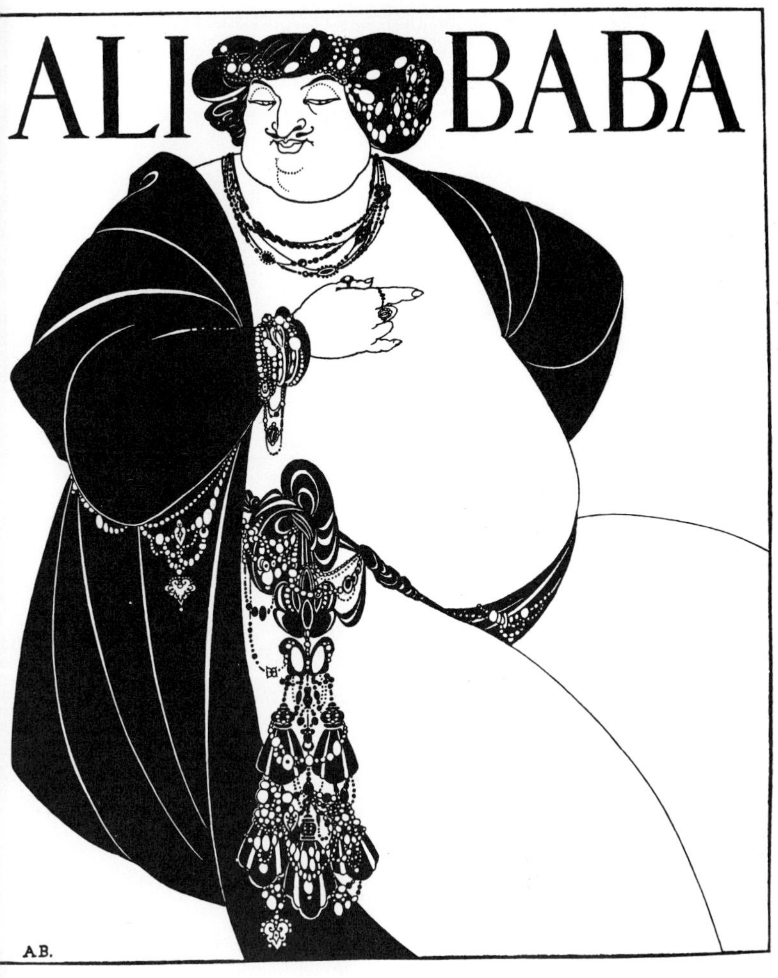
ALI BABA
A.B.

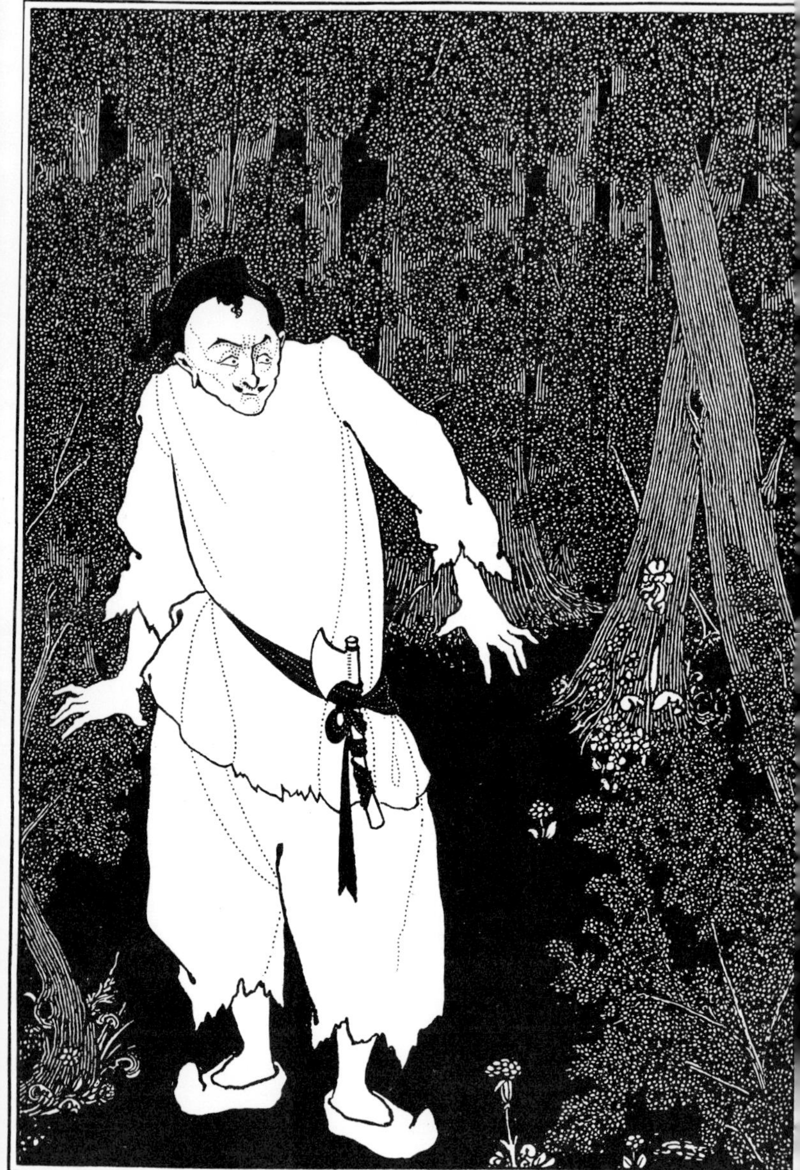

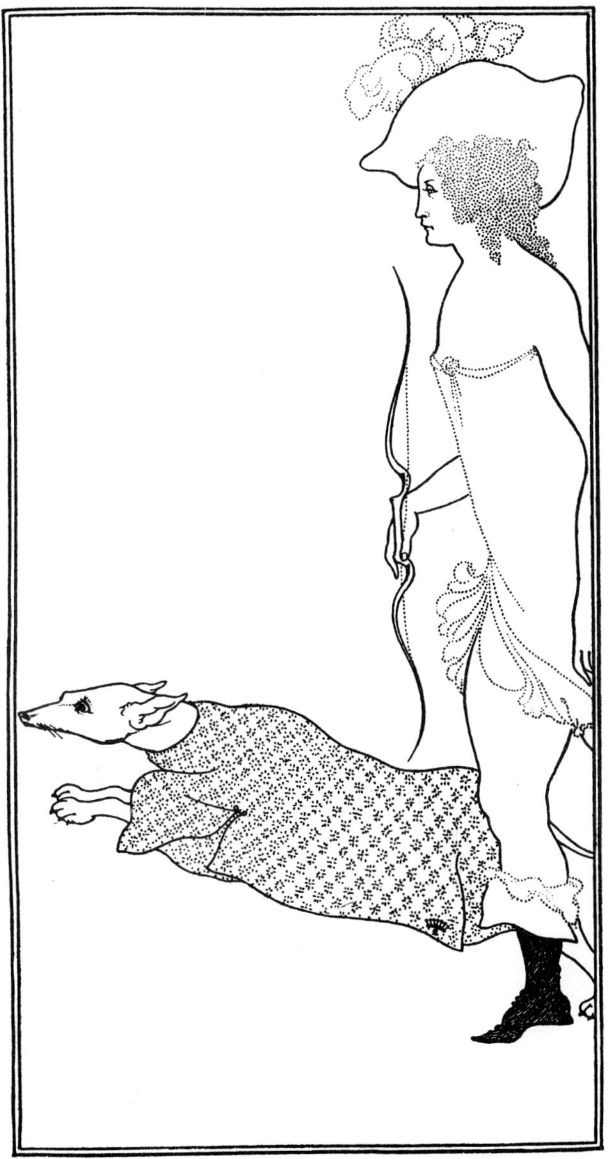

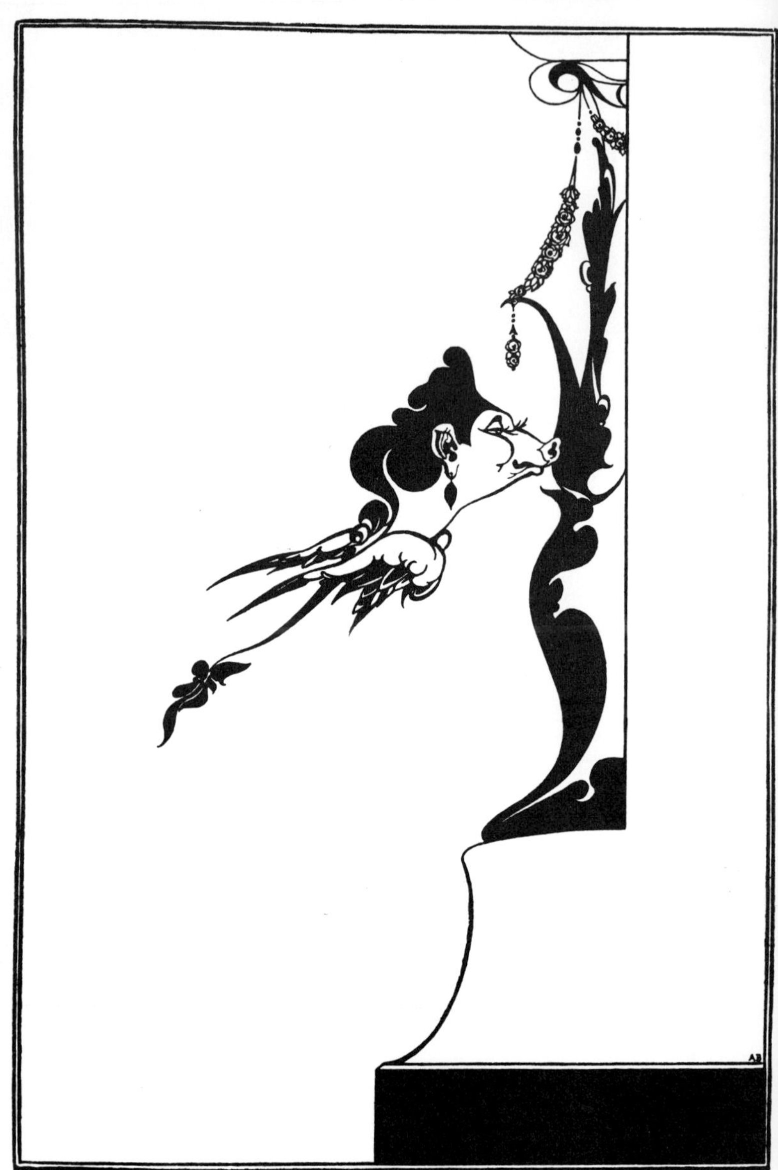
AB

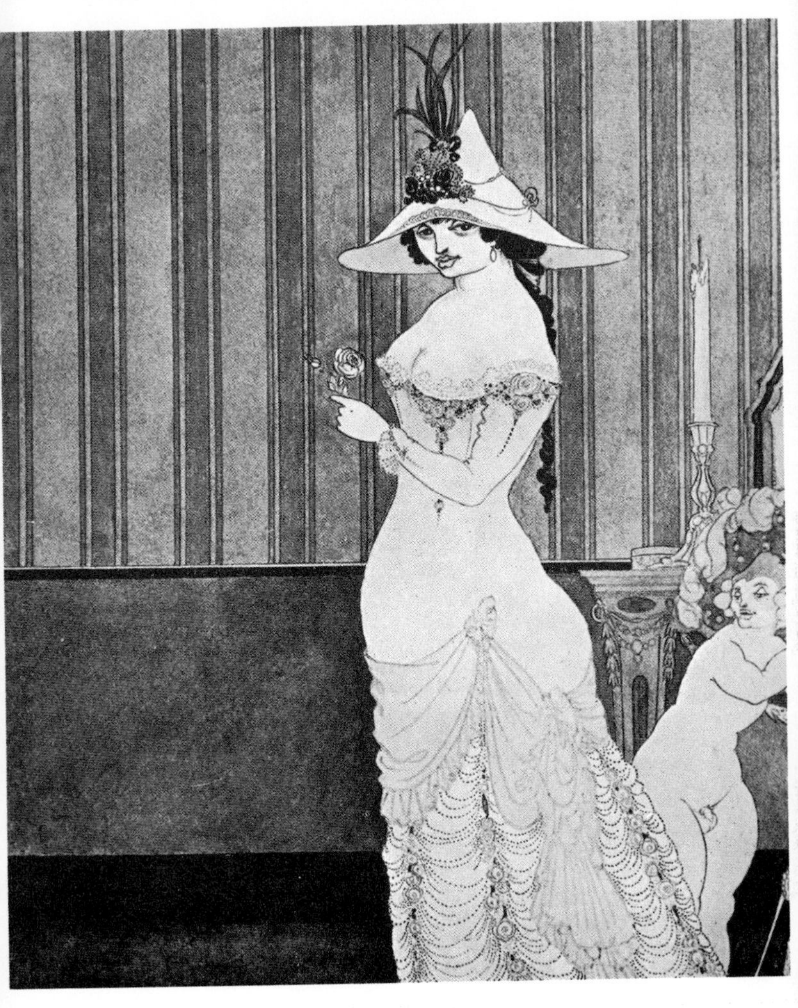

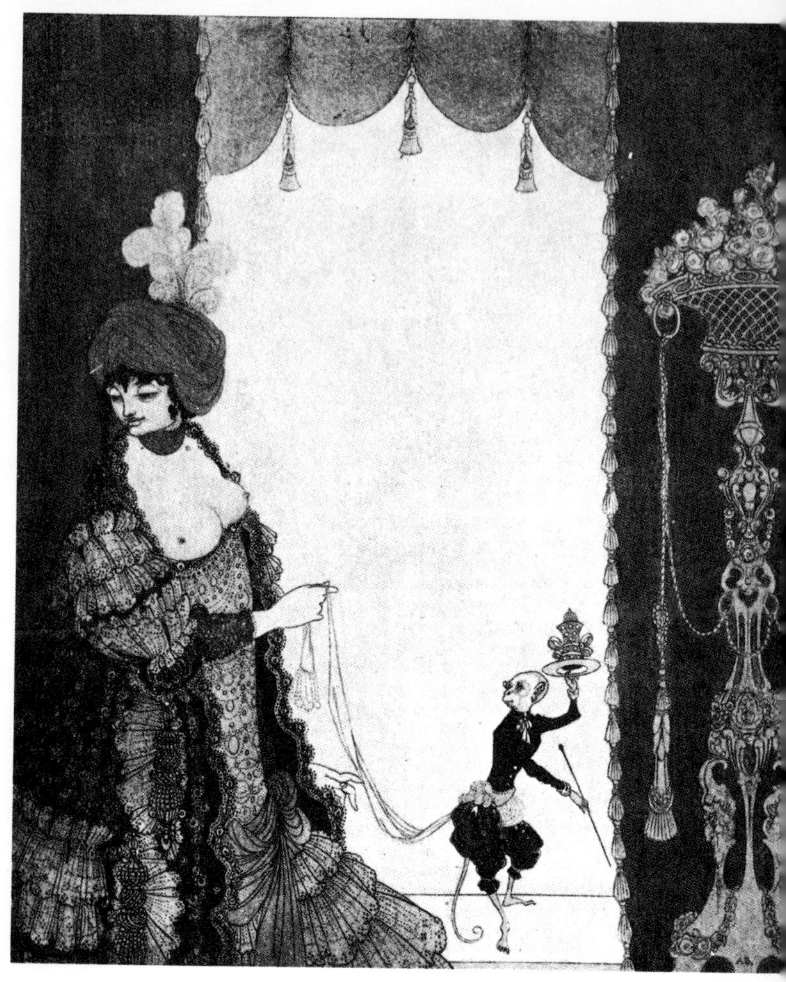

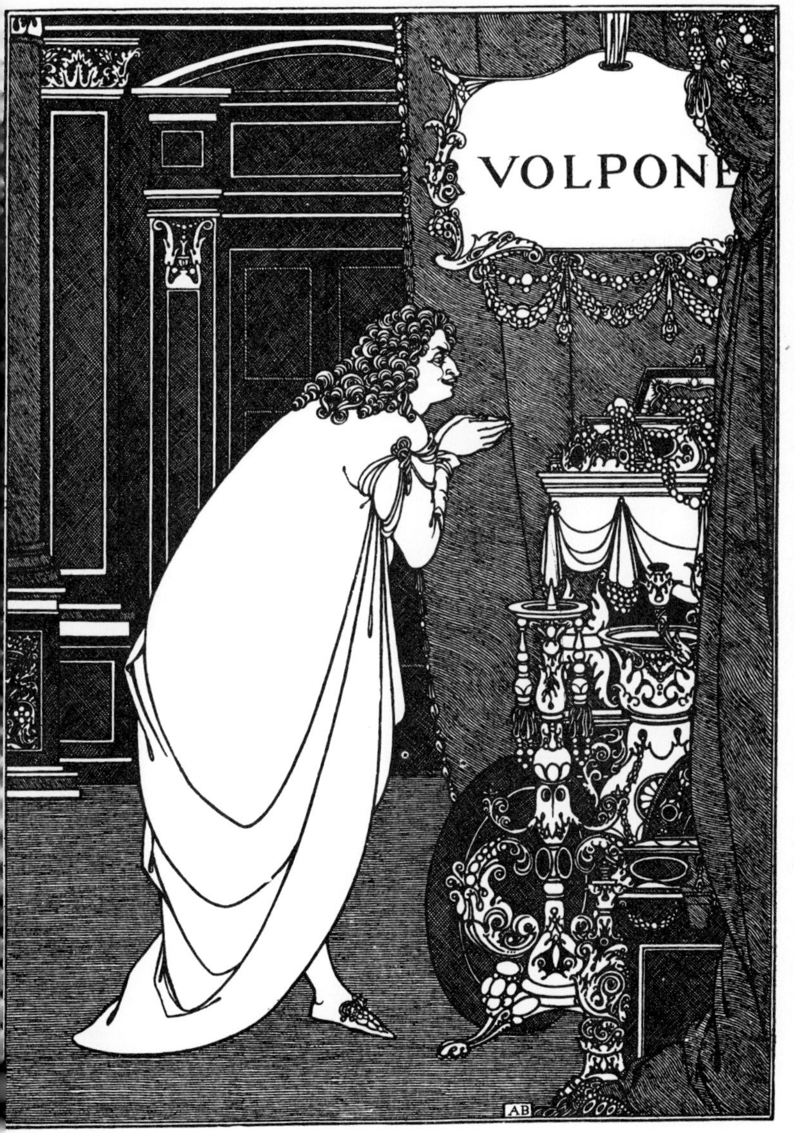
VOLPONE
AB

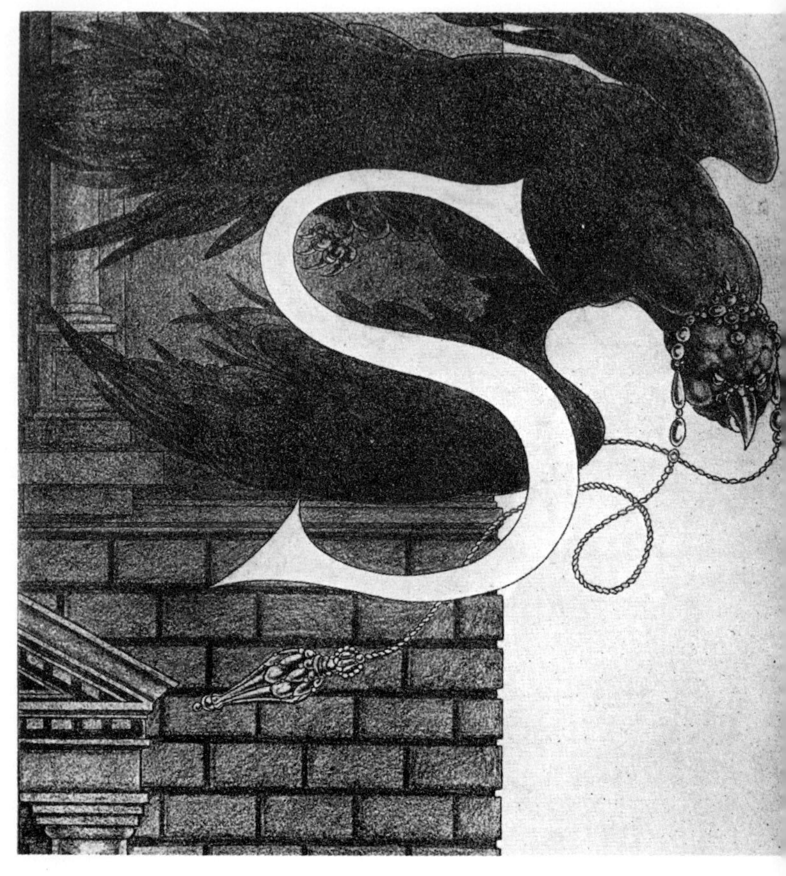
S

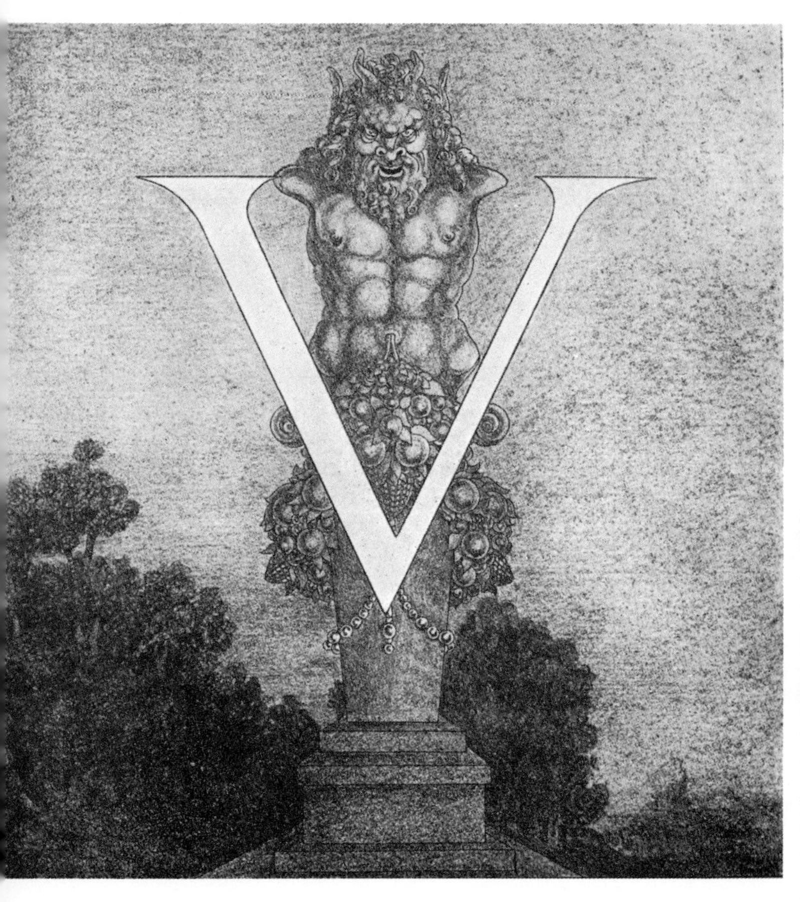
V

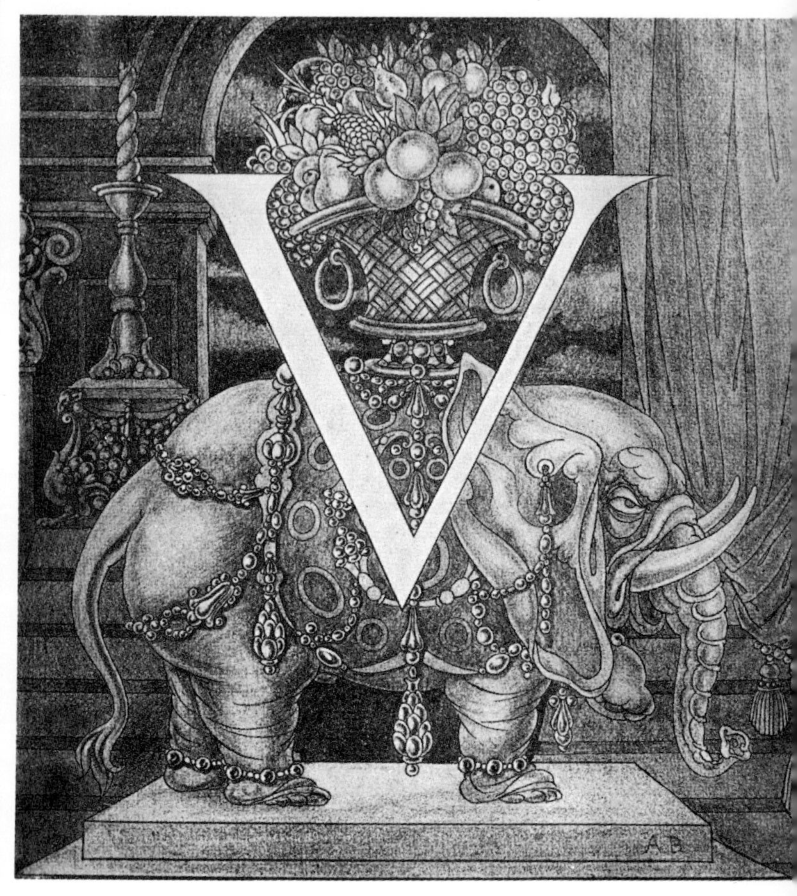

List of Plates

32 Cover design for *Platonic Affections*
33 Eight initial keys, from *Keynotes*
34 Title vignette
35 Title vignette
36-37 Design for the menu of the Playgoers' Club
38-39 Illustrations for Lucian's *True History,* 1894
- 38 *The Snare of Vintage*
- 39 *Lucian's Strange Creatures*. (executed but not published)

40 Poster for the *Pseudonym Library*
41 Sketch of a *Self-Portrait*
42-56 Illustrations for *Salomé* by Oscar Wilde, 1893
- 42 Design for the title page
- 43 Drawing for the table of contents
- 44 *The Woman in the Moon* (In the moon is a portrait of Oscar Wilde)
- 45 *The Peacock Skirt*
- 46 *The Black Cape*
- 47 *The Platonic Lament*
- 48 *Enter Herodias* (In the foreground is a caricature of Wilde)
- 49 *The Eyes of Herod*
- 50 *The Stomach Dance*
- 51 *The Toilette of Salomé* (2nd. draft, replaced 1st. see pl. 54)
- 52 *The Dancer's Reward*
- 53 *The Climax*
- 54 *The Toilette of Salomé* (First draft)
- 55 *John and Salomé* (appears only in later editions)
- 56 End vignette

57-72 From *The Yellow Book,* vol. I-IV, 1894
- 57 Cover design for the prospectus
- 58 *L'Education Sentimentale* (vol. I)
- 59 *Comedy-Ballet of the Marionettes I* (vol. II; the only oil painting by Beardsley is a version of this drawing: *A Caprice*, London, Tate-Gallery)
- 60 *Comedy-Ballet of the Marionettes II* (vol. II)
- 61 *Comedy-Ballet of the Marionettes III* (vol. II)
- 62 *The Slippers of Cinderella* (vol. II)
- 63 Cover design for vol. III
- 64 Title-page drawing (vol. III)
- 65 *La Dame aux Camélias* (vol. III)
- 66 *Self-portrait* (vol. III)
- 67 *Lady Gold's Escourt* (vol. III)
- 68 Cover design for volume IV
- 69 *The Mysterious Rose Garden* (vol. IV)

70 *The Repentance of Mrs. . . .* (vol. IV)
71 Frontispiece for *Juvenal,* sixth satire (vol. IV)
72 Cover design (not used)

73-77 Illustrations for *Venus and Tannhäuser,* 1895
73 Frontispiece (Venus between terminal gods; not used as such)
74-75 Frontispiece and title page (not used as such)
76 *The Return of Tannhäuser to Venusberg*
77 Design for the title-page *(Venus)*

78 Cover design for *The Cambridge A.B.C.* Magazine for lower classmen, 1894

79 *The Scarlet Pastorale*

80 Invitation for the opening meeting of The Princess Ladies' Golf Club, Mitchum, 1894

81 Poster design, 1894

82 Design for an invitation

83 *Isolde,* from *The Studio*

84 Catalogue cover

85 Illustration for *The Mirror of Love,* 1895. Published by Arthur Symon, 1898, Unicorn Press. The drawing was supposedly conceived as a frontispiece for a book by André Raffalovitch.

86 Frontispiece design for *The Full and True Account of the Wonderful Mission of Earl Lavender* by John Davidson, 1895

87 Messalina, 1895 (First printed by Smithers in *A Second Book of Fifty Drawings,* 1899; then in a folio, 1900)

88 Cover design for *Pierrot*

89 Design for the title page of *Pierrot*

90-97 Illustrations for *Lysistrata,* 1896. These drawings appeared in a privately printed edition of Aristophanes' *Lysistrata.*
90 *Lysistrata,* Frontispiece
91 *Lampito (The Toilette of Lampito)*
92 *Lysistrata Haranguing the Athenian Women*
93 *Lysistrata Defending the Acropolis*
94 *Two Athenian Women in Distress*
95 *Cinesias Soliciting Myrrhina*
96 *The Examination of the Herald*
97 *The Lacedemonian Ambassadors*

98-106 Illustrations for *The Rape of the Lock,* by Alexander Pope, 1895-96
98 *The Dream*
99 *The Billet-Doux*
100 *The Toilet*
101 *The Baron's Prayer*